Copyright © 1952, 1970, 1982
by Zong In-sob

First published in 1952
by Routledge & Kegan Paul Ltd.
Broadway House, 68-74 Carter Lane.
London, E.C.4, Great Britain

Second edition 1970
by Hollym Corporation; Publishers

Third edition 1982
Seventh printing 1991
by Hollym International Corp.
18 Donald Place
Elizabeth, New Jersey 07208 U.S.A.

Published simultaneously in Korea
by Hollym Corporation; Publishers
14-5 Kwanchol-dong, Chongno-gu, Seoul, Korea
Phone: (02)735-7554   FAX: (02)730-5149

ISBN: 0-930878-26-4

Library of Congress Catalog Card Number: 82-82600

Printed in Korea

FOLK TALES

from

KOREA

Third Edition

COLLECTED AND TRANSLATED

BY

ZŎNG IN-SŎB
Former Dean of the Graduate School,
The Hankuk University of Foreign Studies,
Seoul, Korea

HOLLYM

Foreword for the Third Edition

Korea is one of the most significant hot spots of international conflicts, politically frustrated in the twentieth century, but its culture had been admitted as one flourished in the Far-East, with its genuine creativeness and also with its unique role of reciprocal exchanges of civilization between the Continent and the Pacific Isles.

This book was primarily prepared in English for the purpose of introducing to the world the roots of its cultural heritage. Thirty years have passed since the first edition was published in 1952 during the Korean War, and it has been well appreciated by readers of the world, particularly by those who are interested in things Korean.

Now I hereby intend to bring out the third edition of it as an international feature. I hope this contribute much to the understanding of once a hermit-nation, but now a developing country in modern times.

ZŎNG IN-SŎB

정 인 섭

(鄭 寅 爕)

May 5, 1982   *Advisor to the Korean Chapter of*
the International P E. N. Club

v

Foreword

Ⅰ VERY gladly comply with Professor Zŏng In-Sŏb's request to
write a Foreword to his 'Folk Tales from Korea'. His book is
sure to arouse the keen interest of the general reading public. At
the same time it will be warmly welcomed by the scholar. As
every student of folklore knows, the literature in western languages
on Far Eastern fairy tales and folk tales is still extremely scanty. It is
therefore a matter of congratulation that we should now be presented, by the same publishers, with a companion volume to
Professor W. Eberhard's *Chinese Fairy Tales and Folk Tales.*

As far as the present book is concerned it may be difficult to think
of anybody better qualified to write it than Professor Zŏng. As
readers will see for themselves, his interest in Korean folk tales goes
back to his early childhood, and, inspired by the highest patriotic
motives, he has kept it up all through his life. In each of his 99 tales
a source is put on record and it can clearly be seen that most of them
are based on oral tradition and so constitute primary source material
from the point of view of folklore studies. While the scholar will be
able to collect further information from the detailed introduction
and the carefully worked-out indexes, the main part of the book has
on purpose been kept free from any learned apparatus so as to
enable the reader to do justice to the primary purpose of all tales.
They are told to be enjoyed. I very much hope that the present
collection will give joy to the general reader as I am sure it has been
a source of permanent joy to the compiler who has concentrated on
this subject for more than thirty years.

W. SIMON

vi

Author's Foreword

KOREA is not a primitive country, it has a long cultural history, which is briefly summarized at the beginning of the introduction. Its people have attained a high level of civilization, and their literacy rate is said to be comparable to that of the inhabitants of Eastern Europe. Their achievements in the cultural field are by no means negligible.

I was born in 1905 in a small farming town, Ŏnyang, in the County of Ulsan, not far from the port of Busan (or Pusan), in the south-east, in the province of south Gyŏngsang, Korea. My mother and my five sisters, including the youngest, Zŏng Bog-Sun, and their friends told me many fairy tales while I was still a child. I heard more from my class-mates at the 'sŏdang', the old type of Korean school, which I attended at the age of seven. When I was eight I went to a primary school of the Western type, but even there I heard tales of old Korea from boys from other villages. My father was a scholar of the classics, with the pseudonym of 'A-Song', or 'Moth-Pine'. He attached great importance to the education of his sons, and so he arranged a special 'bogsŭb bang' or study room in our house, where schoolboys from the village used to come and visit my elder brother, Zŏng In-Mog, and myself, and where we used to exchange stories. The next room was allotted to the farm workers, and there my elder brother and myself sometimes went at night to listen to their stories by the dim light of the oil-lamp.

It was in these circumstances that my interest in folk tales was first awakened. In 1922, however, when I entered Waseda University in Tokyo and began to carry out research in English literature I came across some books about the Irish Renaissance movement, written by W. B. Yeats and others. It was then that I realized that the first step in a revival of literary consciousness in my native land must be a revival of interest in folk tales. So in 1925 I joined the Sĕgdong Hoe, a society for the protection of children, which had been established in Seoul by the late Mr. Bang Zŏng-Hwan, our best story-teller, and I insisted on the necessity of providing for the children fairy tales, nursery rhymes, and children's verses and plays through his magazine *Ŏrini* ('Childhood'). At the same time I and two colleagues, the late Mr. Song Sŏg-Ha, a student of folk-lore, and Mr. Son Zin-Tĕ, a historian, organized the Korean Folk-Lore Society, and began to collect myths, legends, fairy tales, fables, and other stories, together with ballads, folk songs, folk plays, and other items of folk-lore. Two years later, in 1927, I published in Tokyo a book of Korean folk-tales in Japanese under the title of *Ondoru Yawa*, or 'Korean Nights', to show something of the inner life of our Korean people. Many of them are here reproduced in English. At the same time two volumes of *Fairy Tales of Many Countries*, which included some Korean tales, appeared in English under my editorship to encourage a general interest in folk-lore among students of English.

A traditional background of this kind was not sufficient by itself. Something more was needed if our new literature was to rank with those of the civilized countries of the twentieth century. So with several friends studying foreign literatures I had already founded the 'Society for Research in Foreign Literature' in 1926, and had set on foot a movement to translate into Korean foreign literary works in order to introduce to our people the inner lives of people of other countries. This we did through the Society's periodical 'Literæ Exoticæ'.

When I graduated from the University in 1929 I took a post in Yŏnhi college in Seoul, and taught Introduction to Literature and English. Here I attempted to combine the two cultural elements of the traditions of the Orient and the modern civilizations of the West through my professorship there. At the same time I organized with several colleagues the Society for Research in Dramatic Arts, and at its performances I introduced to the public Korean and foreign plays. I also joined the Korean P.E.N. Club, and began to write poetry and literary criticism. I based my work on this same principle of modifying the cultures of the East and of the West and combining them to form a synthetic basis for new inspiration. In 1930 I joined the Korean Philological Society and served on the Committees for the Unified System of Korean Spelling, the Examination of a Standard Vocabulary, and also for the Establishment of a Unified System of Romanization, the Transcription of Korean

Author's Foreword

Speech Sounds in the International Phonetic Alphabet, and the Koreanization of Foreign Sounds. And I founded the Korean Phonetic Association in 1935.

On many occasions during the past twenty years I have translated Korean works into English, or introduced them to English-speaking people in public lectures or in my publications of 'English Literature at Home and Abroad', first edited in 1932, and 'An Anthology of Modern Poems in Korea' (1948). I have at the same time tried to reform the methods of teaching English in Korea, as suggested in my book 'New Methods of Teaching and Learning English in Korea' published in 1949.

This is the outline of my activities to bring about an interchange of ideas between the two worlds. I have never believed in the narrow-minded aphorism that 'East is East and West is West, and never the twain shall meet'. It is my belief, and my experience bears it out, that when they really understand each other East and West can be friends. And so I am confident that my book of folk-tales will make its own contribution to achieving this friendship. The book was prepared for publication after I came to London in 1950, while I was giving lectures on Korean culture in School of Oriental and African Studies, University of London.

In this book I have chosen ninety-nine tales, some of which I collected after the Second World War, when I had been appointed Professor at the Central University and the National University, Seoul. I hope that they will be of some help to English-speaking readers in achieving this understanding between East and West. And folk tales, as the oral literature of the people, provide valuable material for the student of Korean literature, but they are also indispensable for those who wish to know and understand Korean culture, history, religion, philosophy, and even politics and economics.

ZŎNG IN-SŎB

London, 1952   *School of Oriental and African Studies*
University of London

Contents

Part I. Myths

Contents

Part II. Legends

Contents

Part III. Fairy Tales

Contents

Part IV. Fables

Part V. Old Novels

Contents

Appendix

Acknowledgements

I would like to take this opportunity of expressing my heartfelt thanks to W. Simon, Dr.Phil., D.Lit., Professor of Chinese in the University of London and Acting Head of the Far East Department of School of Oriental and African Studies, University of London, who suggested to me the preparation of this work and kindly wrote the Foreword of this book.

I am especially indebted also to Mr. W. B. Eggington, B.A., who read my manuscript and helped me with valuable suggestions.

ZŎNG IN-SŎB

Introduction

I. GENERAL

THE history of Korea dates back 4,303 years to the first king, Dan-Gun, the mythical founder of Korea. Her people are an ancient and homogeneous race, distinct from both the Chinese and the Japanese. The area of the country to-day is 85,228 square miles, but in the days of Buyŏ (*circa* 1333 B.C.–A.D. 494) Korean territory extended as far as the River Sungari in Manchuria. With a population of some thirty millions Korea to-day ranks twelfth among the nations of the world. She has the third largest fisheries in the world, and is the fourth largest producer of rice. She also possesses varied mineral resources and a great hydro-electric power potential. The majestic beauty of the Diamond Mountain which stands midway along the East coast has earned for her the title of the 'Switzerland of Asia'.

In the cultural field Korea was not only the channel through which the civilization of China and the religion of India were transmitted to Japan, but also by the ingenuity of her people made a great contribution to the inventions of the world. The spinning wheel was invented in Korea in 1376, movable type in 1403, astronomical instruments in 1438, the mariner's compass in 1535, the first bomb and the first iron-clad battleship in the world in 1592, and the observation balloon in the sixteenth century. It was in Korea too that the earliest and most continuous records of rainfall were kept. In the fifteenth century Korean scholars compiled an encyclopædia in 112 quarto volumes, three hundred years before a similar work was produced in France. One of the best phonetic alphabets was invented there in 1443, literature flourished, encouraged by the system of Civil Examinations, and the fine arts were brought to a high pitch of development.

The temples of Korea are distinguished by the perfect symmetry

xvii

of their Oriental architecture. Korean pottery has been acknow-
ledged to be superior to that of the rest of the Far East, and her
lacquer ware inlaid with mother-of-pearl is said to be the finest in
the world. The music of Korea too inherits a long tradition of
ancient court music. Korean clothes and food are highly praised by
experts.

These are a few historical facts. The written history of a people
shows us the main currents of their politics and culture, but when
we wish to discover the spirit of their daily life it is to their folk-lore
that we must turn. Folk-lore is a vast storehouse of traditions, such
as folk tales, folk songs, folk dance and drama, proverbs, riddles,
superstititions, and even customs and manners. Of these folk tales
are most widely known among the people of the country and can
most easily be appreciated by foreigners.

Modern Korean literature is a blending of the traditional features
of our native life and the new currents of Western literature. It
deals with almost the same subjects as does modern European
literature, whether in poetry, novels, and plays, or in essays and
criticism, but behind these common themes there are certain
features peculiar to Korea, deriving from our language, customs,
and manners, and our geographical and political situation, which
are not found in the literatures of other countries.

As to the language, which is the basic element of any national
literature, it should be remembered that the Korean national
phonetic alphabet of twenty-four letters (which may be used in
conjunction with Chinese characters, which are ideographic,
arranged and pronounced in the Korean way), is one of the best
scripts ever invented. It is scientifically constructed, very simple in
form, and easy to understand. It is entirely different from the
Chinese and Japanese scripts. Now the Unified System of spelling is
being adopted by schools and the Government, thanks to the
untiring industry of the Korean Philological Association, established
in 1921, with which I have been associated as a member of the
committee, and the Korean Phonetic Association which I myself
founded in 1935. The Romanization of proper names (surnames
invariably precede personal names, and the latter are hyphenated
when they consist of two or more syllables) and Korean terms
adopted in this book is based on the unified system which has been
authorized by these two associations for general use. The original

Introduction

plan of this system was drafted by myself and introduced by me at the 4th International Congress of Linguists held at Copenhagen in 1936.

A, e, i, o, and u are pronounced as e.g. in Italian, a as in 'father', e as in 'bed', i as in 'sit', o as in 'boy', and u as the oo in 'book'. Ŏ is pronounced like the a in 'about' or the ea in 'heard'; ĕ like the a in 'back'; and ŭ is to be pronounced as a vowel somewhere between i and u, the highest central vowel, with lips spread, the international phonetic transcription of which would be ɯ or ɨ. When necessary long vowels are represented by the duplication of the same vowel. B, d, g, and z represent the English sounds of b in 'bed', d in 'do', g in 'go', and j in 'joy' respectively, but they are devocalized when initial, and also devocalized but not exploded when final. Bb, dd, gg, and zz have the non-aspirated and non-voiced glottal values of b, d, g, and j respectively. P, t, k, and cz are articulated like the English p, t, k, and ch respectively, but much more strongly aspirated.

Although, of course, customs and manners have changed greatly through the ages they still exert a great influence on literary production as well as on the daily lives of the Korean people, and many of their basic features can be approached through the tales included in this book. In some ways they are as full of primitive sentiments and mysterious superstitions as the folk tales of other nations, yet the main points suggested in the tales and the emotions which prompted them still predominate in the minds of our people.

Births, marriages, and deaths are described in their genuine Korean traditional forms. Omens and dreams, auguries and divinations, charms and amulets all have a Korean flavour and are not identical with those of China. Many supernatural beings appear, but they do not behave in the same way as those in Japanese stories. For instance, Buddhist monks or priests are not always respected in the Korean tales which are told to-day, despite their possession of magical powers. This is due, as I shall show later, to the historical background of religion in Korea and its changing social status through the ages. Korean fairies, elves, goblins, ghosts, giants, monsters, and other such creatures all have their own peculiarly Korean characteristics. Dragons, animals, and plants behave in many cases in a Korean manner, and certain kinds figure in our stories more often than in those of other countries.

II. KOREA AND ITS NEIGHBOURING COUNTRIES

The geographical location of Korea and its political situation have greatly influenced the literary taste of her inhabitants. Korea has played an important role in the history of the Far East as the bridge between the continent of Asia and the islands of the Pacific. So in her folk tales we can trace several intermingling currents from the surrounding countries of China, Japan, India, Mongolia, Tibet, Manchuria, and Siberia. There are, however, some universal elements which can be found even in European stories. For example, (2) Go Zu-Mong, King of Goguryŏ, can be referred to the Greek myth of Perseus. Another story of the Perseus type is told in Korea in which a toad is the hero who saves a maiden from a serpent or a centipede by breathing its poisonous breath upon it, as the tortoise of China kills a serpent, or a scaly dragon, or the hero of Japanese folk lore kills a serpent, or the knights of Europe rescue damsels in distress. Stories of the type of 'Cupid and Psyche' [compare (6) 'The Three Stars' and (76) 'The Toad Bridegroom'] and the 'Swan Maiden Tales' [compare (11) 'The Heavenly Maiden and the Wood-cutter'] are also found in Korea, as well as in China, Japan, Siberia. and Europe.

Some Korean tales are closely related to stories told in the neighbouring countries, though they are moulded in a Korean style. For instance a tale resembling No. 51, 'A Stone Memorial to a Dog,' was told in China from the fourth century A.D., as was recorded in Volume 5 of the Sou Shên Chi by Kan Pao, of the Chin Dynasty, one of the same type as No. 13, 'The Mud-snail Fairy,' called 'The Virgin Po Sui' is found in Volume 16 of the Sou Shên Hou Chi by T'ao Ch'ien the same dynasty. In the same way No. 59, 'The Story of the Virgin Arang' can be identified with the Chinese legend of the Maiden Chieh San, in Volume 17 of the Yi Chien Chih by Hung Mai of the Sung Dynasty, and tales closely resembling our No. 18, 'The Green Frog,' No. 25, 'The Man who wanted to bury his son', and No. 81, 'Three Corpses, Money, and a Wine-bottle' have been told in China, as in Volume 9 of the Hsü Po Wu Chih by Li Shih of the T'ang Dynasty, in Volume 11 of the Sou Shên Chi by Kan Pao of the Chin Dynasty, and in the Chang Shih Ko Shu by Chang Chih Fu of the Sung Dynasty respectively.

Turning now to Japanese legends, a story of the same type as our

No. 3, 'The Sun and the Moon,' is told in the island of Kyushu, Japan, under the name of 'Soba' or 'Buckwheat' (in 'The Legends of Japan' by Mr. Takagi Tosio, p. 267). In Japan we also find stories of the same type as our No. 86, 'The Bride who would not speak' (Volume 75 of the Japanese work 'Wakan Sanzai Zukai'), and No. 64, 'The Mallet of Wealth' ('Elves and the Envious Neighbour', in Lord Redesdale's 'Tales of Old Japan', p. 160). Moreover the tiger of our story No. 79, 'The Tiger and the Persimmon,' is undoubtedly the monster called 'Toraokame', or 'Tiger-wolf', in a Japanese story of similar type (Takagi Tosio, Studies in the Myths and Legends of Japan, p. 450). This story may well have been introduced into Japan from Korea, as the tiger is not found in Japan, and a modified form of the word 'Wolf' has been added. This type of story seems to be originally derived from 'The Thief, the Monster, and the Monkey', No. 9 of Volume 5 of the Indian 'Panch-Tantra', in which the central figure is a man-eating monster 'Rakchasa'. Therefore an Indian origin may be postulated for certain Korean tales. It is commonly held that No. 8, 'The Great Flood,' No. 82, 'The Aged Father,' No. 17, 'The Deer, the Hare, and the Toad,' and No. 85, 'Lazybones,' are derived from the Buddhist Scriptures of India.

Then our No. 12, 'The Cat and the Dog' can be referred to the Mongolian myth, 'The Story of Sharau' (A Journey in Southern Siberia; the Mongols, their Religion and their Myths, by Jeremiah Curtin, p. 201). In Mongolia too we find a tale of the same type as our No. 72, 'The Nine-headed Giant,' and stories of the same type as our No. 70, 'The Young Gentleman and the Tiger,' are found in East Mongolia, Japan, India, and even in Tibet.

III. CHARACTERISTICS OF KOREAN TALES

Korean folk tales can be classified in many ways. In this book I have divided these tales into five groups, myths, legends, fairy tales, fables, and old novels. By myths I mean those tales which describe the creation of the world and natural beings. Legends include those tales which are derived from anecdotes about individuals which contain some historical facts. Fairy tales comprise innocent stories for children and fables those which point a moral. And finally I have included summaries of three autobiographical novels written by early writers, because these old tales have been told among the people for so long that they have almost become popular folk tales and some of the authors forgotten. In any case they were originally derived from such material as gives rise to legends.

The tales can also be grouped under about fifteen main heads according to their subject-matter or material. That is to say, tales dealing with the Heavenly Kingdom and other celestial matters, genii and mysterious priests, human beings and their activities, ghosts and devils, fairies and goblins, giants and dwarfs, magicians and geomancers, dragons and the kingdom under the sea, animals and birds, insects and worms, fish and shells, trees and grass, stones and mountains, rivers, lakes and seas, and stories about eggs. This list does not, of course, claim to be complete. Other types may certainly be found. All these types are often interwoven one with another and it is often difficult to draw clear distinctions between them.

In Korea we find almost every kind of myth, such as Creation Myths, Sun and Moon Myths, Star Myths, Flood Myths, Myths of Places of Rewards or Punishments, Myths of the Underworld, or Place of the Dead, Soul Myths, Hero Myths, Dualistic Myths of the Good God fighting the Bad God, Myths regarding Taboo and Myths of Animals. The Myths of Korea are not, however, on the grand scale of the myths of Greece or some other Western countries, but they are elaborately designed stories, and more or less independent of one another. They explain how the Sun and Moon originated, as in No. 3, 'The Sun and the Moon,' or came to have eclipses, as in No. 4, 'The Fire Dogs'; they tell of the stars, as in No. 5, 'The Seven Stars of the North,' and No. 6, 'The Three Stars'; of mountains and rivers, as in No. 7, 'The Mountain and the River'; why the ant has such a slender waist, as in No. 16, 'The Ants and the Hare'; why the bedbug is so flat and the louse has a spot on his back, as in No. 20, 'The Bedbug, The Louse, and the Flea,' and so on.

In those myths and legends which tell of the foundation of kingdoms and dynasties, eggs often play an important part, and the heroes are born from them. Go Zu-Mong, the first King of Goguryŏ (in No. 2), was born from an egg, the founder of the Silla Dynasty was born from a big egg, and the heroes of Gara also came from eggs. Many Korean legends, fables, and old novels tell of the wisdom of magistrates, governors, and Royal Inspectors in solving legal problems. On the other hand they also often tell of their wickedness and cruelty which bring great suffering to the people (Nos. 13, 31, 55, 57, 59, 83). The Civil Examinations often figure in the tales, since they formed the first obstacle in the path of those who aimed at attaining high rank in the government or an honoured position in society (Nos. 30, 39, 56, 57, 60). Another noteworthy feature of the Korean legends is geomancy, which even now exerts an influence on the popular mind (Nos. 23, 24, 29, 59, 62). There are many love stories which show how social conditions prevented social contact between men and women, and other tales tell of the sorrows of women kept in strict seclusion from the outer world (Nos. 58, 86, 87, 88, 92, 93). The victims of the system are seen to form illicit associations contrary to the restrictions of the caste system (Nos. 28, 52, 63, 88, 98, 99). Many fables, full of irony and humour, reveal to us the delicate sensibility of Korean domestic life, in which charm is mingled with tears (78, 80, 82, 84, 89, 90, 95).

The typical Korean goblin called 'doggabi' very often appears in fairy tales. It usually takes pleasure in making people happy, but sometimes it brings trouble to men (Nos. 61, 64, 66, 67). Some people believe that the goblins are the spirits of good people who have died but for some reason have not been permitted to go to the world of the blessed, and so wander through this world. And the Korean believes that ghosts are the spirits of those unhappy men or of wicked men who have been refused entrance into the other world and are waiting for their release from this world.

As in the folk tales of other countries animals have the power to transform themselves into men. Dragons, tortoises, dogs, bears, deer, hares, carp, and toads are usually represented as good, and tigers, foxes, serpents, and centipedes as bad, although there are exceptions to this rule. The most typical animal is the tiger. Tigers must at one time have been very common in the mountains of Korea, and the tiger was commonly worshipped as the 'God of the Mountain', or the 'Lord of the Mountain' or the 'Sacred Spirit of the Mountain', because of its character, fierce, yet full of mystery. The tales of tigers can be divided into five categories: (1) the tales of its ferocity, as in No. 3, 'The Sun and the Moon,' No. 71, 'Four Sworn Brothers,' No. 78, 'The Ungrateful Tiger,' No. 44, 'The Tiger and the Dwarf,' etc.; (2) tales in which it expresses gratitude, as in No. 45, 'The Tiger's Grave,' No. 47, 'The White Eared Tiger,' etc.;

(3) Tales that tell of its marriage with men, as in No. 48, 'The Tiger Girl,' and others; (4) tales of its revengefulness, as in No. 46, 'Hong Doryŏng, the filial Tiger,' and others; (5) tales that depict the tiger as a rather innocent, humorous animal, as in No. 65 'The Three Sons,' No. 69, 'The Old Tiger and the Hare,' No. 70, 'The Young Gentleman and the Tiger,' No. 79, 'The Tiger and the Persimmon,' and others.

IV. FOLK-BELIEFS

In a description of the main characteristics of the folk tales of Korea it is essential that a survey of the folk-beliefs of the Korean people should be included. The folk tales can also be classified under the six religious currents in Korea, Shamanism, Buddhism, Confucianism, Taoism, Christianity, and Man-God religion.

Korean Shamanism, the typical form of which is called 'Balg', is one of the basic elements in Korean folk-lore. It is a form of nature-worship. The people of Korea attribute spirits to heavenly bodies and natural phenomena, such as the sun, moon and stars, the wind, clouds, rain, etc., and they also worship mountains, streams, caves, stones, animals, trees, and other things. It is indeed a form of pantheism, but they believe that above all these there stands a supreme ruler, called 'Hanŭnim'. This name is compounded of two words meaning 'Heaven' and 'master', i.e. 'Lord of Heaven,' who figures in such stories as No. 1, 'Dan-Gun, the First King of Korea.' The Korean people recognize him as the Celestial Emperor of the Heavenly Kingdom, who sends the sunlight and the rain, and strikes the wicked with lightning, or visits other punishments upon them, and rewards the good according to their merits, but they never worship him in the form of an actual idol. All other natural objects which are worshipped in personified forms are in the final analysis measured against this unrevealed higher standard of Hanŭnim.

Besides this Heavenly Kingdom and the human world there are three other regions, the Kingdom of Darkness that figures in No. 4, 'The Fire Dogs,' the Underworld in No. 72, 'The Nine-headed Giant,' and the Dragon-Kingdom under the Sea. The guiding principle on which men are to act is that good deeds will be rewarded and evil punished. After death the good men will become good spirits and admitted to live in the Heavenly Kingdom, while bad men will be evil spirits, condemned to suffer in the Kingdom of

Darkness or the Underworld. The Dragon Kingdom is conceived as a sort of underwater Utopia which men may sometimes have the good fortune to visit for a short time, as in No. 12, 'The Cat and the Dog,' or No. 73, 'The Mountain Witch and the Dragon-King.' The tenets which guided the Korean people in their daily lives and their domestic virtues were based on these ideas, and from the time of the first king, Dan-Gun, through the succeeding dynasties of the early period, the theme of political development was 'to spread righteousness among the people'. There were elements of democracy in the administration, although the kings wielded absolute power. Finally, it is worth noting that farming, which has been the basic industry of Korea for thousands of years, and the occupation of 80 per cent of the population, is closely bound up with Korean Shamanism. Shamanistic folk-beliefs have also been greatly influenced by chivalry, as in Nos. 32, 34, 35, 73, 97.

Buddhism was introduced into Korea in A.D. 372, and soon achieved widespread popularity, for it had some pantheistic features which could easily be reconciled with the shamanistic elements of Korean beliefs. The Buddhist idea that the present life has been determined by the past and the future is being determined by the present is commonly found in Korean folk-beliefs. Moreover the Government built many large temples throughout the country, and gave Buddhism an important national role as the principle of administration, and it became the mould of popular thought for about a thousand years. (See Nos. 27, 36, 37, 38.) The negative and pessimistic elements of Buddhism, which had prevailed in the years following its introduction were gradually replaced by an optimistic utilitarianism, as the faith became completely assimilated. Learned and virtuous priests exerted a powerful influence on the spiritual lives of men and women, and many a time outstanding men retired to temples in the mountains for their literary and military education, a custom which enters into some tales, e.g. Nos. 39, 40, 57.

Unfortunately, in later times Buddhism degenerated, owing to the luxury of temple life and the worldly ambitions of corrupt priests who meddled in politics. Under the Yi dynasty, which came to power in 1392, Buddhism was suppressed by the government, partly for political reasons, when they attempted to give a new impetus to the national spirit. As a result it ceased to exist as an influential religion. So we find that priests and monks in Korean

Introduction

folk-tales are often treated with disrespect and with great irony, as mentioned above. The tales called 'Three Stars' (No. 6), 'The Tiger Priest' (No. 49), and 'The Two Brothers and the Magistrate', (No. 55), will illustrate this point.

Subsequently the new government gave great encouragement to the development of Confucianism, and for four or five hundred years after the decline of Buddhism it was the dominant religion of Korea. It cannot, of course, be properly called a religion, as it does not prescribe the worship of any god, and human activities begin with birth and end with death. It did, however, exert a powerful influence on the standards of political and individual conduct, and Confucian principles are an important element in many tales. Many tales interpret its ethical principles, the basic motives of human life, the 'Five Principles of Conduct', loyalty to the King (Nos. 1, 7, 35), filial respect for one's parents (Nos. 5, 18, 25, 26, 46, 50, 82), harmony of husband and wife (Nos. 13, 23, 47, 54, 57, 63, 87, 96), respect for elders (Nos. 15, 17, 68, 84, 97), and true friendship (Nos. 35, 70, 71). Sometimes they are closely interwoven with Buddhist elements, whose imaginative character appeals to illiterate woman, and so has resulted in their preservation to the present day. Confucianism is, on the whole, deemed a man's religion, by reason of its learned background. The ideas of virtue, justice, etiquette, wisdom, and trust found their way into our political thought and popular customs relating to birth, marriage, death, funerals, festivals, and other ceremonies were formulated according to the classical standards of Confucianism, though in a modified Korean form.

Education and the Civil Examinations were standardized on rationalistic Confucian lines, and all unorthodox elements, whether of Buddhism or Taoism or anything else, were rejected. Society was dominated by the gentleman, or 'yangban', or the nobleman, whose privilege it was to receive the traditional training. The ordinary people, especially those who were born humble, were rigidly controlled by the caste system. It was easy for those who suffered injustice, or who were exiled for political or other reasons, to turn to a life of retirement in a Buddhist temple. There they might ease their feelings of pessimism, or long for the supernatural exultation of Taoism, or even plan adventures or revenge, as in No. 98, 'The Story of Hong Gil-Dong,' and No. 99, 'The Legend of Zŏn U-Czi.'

Taoism in Korea did not develop as a distinct religion and there was no period when it flourished under official protection, as Buddhism and Confucianism did. But certain elements of Taoism, such as geomancy, divination, diagrams, and prophecy, exerted an influence on Shamanism, Buddhism, and even Confucianism and the Man-God religion, and appear in many of our folk tales. (See Nos. 29, 30, 32, 33, 34, 35, 73, 98, 99.)

Christianity was introduced into Korea in 1653, and its ideals of love, humanity, and eternal life were a new experience for the people. When the new religion established churches, schools, and hospitals on the European pattern a large number of men and women turned to it. The traditional acceptance of many superstitions gradually died out among the believers, but the people in general still clung to the customs and manners they had known for generations. So Christian elements were not readily absorbed into popular folk tales, although it is possible that some stories of Christian miracles worked by Koreans may have been current among the native Christians. In other words, although in later times Christianity became the most influential religion among educated people it never produced folk tales of its own that could appeal to the Korean people in general.

Finally in 1860 Czoe Zĕ-U founded a reactionary religious movement, the 'Dong Hag', or 'Eastern Doctrine', whose avowed aim was to save the people from the danger of exploitation by the Western religion. In practice his doctrine combined the original ideas of Shamanistic belief with those of Confucianism, Buddhism, and Taoism, as its founder himself declared, and even some Christian elements. It might be described as a kind of potimistic fatalism. The basic idea of this religion is that the present world is the result of the past, and the world of the future will be created anew from the present. That is to say, the past ends with yesterday, and a new life will begin to-day, created by a new religion which will soon lead men to an ideal society. It does not aim at a life after death, but at a happy life in this world. The Saviour will come as the disciple of Heaven, the true absolute form of the Universe, and by His Salvation every man shall become a god in this world, and live in Paradise in this world. Czoe's followers insisted on the doctrine that 'Man is God'. On several occasions they fomented armed risings in various provinces to persecute Christians. They later formed an influential political and religious group to work for the independence of Korea against Japan, with the new title of Czŏndo Gyo, or Religion of the Way of Heaven, under the leadership of Son Byŏng-Hŭi. This religion produced some historical anecdotes which can be found in the history of Korea, rather than in the popular folk tales.

These five religions, Shamanism, Buddhism, Confucianism, Taoism, and the Man-God Doctrine have each given rise to a number of sects, each with its own individual title, in the same way as Christianity has produced sects. It is possible that they will in the future be the source of yet more popular folk tales. Moreover, the situation of Korea since the Second World War may give rise to folk tales, for example on the subject of the 38th Parallel, which could hardly happen in other countries. Already many stories of gallantry and suffering have been born of the conflict between South and North, a conflict brought about by the clash of world ideologies. As yet this new type of folk tale may not have become true popular folk tales, but I have no doubt that they will do so in time.

PART ONE
MYTHS

(BUYŎ)

MANCHURIA

(GOGURYŎ)

Amnog-gang (Yalu)

Dŏman

RUSSIA

Bĕgdu

Czŏnzi
(Yongdam)

XIII

Ŏdĕzin

Myŏngczŏn

XI

XII

Myohyang
(Tĕbĕg)

Zŏngpyŏng

Hamhŭng

Dĕdong

X

Zŏngpyŏng

Pyŏngyang

Guwŏl
(Asadal)

IX

Gumhwa

Gosŏng

Gŭmgang
(Diamond)   Eastern Sea

Gĕsŏng

Ganghwa

Yangzu

SEOUL

VIII

Yellow Sea

Suwŏn

Namyang

VII

Yŏngwŏl

II GYŎNGSANG BUG-DO
I GYŎNGSANG NAM-DO

Zinczŏn

Mungyŏng

V   VI

Andong

VII GYŎNGGI-DO
VI CZUNGCZŎNG BUG-DO
V CZUNGCZŎNG NAM-DO
IV ZŎLLA BUG-DO
III ZŎLLA NAM-DO

Buyŏ

Tĕzŏn

Sŏnsan

Ogczŏn

Gunwi

Unzin

Gŭmsan

II

Yŏngczŏn

Gŭmze

Zŏnzu

Dĕgu

Gyŏngzu

IV Zangsu

Hyŏbczŏn

Ŏnyang

Miryang

Ulsan

Yangsan

Gwangzu

Zinzu

I Gimhe

Gupo

III Guryĕ

Saczŏn

Masan

Busan

Nazu

Mogpo

Tongyŏng

Zanghŭng

KOREAN STRAIT

ZEZU

JAPAN

KYUSYU

XIII HAMGYŎNG BUG-DO
XII HAMGYŎNG NAM-DO
XI PYŎNG-AN BUG-DO
X PYŎNG-AN NAM-DO
IX HWANGHĔ-DO
VIII GANGWŎN-DO

KOREAN MAP OF TALES

I

Dan-Gun, First King of Korea

THERE was once a wise and brave Prince, Hwan-Ung by name, son of the Heavenly King. The Prince asked his father to grant him the Beautiful Peninsula of Korea to govern. The King granted his wish, and he was dispatched to the Earth, bearing three Heavenly Seals, and accompanied by three thousand followers.

The Heavenly Prince arrived under the sacred sandalwood tree on the Tĕbĕg Mountains, and ascended the throne. There he established the Sacred City. There were three ministers to carry out his orders, Pung-Bĕg (Earl Wind), U-Sa (Chancellor Rain), and Un-Sa (Chancellor Cloud), who were charged with the supervision of about three hundred and sixty officials, who controlled all things, such as grain, life, sickness, the determination of good and evil.

At that time a bear and a tiger were living in a big cave near the sandalwood tree. They wished ardently that they could become human beings. Every day they prayed so earnestly before the tree that the Heavenly Prince, who was now the ruler of the land, was moved by their sincerity, and, giving them twenty bulbs of garlic and a bundle of mugwort, he said to them, 'Eat these, and confine yourselves deep in your cave for one hundred days, and then you will become human.'

So the bear and the tiger took the garlic and the mugwort and went into their cave. They prayed earnestly that their wish might be granted. The bear patiently endured weariness and hunger, and after twenty-one days became a beautiful woman, but the tiger ran away, for it could not tolerate long days sitting quietly in the cave.

The woman was overjoyed, and visiting the sandalwood again

3

she prayed that she might become the mother of a child. Her ardent wish was appreciated, and before long she became Queen, and gave birth to a prince, who was given the royal name Dan-Gun, or the Sandalwood King.

The people of the country rejoiced at the birth of the prince, Dan-Gun, who reigned afterwards as the first human king of the peninsula. When he came to the throne he established a new capital at Pyŏngyang, and gave the kingdom the name of Zosŏn (Chosŏn—Land of Morning Calm). This was four thousand two hundred and eighty-three years ago. As the King's real name was Wang-Gŭm, the capital was also known as the Castle of Wang-Gŭm.

He later removed the capital to Mount Asadal (now Mt. Guwŏl in Hwang-Hě Province), where there is now a shrine called Sam-sŏng (Three Saints, Hwan-In, the Heavenly King, Hwan-Ung, the Heavenly Prince, and Dan-Gun, the first human King). It is said that when Dan-Gun abdicated and left his throne to the next king he became a San-sin (Mountain God).

In the Tĕbĕg Mountains, now called Myohyang-San, where the Heavenly Prince descended and the first King was born, there is even to this day a cave, known as the cave of Dan-Gun. There are historical relics of Dan-Gun on Mt. Mai, in Island Ganghwa, near Seoul, also.

From *Samgug Yusa* and *Ondoru Yawa*.

2

Go Zu-Mong, King of Goguryŏ

IN ancient times there was a kingdom called Buyŏ whose territory included the Korean peninsula and the whole of Manchuria. The King of this land, Hĕburu, by name, though he had reached an advanced age, was yet without an heir. He therefore prayed constantly to the gods of the mountains and rivers that he might be granted a son. He was out riding one day, and when he came to a pool called Gonyŏn, his horse stopped, and neighed mournfully at a big stone. He ordered his attendant to turn the stone over, when,

Go Zu-Mong, King of Goguryŏ

lo and behold, there appeared beneath it a little boy in the form of a golden frog. The King was overjoyed to find the boy, and, thinking that he must be a gift from a god, he adopted him as Prince. And he called him Gŭm-Wa (Golden Frog).

One day one of the King's ministers, Aranbul by name, came to the King and told him that a god had appeared to him in a dream and advised him that they should move to a more fertile land, called Gayŏbwŏn, near the Eastern Sea. So the King moved his kingdom thither, and renamed it Dong-Buyŏ (East Buyŏ). And after his death the Prince, Gŭm-Wa, succeeded him, but in his former territory a pretender called Hĕmosu took the throne, claiming that he was of divine ancestry.

One day the new King was travelling in the land of Ubalsu, south of Mount Tĕbĕg, when he happened to meet a woman, by name Yuhwa, daughter of Habĕg (Lord of the River). The King asked her about herself, and she answered, 'I once met a man called Hĕmosu. He said he was the son of a god. We stayed one night together in a house by the Yalu River, near Mount Ungsim, but after that he never came back. And for this illicit liaison my parents cast me out.'

On hearing her story the King was deeply moved, and he took her and confined her in a room. Sunbeams came streaming in towards her. Though she tried to avoid them she could not, they still fell directly upon her. She soon became pregnant, and in the end she gave birth to an enormous egg, as big as five *dwoe* (a unit of dry measure).

The King was most displeased by the birth of an egg, and threw it to the dogs and the pigs, but they would not eat it. He cast it out on the streets, but the cows and horses avoided it. He had it taken out into the fields, but the birds tended it under their wings. So he took it back and tried to break it, but it was not to be broken, and so finally he returned it to the mother. She wrapped it in soft cloth and placed it in a warm part of the room. Before long it hatched, and a boy was born from it. He appeared from birth to be very strong and healthy. His mother was very happy, and tended him with great care.

When the boy was six years old he could already shoot with the bow, and soon became so skilful that he outstripped all rivals. He was thereupon given the name of Zu-Mong, because from the earliest times the champion archer had been called so.

5

The King had seven sons. The eldest, Děso, was jealous of Zu-Mong, and said to his father, 'Zu-Mong was born from an egg. I think he is a dangerous character. I advise you to get rid of him at once, for if you do not he may sow seeds of trouble.' But the King ignored this suggestion, and appointed Zu-Mong to the care of his horses. Zu-Mong fed the better horse sparingly, in order that it might become thin and weak, and on the other hand he fed the other lavishly that it might become fat and appear to be strong. This he did because he already suspected the malice of others toward himself, and wished to be prepared for what might happen in the future.

One day the King decided to go hunting, and, riding the fat horse himself, bade Zu-Mong ride the thin one. In the field the King was hindered in his hunting by the slowness of his horse, whereas Zu-Mong was most successful even with the poor bow and arrows that he had, since the horse he rode was really the better one.

Now the King was anxious about possible dangers, and, influenced by the malicious designs of the Princes and his ministers, was inclined to have Zu-Mong killed. His mother Yuhwa guessed this evil intention, and earnestly advised her son to escape. He fled with three followers, Zoi, Mari, and Hyŏbbu, and came to the river Ŏmczesu. But there was no bridge, and they were hotly pursued by the King's men. So Zu-Mong prayed to the River God, 'I am the son of a god, and of the daughter of Haběg. I am beset by the gravest of dangers. Save me, oh, please save me!'

Then marvellous to relate, there came swimming in the river a great crowd of fish and tortoises, and they formed a bridge with their backs. So they crossed the river with ease, but their pursuers could not follow, for the fish and tortoises immediately swam away.

Zu-Mong and his followers went on their way and came to the valley of Modun, where they met three wise men, Zěsa, Mugol, and Muggŏ. He asked them to assist him in founding a new kingdom. The three wise men agreed and followed him, and he bestowed on them the family names of Gǔgsi, Zungsil, and Sosil respectively.

So Zu-Mong went to Zolbonczŏn with his three followers and the three wise men, and founded a new capital there, for it was a fertile spot, surrounded by steep mountains and traversed by a beautiful river. Until such time as he might be able to build himself a palace he built temporary dwellings of thatched houses on the banks of the

The Heavenly Hostess and Host (p. 7)

Dog (pp. 11, 25, 92, 93)

Cock (p. 21)
Butterflies (p. 39)

Deer (pp. 21, 33, 94)

Hares (pp. 33, 157)
Turtle (p.77)

A Woman Being Kidnapped (p. 29)

Bullyu River. His kingdom he called Goguryŏ, and took as his family name the first syllable Go.

Thus Go Zu-Mong became the first king of Goguryŏ, two thousand three hundred and two years ago.

From Samgug Sagi, Vol. 13.

3

The Sun and the Moon

LONG, long ago there lived an old woman who had two children, a son and a daughter. One day she went to a neighbouring village to work in a rich man's house. When she left to come back home, she was given a big wooden box containing buckwheat puddings. She carried it on her head, and hastened back to her waiting children. But on the way, as she passed a hill, she met a big tiger.

The tiger blocked her path, and opening its great red mouth asked, 'Old woman, old woman! What is that you are carrying on your head?' The old woman replied fearlessly, 'Do you mean this, Tiger? It is a box of buckwheat puddings that I was given at the rich man's house where I worked to-day.' Then the tiger said, 'Old woman, give me one. If you don't, I will eat you up.' So she gave the tiger a buckwheat pudding, and it let her pass the hill.

When she came to the next hill the tiger appeared before her and asked her the same question, 'Old woman, old woman, what have you got in that box you are carrying on your head?' And, thinking it was another tiger, she gave the same answer, 'These are buckwheat puddings I was given at the rich man's house where I worked to-day.' The tiger asked for one in the same way. And the old woman gave it a pudding from her box, and it went off into the forest.

The tiger then appeared several more times and made the same demand, and each time she gave it a pudding, until there were no more left in the box. So now she carried the empty box on her head, and she walked along swinging her arms at her sides. Then the tiger appeared again, and demanded a pudding. She explained that she had none left, saying, 'Your friends ate all my buckwheat puddings. There is nothing at all left in my box.' Thereupon she threw the box

7

away. Then the tiger said, 'What are those things swinging at your sides?' 'This is my left arm, and this is my right arm,' she replied. 'Unless you give me one of them, I will eat you up,' roared the tiger. So she gave it one of her arms, and it walked off with it. But not long afterwards it appeared in front of her again, and repeated its threats. So she gave it her other arm.

Now the old woman had lost all her puddings, her box, and even both her arms, but she still walked along the mountain road on her two legs. The greedy tiger barred her way once more and asked, 'What is that, moving under your body?' She answered, 'My legs, of course.' The tiger then said, in a rather strange tone, 'Oh, in that case, give me one of your legs, or I will eat you up.' The old woman got very angry, and complained, 'You greedy animal! Your friends ate all my puddings, and both my arms as well. Now you want my legs. However will I be able to get back to my home?' But the tiger would not listen to her, and persisted in its demand. 'If you give me your left leg, you can still hop on your right leg, can't you?' So she had to take off her left leg, and throw it to the tiger, and then she set off homewards, hopping on her other leg. The tiger ran ahead of her, and barred her way again. 'Old woman, old woman! Why are you hopping like that?' it asked. She shouted furiously, 'You devil! You ate all my puddings, both my arms, and one of my legs. However can I go home if I lose my right leg too?' The tiger answered, 'You can roll, can't you?' So she cut off her right leg, and gave it to the tiger. She set out to roll over and over along the road. Then the tiger rushed after her, and swallowed what was left of her in a single gulp.

Back at the old woman's home her two children waited till nightfall for her to return. Then they went inside and locked the door, and lay down hungry on the floor, for they did not know that a tiger had eaten their mother on her way home.

The cunning tiger dressed in the old woman's clothes, and put a white handkerchief on its head. Then, standing erect on its hind legs, it walked to the old woman's house and knocked at the door. It called to the two children, 'My dears, you must be very hungry. Open the door. I have brought you some buckwheat puddings.' But the children remembered the advice their mother had given them when she went out in the morning, 'There are tigers about. Be very careful.' They noticed that the voice sounded rather strange, and so they did not open the door, and said, 'Mother, your voice sounds rather strange. What has happened to you?' So the tiger disguised its voice and said, 'Don't be alarmed. Mother is back. I have spent the day spreading barley to dry on mats, and the sparrows kept flying down to eat it, so that I had to shout loudly at them all day long to drive them away. So I have got rather hoarse.' The children were not convinced, and asked again, 'Then, Mother, please put your arm in through the hole in the door, and let us see it.' The tiger put one of its forepaws in the hole in the door. The children touched it and said, 'Mother, why is your arm so rough and hairy?' So the tiger explained, 'I was washing clothes, and I starched them with rice paste. That must have made my arm rough.' But the children peeped out through the hole in the door, and were surprised to see a tiger there in the darkness. So they slipped quietly out the back door, and climbed a tall tree and hid among the branches.

The tiger waited for a while, but as it got no further reply from inside, it broke into the house, and searched in vain for the children. It came out in a furious temper, and rushed round the house with terrible roars, till it came to an old well underneath the tree. It looked down at the water, and there saw the reflections of the two children. So it forced a smile and tried to scoop up the reflections, and said in a gentle voice, 'Oh, my poor children. You have fallen into the well. I haven't got a bamboo basket, or even a grass one. How can I save you?' The children watched the tiger's antics from above, and could not help bursting out laughing. Hearing their laughter it looked up, and saw them high in the tree. It asked in a kindly voice, 'How did you get up there? That's very dangerous. You might fall into the well. I must get you down. Tell me how you got up so high.' The children replied, 'Go to the neighbours and get some sesame oil. Smear it on the trunk and climb up.'

So the stupid tiger went to the house next door and got some sesame oil and smeared it thickly on the trunk and tried to climb up. But of course the oil made the tree very slippery. So the tiger asked again, 'My dear children. You are very clever, aren't you? However did you get up there so easily, right to the top? Tell me the truth.' This time they answered innocently, 'Go and borrow an axe from the neighbours. Then you can cut footholds on the trunk. 'So the tiger went and borrowed an axe from the house next door, and, cutting steps in the tree, began to climb up.

9

The children now thought that they would not be able to escape from the tiger, and in great terror prayed to the God of Heaven. 'Oh God, please save us. If you are willing, please send us the Heavenly Iron Chain. But if you mean us to die, send down the Rotten Straw Rope!' At once a strong Iron Chain came gently down from Heaven to them, so that they could climb up without difficulty.

When the tiger reached the top of the tree the children were gone. It wanted to follow them, so it too began to pray, but in opposite terms, because it was very afraid that it might be punished for its misdeeds. 'Oh God of Heaven, if you would save me, send down the Rotten Straw Rope, I beg of you. But if you mean me to die, please send down the Heavenly Iron Chain.' By praying in this way, it hoped that the Iron Chain would come down, and not the Straw Rope, for it expected that as a punishment it would receive the opposite of what it had prayed for. But the gods are straightforward, and always willing to save lives by answering prayers directly, and so it was the Rotten Straw Rope that came down after all. The tiger seized the rope, and began to climb up it, for in the darkness it could not see that it was not the chain. When it got a little way up the rope broke, and so it fell down to the ground. It crashed down in a field of broom-corn, where it died crushed and broken, its body pierced through by the sharp stems of the corn. From that day, it is said, the leaves of broom-corn have been covered with blood red spots.

The two children lived peacefully in the Heavenly Kingdom, until one day the Heavenly King said to them, 'We do not allow anyone to sit here and idle away the time. So I have decided on duties for you. The boy shall be the Sun, to light the world of men, and the girl shall be the moon, to shine by night.' Then the girl answered, 'Oh King, I am not familiar with the night. It would be better for me not to be the moon.' So the King made her the Sun instead, and made her brother the moon.

It is said that when she became the Sun people used to gaze up at her in the sky. But she was a modest girl, and greatly embarrassed by this. So she shone brighter and brighter, so that it was impossible to look at her directly. And that is why the sun is so bright, that her womanly modesty might be for ever respected.

Ondoru Yawa, told by O Hwa-Su ; Ŏnyang (1911).

4

The Fire Dogs

THERE are many countries in Heaven, just as there are in the world below. One of them is called Gamag Nara, the Land of Darkness, and its inhabitants keep many horrible dogs. They are known as Fire Dogs. The King of that land is greatly concerned before all else that his realm is so dark. So from time to time he sends his dogs to the world of men to try to steal the Sun or the Moon.

Once upon a time the King summoned the fiercest of his Fire Dogs and ordered it to go and steal the Sun and bring it to him. So the Fire Dog went off, and tried to seize the Sun in its mouth, but it was too hot. It snapped at it again and again, but in the end it had to give up, and returned without its prey. The King was very angry, and reprimanded the dog severely for its failure. Then he turned to the next fiercest dog, and sent it to try to steal the Moon, for he thought that it might not be so hot as the Sun. The Moon would not give him as much light as the Sun of course, but he thought it would be better than nothing. But when the dog tried to bite the Moon, it was so cold that it froze its mouth. It tried repeatedly to grasp it with its teeth, but in the end was obliged to spit it out. And so the second Fire Dog too had to return without the prize.

Despite these failures the King of the Land of Darkness never gave up hope, and to this day he often sends out his Fire Dogs, but they always fail in the end.

It is said that eclipses of the Sun and Moon are caused in this way by Fire Dogs from the Land of Darkness. It is the parts of the Sun or Moon that they bite which show dark during an eclipse.

We cannot watch an eclipse of the sun directly because it is so dazzlingly bright, but it can easily be seen in the reflection of the sun in a basin of water in which a little black ink has been dissolved. An eclipse of the moon can also be watched in the same way. We can easily see on the inky surface of the water the Fire Dog biting the sun and then spitting it out again.

Told by Zŏng Tĕg-Ha ; Ŏnyang (1912).

11

5

The Seven Stars of the North

ONCE upon a time there lived a widow, who had seven most filial sons. Every winter they used to cut wood in the mountains so that they could keep a fire burning constantly under the floor of their house and make it warm enough for their aged mother to sleep warm at night. But she always looked very cold and sad. However much wood they burnt, she always felt the cold. In fact, she always complained of the cold, even in the hottest midsummer months.

One night the eldest son woke up, and saw that his mother was not in the room. He waited in great anxiety for her to return, though he pretended to be asleep. Just before dawn she came creeping stealthily back, so that her sons should not notice her.

When she went out the next night her eldest son followed her secretly. When she reached a stream on the outskirts of the village she girded up her skirts and waded across, muttering to herself, 'Oh, how cold it is,'—for it was winter—and went to a poor thatched cottage on the other side. She stood before the house and called, 'Father, are you at home?' An old man came out and welcomed her, saying, 'Come in, Mother.' He was a poor widower who earned a living by weaving straw sandals.

The eldest son now understood what was in his mother's heart. So he hurried home and woke his brothers, and told them what he had seen. Then they all went out together and set stepping stones in the stream. They went back home and slept as if nothing had happened.

When their mother came to the stream on her way home she was very surprised to see the stepping stones which had not been there before. Of course she did not know that her sons had put them there. She was deeply grateful to whoever had set them in the stream, and prayed to Heaven, 'May those who put these stepping stones in the stream become the Seven Stars of the North.'

So when the seven filial sons died they were set in Heaven as the Seven Stars of the North, just as their mother had prayed. And they formed the constellation that is known in the West as the Great Bear.   Told by Son Zin-Tĕ; Gupo (1926).

12

6

The Three Stars

LONG ago there lived a rich man who had one daughter. One year
he went up to the capital to take a Government post, and left his
daughter in charge of the house in his absence.

One day a Buddhist monk came begging alms. The daughter told
the maid to give him a little rice. But the monk asked her to fill the
bowl right up, and so she told the maid to do so. Yet however much
she put into the bowl it could not be filled. She fetched all the rice
from the storeroom, and even unhulled rice and millet, and yet the
bowl could not be filled. The maid was very puzzled, and she
asked, 'How can it be filled?' The monk answered, 'If the daughter
of the house comes and tries herself, she will be able to fill it without
difficulty.' So the daughter of the house came to the monk and tried
to fill the bowl, but even she could not fill it completely. Then the
monk said, 'If you pick up each grain separately nine times with
silver chopsticks you will fill it.' So she did as he suggested, but still
without success. 'If you take off your undergarments in a pit, and
then try, you will succeed,' said the monk. So she did so, but even
so the bowl was not filled.

Meanwhile the sun had set, and the monk earnestly begged her to
give him lodging for one night. She refused his request, with the
excuse that there was no guest room in the house, but he still
persisted in his request, and would not leave the house. He said that
he would be satisfied to sleep in the stable, and this she allowed him
to do. About midnight he came and said, 'It is too cold in the stable,
will you not let me sleep in the corner of the kitchen?' She took pity
on him, and let him move into the kitchen. But a little later he came
and said, 'I cannot stand the cold here either, let me come and sleep
in the annexe of your room.' This too she allowed him to do. Very
soon, however, he came and said, 'It is too cold here too. Please let
me sleep behind the screen in your room.' Even this she allowed him
to do. And so it came about that the monk slept in the same room.

When she awoke next morning the monk had gone. On her
father's return, some time later, all the servants went out to welcome
him, but she could not go, for she was with child. On hearing this

13

her father was very angry, and dètermined to kill her. She was taken into the garden and bound, and a servant was ordered to cut off her head. But when he lifted the axe, the handle broke in two, and it fell behind him. He took a sword, and tried to kill her with that, but when he flourished it over her head the blade snapped in half. Her father then had an underground cell made, and she was cast into it. He kept the key himself, and gave orders that no food should be taken to her, so that she might starve to death.

From that time the monk appeared in the underground cell every night. No one knew whence he came, or how he was able to get into the cell. He took food to the girl, and in due course she gave birth to triplets.

Some years later her father ordered the cell to be opened. He expected he would find only a skeleton. Great was his amazement to find his daughter alive, with three children sitting reading beside her. So he asked her how it had come about and she told him the whole story. So he sent for the monk, and when he came he asked him 'Are these three children yours?' 'Yes,' replied the monk, 'and I will prove it.' He lifted up the sleeve of his robe. 'If these three children pass through my sleeve without touching it, that will prove that they are indeed my sons.' Then the children passed through his sleeve without touching it. The monk said again, 'Let them put on wooden sandals and walk on white sand. They will leave no trace whatever on the sand.' This they did, and walked on sand without marking it. So the truth was proved, and the father recognized the marriage of the monk with his daughter. And the monk was seen to be a miracle-working Buddhist.

When they died his three children were set in Heaven as the three stars of the constellation Vega. They rise in a vertical line, and set in a horizontal line, just as the children were born one after the other downwards from the womb, and were buried in three graves side by side.   Told by Son Zin-Tĕ; Gupo (1926).

7

The Mountain and the Rivers

LONG, long ago, when food ripened on the Food Tree, and clothes ripened on the Clothes Tree, there lived a giant. He was so big that even his ears were six hundred feet long. He could not wear clothes, because there was not cloth enough in the whole land to cover his body. So he went almost naked the whole year long, and in winter he suffered bitterly from the cold weather.

The King in those days—it was, of course, even before the time of Dan-Gun—was very sorry indeed for the poor giant, and had as much cloth as could be found collected from all the provinces, and ordered all the tailors to make a robe for him. After many months they finished the robe, but even so it was too short. Nothing more could be done as there was no more cloth, and so it was bestowed upon the giant as a gift from the King.

The giant gladly put on the robe, and danced for joy on the lofty mountain pass of Sĕzĕ. Suddenly the whole land was darkened, for as he danced his robe cut off the sunbeams. All the crops failed in the darkness, and the people appealed to the King to send the giant away. The King was very angry, and ordered his army to expel the giant beyond the borders of the land. A party of the mightiest warriors set out to carry the royal message to him. When they reached the summit of the mountain pass where he was standing they all shouted together in a loud voice, but the giant could not hear them, his ears were so far from his feet. So they climbed up his legs, and after many months they reached his navel. Once more they shouted, 'HO, GIANT! Your robe cuts off the sunlight, and the crops do not ripen. His Majesty has ordered that you be expelled beyond the borders of the land.'

So the giant was driven out into the barren fields of Manchuria. Soon he became very hungry and thirsty, and ate the soil of the fields, and drank the water of the sea. Then his stomach began to roar like a mighty flood, and instantly his bowels were loosened. And his excrement became a range of mountains, the highest mountain in Korea, Bĕgdu-San (White Head Mountain). And when he made water two mighty channels were cut, one before him, and one behind. These are the two greatest rivers of the northern frontier of Korea. One is the Amnog-Gang (Yalu River), the longest river in Korea, and the other great river is the Duman-Gang (Tumun River). There is a great lake on top of the mountain where both these rivers rise, called Czŏnzi (Heaven Lake) or Yong-Dam (Dragon Pool). This lake was formed by the giant making water there.

Ondoru Yawa, told by Bang Zŏng-Hwan ; Seoul (1925).

15

8

The Great Flood

ONCE upon a time there stood a big laurel tree. A fairy often used to come down from Heaven and rest there. She bore a son, whose father was the tree, and when he was seven years old she went up again to Heaven.

One day there was a great storm, and the rain continued for many months, so that the whole Earth was flooded as if by a raging sea. The flood even began to drown the great laurel. So the tree said to its son, 'My boy, you are my son. I am afraid I shall fall, so then you must ride on my back. In that way only can you be saved.' Soon afterwards the tree was uprooted by the waves, so the boy climbed on to the back of his father the tree, and the tree remained floating on the water for many days.

One day a great crowd of ants came drifting by. They shouted, 'Oh, Son of the Tree! Save us, please save us!' So the Son of the Tree asked his father, 'Father, may I save them?' And the tree replied, 'Indeed you may.' The son called to them, 'Get on to the tree.' So the ants gladly climbed on to the branches and leaves of the laurel. Then a group of mosquitoes came past, and wearied with much flying, appealed to the boy, 'Oh, Son of the Tree! Please save us, we implore you!' So the Son of the Tree asked his father if he might save them. It gave its consent, and the mosquitoes alighted on the branches of the tree. Then a boy of his own age, who was floating on the water, shouted, 'Oh, my friend! Save me, please save me!' So the son asked his father the tree for permission to help the boy, but the tree said, 'No!' The boy shouted desperately in his distress, and the son asked his father again, but the answer was the same. Now the boy was screaming for help, for he was near to drowning, so the son asked his father a third time, 'Father, do let me save the boy.' This time the tree replied, 'Do as you like,' and so the son shouted to the poor boy, 'Get on to this tree!' And so the boy was saved too.

At last the great laurel tree, carrying the two boys, the ants and the mosquitoes, came to an island. It was the summit of a lofty mountain, as high as Mt. Bĕgdu. The ants and the mosquitoes then

16

went away, after bidding farewell to the boy, and expressing their gratitude, 'Thank you, Son of the Tree. You saved our lives, and we are deeply indebted to you. Good-bye!'

The two boys, who were very hungry, went and found a house, where there lived an old woman and her two daughters. One of them was her own daughter, and the other a foster-child. She received the two boys kindly, and gave them work in the farmyard. There was no one else left alive, as all the other people had been drowned in the flood.

Now the rain stopped, the waters subsided, and they started farming again. The old woman thought it would be advisable to arrange marriages between the young people, and decided to match her own daughter with the cleverer boy, and her foster-daughter with the other.

The second boy detected the old woman's plan, and decided to take advantage of his opportunity. He said to the old woman maliciously, 'The Son of the Tree is a most unusually clever boy. Though you scatter a great bag of millet grains on the sand he can pick it all up within half an hour. Let him try it, and you will see for yourself.'

So to test his skill the old woman scattered a great bag of millet on the sand, and bade the son of the tree collect it again. He refused at first, but she repeated her demand, and in the end he had to agree. He tried to pick the grains up one by one, but he was so slow that it seemed unlikely that he could finish in half a year to say nothing of half a day. So with his head bowed in despair he wondered miserably what he could do.

Then he felt something biting his heel. It was a big ant, and it said to him, 'I am one of the ants you saved from the flood. Why are you so sad?' The boy told it what a difficult task he had been set, and then the ant brought thousands of its friends and picked up all the grains, so that the bag was filled in a few minutes. But the other boy was jealous, and watched the scene from a distance. He went and told the old woman that the task had not been done by the Son of the Tree himself.

So the old woman could not decide which of the boys she favoured, and said to them, 'I love both of you equally, and so I cannot decide which of you should marry my daughter, and which my foster-daughter. Now I have a plan. You shall choose your own destiny. There will be no moon to-night, for it is the last day of the

17

month. You must go and wait outside the gate in the dark, and I will put one of the girls in the east room and one in the west room. Then I shall call you, and you may enter whichever of the rooms you may choose. Thus you shall make your own choice, and you will not be able to complain at the result.'

After supper the two boys went and waited outside. After a while the old woman called them to come in. In the summer night the Son of the Tree stood wondering which room he should enter. Just then he heard a big mosquito flying near his head. It came and whispered in his ear, 'Son of the Tree! Go to the east room, the east room!' So he went to the east room, and there he found the old woman's beautiful daughter. And the other boy found her foster-daughter in the west room.

It is said that these two couples had many children, and that they are the ancestors of the whole human race to-day.

Told by Gim Gi-Tĕg; Tong-Yŏng (1913).

9
The Jewel of the Fox's Tongue

THERE was a big school in a country village long ago. There were a hundred pupils at this school, and they used to study at night, reading aloud at the top of their voices. Sometimes, when it was too late for them to go to their homes, they used to sleep together in a big room.

Late one night they were all sleeping soundly, except the youngest boy, who was just seven years old. He heard strange footsteps outside, and pricked up his ears. Amid the loud snores of his friends he could hear faintly, yet clearly, the voice of a woman counting the shoes outside—one, two, three, four . . . and so on up to one hundred pairs. Then a beautiful girl quietly opened the window and crept stealthily into the room. The youngest boy was very frightened, and crept silently to the furthest corner of the room. He saw the girl begin to count the pupils, starting from the doorway. She kissed each of them on the lips, and then, strange to say, each of them stopped breathing and died as soon as she kissed him. When she came near the corner where the youngest boy was hiding he crept over to the opposite corner to escape from her, and there found his friends lying stiff and cold. He lay down among the dead bodies trembling with fear and utterly horror-struck.

When she reached the end the girl turned and sighed, 'Only ninety-nine! There is one missing. It is very strange.' So she went outside and began to count the shoes again, one, two, three, four . . . up to one hundred pairs. She counted them several times, from the right and from the left, so as to make absolutely certain. 'There are exactly one hundred pairs of shoes. Let me count the boys in the room again.' So she came in and counted them again, and still found only ninety-nine, for the youngest boy succeeded in avoiding her again. In the end she gave up, and said with a sigh, 'If only I could find one more, it would make one hundred, and I could go up to Heaven. But they are one short. Whatever shall I do?' Then suddenly a cock crowed. 'Oh, I must be going,' she cried, and rushed out of the room into the fields.

The youngest boy was very brave, despite his tender years, and he followed her to see where she would go. She hastened to the graveyard on the mountain near the village, and disappeared behind a large rock. The boy turned back towards the village, when suddenly the girl appeared in front of him again, and taking him by the hand, led him back to the rock. She seemed very glad to meet him, and taking him on her knee, patted him on the shoulder in a very friendly fashion. He sat and looked at her, wondering who she could be. Her clothes were not very neat or clean, but she was very pretty. 'Who are you?' he asked, but she smiled and made no reply. Then she embraced him and tried to kiss him on the lips. But he had realised that she could not be a real woman, but rather perhaps a goblin or a fox. He thought of his friends who had died of her kiss, and tried to keep her from kissing him, but in vain. Then she rolled a jewel from her mouth to his, and sucked it back. She did this again and again, rolling the jewel from her mouth to his and back again, until his face gradually became pale and wan. She was absorbing human energy from him.

Suddenly the boy remembered an old belief. 'If a man swallows the jewel which a fox always carries on her tongue, then if, before it dissolves, he looks up at the sky, he will possess all the wisdom of Heaven, and if he looks down on the ground he will possess all the wisdom of the Earth.' So a plan formed in his mind, and when the jewel rolled into his mouth, he swallowed it and slipped down on to the ground. He meant first to look up at the sky, and then down at the ground, but the frightened girl pulled his chin down to try and get her jewel back, and so he was forced to look only at the ground.

Then the boy shouted at the top of his voice to attract the attention of any of the villagers who might be passing. The girl disappeared immediately. It was still dark, though the dawn was near. There was no answer and no one came. He fell down in a faint, and lay there unconscious for some time.

When he got home in the morning his parents were greatly surprised to hear his story. The other ninety-nine boys were lying dead, but their parents did not believe his explanation of their fate. So he decided to catch the fox that lived in the mountain graveyard, for now he knew all the wisdom of the Earth.

All the villagers followed him with spears and arrows. They surrounded the graveyard, and searched it with great care. The boy told them to examine the rock where he had come during the night. Suddenly a fox with nine long tails, and dressed in woman's clothes, ran out of the cave beneath the rock. They killed it on the spot. In the cave they found a large pile of women's clothes. There were tunnels running underground into the graveyard, so that the fox had been able to go and eat the bodies in the graves. It had taken the beautiful dresses from the women so that it could disguise itself as a pretty girl.

From that day men have possessed the wisdom of the Earth, but not the wisdom of Heaven.

Ondoru Yawa, told by Zŏng Yŏng-Ha ; Ŏnyang (1913).

10

Onions

IN the very earliest days of human history there was a time when men used to eat one another. This was because in those days men often appeared in the form of cattle, and so were slaughtered for food.

At last a certain man set out in quest of a better world. In his wanderings he met a leper, who asked him the reason for his journey. He answered 'This world is horrible and I hate it, for men eat one another. I am on my way to seek a better world, where men may not do such evil things.' To this the leper replied, 'Your quest will be in vain, for wherever you may go you will find that men everywhere behave in the same way. So I would advise you to go back to your native place.' Then the wanderer replied, 'I cannot go back now, for if I do they will assuredly kill me. Whatever shall I do?' The leper said, 'My advice to you is that you should eat onions. Any man who does so will thereafter appear in human form, even though he has previously appeared in the form of an ox.'

So then the traveller hastened homewards. As he drew near his home he met some of his friends, and greeted them cheerfully, 'Hullo, how do you do? I haven't seen you for some time.' Thereupon the others said, 'The lowing of this ox is most remarkable,' and instantly they seized him. He was greatly alarmed, and said, 'No! I am not an ox. I am your friend, and my name is . . .' But the others did not understand what he was saying, and said to one another, 'This ox is bellowing too much. Isn't he making a din? We had better kill him at once.' With these words they tied him to a post.

Just then it happened that a young girl passed by, carrying a basket full of onions on her head. With a great effort he managed to snatch one and swallow it. When he had eaten it all he immediately changed into human form. The others were astonished, and said, 'What, so it is you, our dear friend. We are very sorry indeed. We did not realize it was you.'

So then he told them all about the miraculous powers of onions, and advised them to eat them. From that day men began to eat onions, and thereafter always appeared in human form. And it is said that the cultivation of onions was encouraged in order that men might not eat one another any more.

Told by Zŏng Yŏng-Ha ; Ŏnyang (1915).

II

The Heavenly Maiden and the Wood Cutter

ONCE upon a time there lived a young man whose home was in northern Gangwŏn Province, near the foot of the Diamond Mountain. He was very poor indeed, and in order to live he used to go every day to the mountain to cut firewood and sell it to the neighbours. All the other young men of his age were married, but he was so poor that he could not find a bride. He was an honest and conscientious young man, who worked very hard and never complained of his hard lot. The villagers used to say, 'Even though the sun may not appear there is never a day when the sound of his axe is not heard on the mountain.'

One day when he was cutting firewood on the mountain as usual he heard something running towards him over the fallen leaves. This was most unusual, and he stopped work for a moment. He saw a terrified young deer running towards him. When it reached him it implored him earnestly to help it, for it was in great danger. He was touched, and immediately hid it under the pile of firewood he had cut. Then he went back to work as if nothing had happened.

Almost at once a hunter came panting towards him, and said to him, 'My man! I have been chasing a deer, and it ran up here somewhere. Have you seen it?' The burly hunter stood in front of the woodcutter, with his bow and arrows in his hands. He was familiar enough with the mountain paths, but among the trees and on the steep slopes he moved only with difficulty. So the woodcutter looked at him and said, 'Yes, I did see it. It came running past and went off down the valley over there. I couldn't say where it went after that.' So the hunter rushed back down the mountain without delay.

Then the young deer came out from under the pile of wood where it had been hiding, not daring to breathe, and thanked the woodcutter for his kindness. Weeping in its gratitude it said to him, 'You saved my life from deadly peril, and I am most deeply grateful to you. To repay your kindness I will tell you something that will bring you great success and happiness. Go up the Diamond Mountain to-morrow afternoon before two o'clock and when you come to the lakes that lie between the peaks at the foot of the rainbow there conceal yourself among the bushes by the water's edge. Then you will see eight Heavenly Maidens come down from the corner of Heaven to bathe in the lakes. While they are bathing they will hang their silken under-garments on the pine trees by the shore. Do not let them see you, but go secretly and hide one of these garments. Then when they finish bathing one of them will not be able to return to Heaven. Go to her and welcome her, and she will go with you. You will live happily with her, and children will be born to you, but you must not return her heavenly under-garment to her until you have four children.' With these words the deer vanished, leaving the young man overjoyed at what he had heard.

The next morning the young man got up very early, and climbed to the peaks of the Diamond Mountain, where there were eight beautiful lakes. The mountain is so beautiful that there is an old proverb which says, 'Do not speak of scenic beauty until you have seen the Diamond Mountain.' It is a spot far from the bustle of everyday life, and has been held sacred from the earliest times, so that great temples have been built there. Precipitous peaks soar into the blue sky and trees that have been growing for untold centuries form dense forests where the light of day scarcely penetrates. Streams as clear as crystal flow among the rocks in the valleys, and here and there are lakes and waterfalls, melodious with the songs of birds and the cries of animals.

The young man concealed himself among the bushes and waited. Suddenly in a corner of the sky the clouds began to seethe, and eight Heavenly Maidens came floating down to the lakes at the rainbow's end. They chattered merrily to one another, and all at once took off their clothes and hung them on the pine trees. Then each leapt into the clear water of one of the eight lakes. As they disported themselves naked in the water the woodcutter gazed spellbound at such etherial beauty. After a while he came to his senses and recalled the advice that the deer had given him. He crept stealthily to the pine trees where they had hung their clothes, and took the under-garments of the youngest Maiden, still unnoticed.

Towards sunset the Heavenly Maidens prepared to return to Heaven. They began to put on their clothes again, but to the astonishment of all the youngest Maiden could not find her under-garments. The others could not wait for her, so they climbed up the rainbow to the sky and left her behind. She stood there utterly bewildered, wondering where to find her clothes, when she suddenly saw the young woodcutter standing before her. It was nearly dark, and the young man apologized profusely for the trouble he had caused her, and begged her to forgive him. He was very kind and attentive to her, and he took her to his home.

At first the Heavenly Maiden found the customs of life on earth most confusing, but she soon settled down happily to the routine of domestic life. The months passed happily by, and then she gave birth to a son. Her young husband was overjoyed and loved her with all his heart, and his mother too rejoiced at their happiness. The Heavenly wife seemed utterly contented and lived in harmony with her family. When their second child was born they were happier than ever. One day the wife asked her husband to return her Heavenly under-garments. 'I have borne you two children. Can't you trust me now?' But her husband refused, for he was afraid that she might carry his children off, one in each arm. When their third child was born she implored him earnestly again to return her garments. She served him delicious food and wine, trying to allay his suspicions. 'My dearest husband! I have three children now. Please just let me see my garments. I can hardly betray you now, can I?' The young man was sympathetic to his wife's feelings, and now showed her the garments which he had kept hidden so long. But alas! When she put them on again she regained her magic powers, and at once went up to the sky, holding one child between her legs and one on each arm.

Her husband was stricken with grief and reproached himself for not having followed the deer's advice to the end. He went out to the mountain to cut firewood, and sat at the same place where he had seen the deer before, hoping that it might reappear. By good fortune it passed that way, and he told it his sad story. The deer said to him, 'Since the day you hid the Heavenly Maiden's clothes, they do not come down to bathe there any more. So if you wish to find your wife and children you must go to them yourself. Happily there is a way. Go to the same lake to-morrow, and wait until you see a bottle-gourd come down on a rope from Heaven. They drop it to fetch up water from the lake for bathing. You must seize it and empty the water out quickly. Then get on to it yourself. They will pull it up at once, for they will not realize that you are on it. That is the only way you will be able to see your family in Heaven.' When it had told him this the deer disappeared.

The woodcutter took its advice, and was able to go up to Heaven. When he arrived there the Heavenly Maidens said, 'This smells like a man!' and, finding him in the gourd, asked him why he had come. He told them, and they took him before the Heavenly King. There he met his wife and children, for she was the daughter of the Heavenly King.

The King allowed him to stay, and he lived very happily in the

Heavenly Kingdom. He had the most delicious food to eat every day, and the most beautiful clothes to wear, and there was nothing at all to worry him. One day, however, he thought regretfully of his mother whom he had left alone on earth, and told his wife that he would like to go and visit her once again. But his wife begged him not to go, for if he once met his mother he would not be able to come back to Heaven again. But he persisted in his request and promised he would come back without fail. So in the end she yielded to his entreaties and said, 'I will get a dragon-horse for you. You will ride on it and it will take you down to the earth in the twinkling of an eye. But whatever you do, do not dismount from it, for if your feet once touch the ground you can never come back to me.'

The woodcutter mounted the dragon-horse, and went down to his mother's house. His mother was overjoyed to see her son again after his long absence. They chatted happily together, and when he bade her farewell, still astride the dragon-horse, his mother said, 'I have cooked some pumpkin porridge for you. Please have just one bowl.' He could not disappoint her kindly thought, and took the bowl she offered him. But the bowl was so hot that he dropped it on the horse's back. The horse started in alarm and reared violently throwing him to the ground. Neighing loudly the dragon-horse flew up into the sky and disappeared.

So the woodcutter never went back to Heaven and used to stand every day in tears looking up at the sky. At last he died of his grief, and was transformed into a cock. So tradition says that the reason why cocks climb to the highest part of the roof and crow with their necks stretched out towards Heaven is that the woodcutter's spirit has entered into them, and seeks the highest place it can find.

Ondoru Yawa, told by Zŏng Dŏg-Bong; Ŏnyang (1913).

12

The Cat and the Dog

ONCE upon a time an old man and his wife lived in great poverty in a little hut by the seashore. The old man used to go out and catch fish in the sea every day, and his wife used to take it to the market and sell it.

The Cat and the Dog

One day the old man went to the seashore as usual and threw his line into the water. But though he sat there the whole day long he did not get a single bite. Just as he was thinking of giving up and going home he made one last despairing cast. He was surprised to find that he had hooked a heavy fish. He drew it out and saw that it was a big carp. Strange to say the fish looked sorrowfully at him and seemed to be weeping and begging him to let it go. He thought it must be a sacred creature and immediately set it free in the sea. It turned several times to gaze at him with deep gratitude in its eyes and then sank beneath the waves.

Next morning the old man went back to the same spot to fish. He had not been there long when a young boy wearing a straw hat appeared before him. 'The Dragon King beneath the sea has sent me to you as his messenger,' he said, raising both his hands in respectful salutation. 'He is most grateful to you for sparing the young Prince's life yesterday. So he has sent me to invite you to come to his Palace. Please come with me now.'

The boy turned to face the sea and murmured an incantation. The waves parted and a wide road appeared between them. Then the boy set off down this road and the old man followed him. They travelled far into the sea, and at last they came to a great palace. Before the gate stood attendants in gorgeous robes. They passed through the gate and along a wide path flanked with richly ornamented buildings, more beautiful than the old man had ever seen. At last they came to an edifice more splendid than all the rest. Here a most dignified person was waiting to greet him, dressed in shining robes and wearing a golden crown. The old man guessed that he must be the Dragon King. The King hurried forward at the old man's approach, and with a low obeisance said, 'Welcome to my Palace. I have been waiting for you.'

So the old man was received into the Palace of the Dragon King, and there he stayed as an honoured guest. Every day he was entertained with lavish feasts, with food more delicious than any he had ever tasted. All the time the Palace was filled with the strains of sweet music, played on instruments encrusted with pearls and precious stones, and angelic maidens danced to the music. Many happy days the old man spent there in the Palace, far from the cares and weariness of the world of men.

But at last he began to think longingly of his aged wife, left alone
26

in their cottage, and worrying over his prolonged absence. So he went to the Dragon King and begged him to let him return home. The King was unwilling to let him go, but the old man repeated his request so fervently that in the end the King reluctantly consented.

On the morning of his departure the young Prince whose life he had spared came to him and said, 'Father will offer you a gift before you go. When he asks you what you would like, you had better tell him that you prefer the iron measure that stands in the jewel box beside the throne. It is the most precious treasure in the whole kingdom. If ever you want anything, you have but to ask the measure for it, and it will bring it to you at once.'

So when the Dragon King asked the old man what he would like to take as a gift he replied that he would like the iron measure, as the Prince had advised him. The Dragon King was taken aback at this request. 'That is the only thing I cannot give you. Ask anything else at all, and it shall be given to you.' But the Prince, standing beside the throne, said to his father, 'Father, he saved my life. Which do you value more, your son, or this measure? Please give him what he asks.' So the Dragon King presented the measure to him and said, 'Farewell, my friend. May Fortune always smile upon you.'

So the old man returned to his home with the measure. His wife was overjoyed to see him safe and sound. He told her the secret of the measure, and they immediately asked it to bring them a good house, in place of the thatched cottage they were living in. No sooner had they made their request than they found themselves in a magnificent house with a tile roof. Then they asked the measure to bring them food, and from that time it was constantly full of rice. In a very short time they became rich.

One day, when the wife was alone in the house, an ill-natured woman who kept a shop in a village across the river came to her and asked her to buy a jewel. 'I don't need money,' she said. 'You can pay me with rice. I have heard that you have a magic measure that is always full of rice. There are no secrets in the world, you know. You know the proverb that says "Rats listen to what you say at night, and birds to what you say in the daytime." How lucky you are to have such a wonderful measure.'

The guileless old woman selected one of the jewels, and then went and fetched the measure from the secret hiding place where they kept it. From it she took as much rice as the woman demanded.

27

The Cat and the Dog

That night, while the old couple were asleep, a thief broke into the house and stole the iron measure from its secret hiding place. They strongly suspected the woman shopkeeper of the crime, but they could find no evidence to prove it. The old man was very sad at his loss, and reproached his wife for her stupidity. And from that day their fortunes gradually declined, until once more they were very poor. So poor did they become that they could no longer feed their cat and dog, to which they were greatly attached.

The cat and the dog were very sorry for their master and mistress in their distress, and resolved to find the iron measure. One day they saw the woman shopkeeper swimming across the river. So they followed her to see where she would go. At last they saw her come to a big house in the mountains. They saw her go in and come out carrying rice which she took home. They saw her do this every day following. The house belonged to a relation of hers who was a notorious thief.

One evening the cat and the dog crept stealthily through the gate, and in the back garden they found a big stone storeroom. They saw the thief come out carrying a bag of rice and lock the door behind him. They guessed at once that the measure must be in the storeroom. That night the dog kept watch in the garden and the cat went and found a rat by the storeroom and demanded that it tell it where the King of the rats was. The rat went and brought the King of the rats to the cat, who asked him, 'Do you know if there is an iron measure here which is always full of rice?' And the King of the rats replied, 'Yes, it is kept in a strong stone chest in this storeroom.' So the cat ordered the King of the rats to go and get the iron measure for it. 'You must bring it to me before morning, or I will kill you,' he said.

So the King of the rats summoned thousands of his subjects and set to work. He divided them into two armies, one under the command of the General of the Rats Songgod-Nyi, or Awl-teeth, and the other under the command of General of the Rats Tob-Nyi, or Saw-teeth. They had no difficulty in getting inside the storeroom, for they could go through the holes they always used, but they found it extremely difficult to break into the locked stone chest. Whetting their teeth as sharp as they possibly could the whole army of rats slaved through the night, carving and sawing away with might and main. Some of them were overcome by their exertions,

28

and died with blood spurting from their mouths. At last they succeeded in breaking into the chest. They took the iron measure out and delivered it to the cat before dawn. The cat received it gratefully and then set out for home with the dog.

When they came to the river the cat rode on the dog's back holding the measure in its mouth. Then the dog swam across the river with the cat on its back. But the dog was anxious for the safety of the measure and asked the cat, 'Have you still got it?' The cat did not reply, so the dog asked again. It asked three or four times and yet the cat did not answer. So the dog stopped swimming and barked angrily, 'Why do you not answer me?' This time the cat had to say something and replied, 'Yes, of course I have it.' But it had to open its mouth to speak, and so it let go of the measure, which fell into the water.

When they reached the bank the dog, ashamed of having asked such a silly question, sneaked off home with his tail between his legs. But the cat wandered along the river bank to find someting to eat, for he was hungry. He saw a fisherman throw away a fish which he had found dead in his net. So he went and picked it up and took it home and gave it to his master. The old woman cut it up and found the measure inside it. Evidently the fish had died from swallowing the measure. As a reward for its services the cat was then allowed to sleep in its master's room, but the dog was ordered to stay outside as a punishment for its stupidity. It was very displeased at such treatment, and from that day to this cats and dogs have glared and growled at one another whenever they have met.

Told by Zŏng Dŏg-Bong ; Ŏnyang (1915).

13

The Mud-Snail Fairy

LONG, long ago there was a poor bachelor who lived alone in a thatched cottage. He was an honest and hardworking farmer and toiled every day in the fields.

One day as he dug the barren ground as usual he began to ponder on the future. He was all of thirty years old, and yet because of his poverty there was no prospect that he would ever be able to marry. So he sighed sadly to himself as he worked, 'While I dig in this field, with whom shall I live?' Then a woman's voice answered, 'You will live with me.' He looked around, but he was quite alone. He spoke again, and once more the woman answered him. Then he spoke a third time, and the woman made the same answer. The voice seemed to be coming from a particular spot on the ground, so he went and dug there. Buried in the ground he found a big mud-snail. In the evening he took it home and tossed it into a corner of the kitchen.

When he entered the kitchen in the morning to cook breakfast he was astounded to see a small table set and steaming rice and other delicious dishes on it, waiting to be eaten. He ate thankfully, and wondered who on earth could have come and prepared such an excellent breakfast for him. Then he went out and toiled in the fields all day. In the evening he came home, and once again he found a meal waiting on the table for him, ready for him to sit down and feast on a marvellous array of good things. He was delighted by this unexpected attention, and made up his mind to find out who this unknown benefactor might be. Late that night he went and hid himself in the kitchen to watch. Early in the morning he saw a beautiful girl come out of the mud-snail. She cooked the breakfast, set the table, and then retired into the snail shell again.

On the third morning he rushed out from his hiding place just as she was about to squeeze into her snail shell again, and took her by the hand. 'Please stay with me and be my wife,' he implored her. 'I am a fairy from Heaven,' she told him, 'but a false accusation was made against me, and the Heavenly King sent me in exile to the world of men. Destiny brought me to your field and to your house. But the time has not yet come for me to marry you. Please wait two months longer.'

The impatient young man refused to be put off a single day. So she was obliged to become his wife at once and they lived happily together from that day in his cottage. But one day the husband fell ill, and could not go out into the fields. So his wife set out to till the fields in his place. It happened that the local magistrate passed that way, so she went and hid in the woods in great alarm. But the magistrate noticed a mysterious light in the woods and sent his men to investigate. They found a beautiful woman there and went and told their master. So he ordered them to bring her to him, and they went and asked her to go with them. She begged to be excused, and sent her golden hairpin to the magistrate as a present. When the attendants returned to their master he would not accept it, but sent them again to bring her to him. Once more she begged to be excused, and sent him her gold ring. Again the magistrate refused to accept it, and summoned her once more. Then she sent her jacket to him, if only he would respect her chastity, and then her trousers. Still he insisted that she be brought to him, and at last she was obliged to submit, and was led before the magistrate clad only in her drawers and weeping in her shame.

Her sick husband hastened to the magistrate and appealed to him to let his wife go, but to no avail. Mad with indignation the husband rushed headlong at a pillar and killed himself. As his body fell lifeless to the floor his spirit soared up into the air in the shape of a blue bird. Every morning and evening thereafter the blue bird came and perched in a tree by the magistrate's residence and sang in mournful tones. His wife refused to eat, and soon starved to death, but preserved her chastity intact. It is said that her spirit became a bamboo comb, so that wives might be reminded of their obligation to remain chaste every time they combed their hair.

Ondoru Yawa, told by Zŏng Dŏg-Zo; Ŏnyang (1912).

14
The Sheep is the Cousin of the Ox

ONE day God decided to destroy all the useless creatures in the world. He thought that the ox could be well dispensed with, but on further reflection he decided that it served a useful purpose in ploughing the fields. So he decided to spare it.

Then he turned to the sheep. 'You are a useless animal,' he said. 'You never do anything but eat.' But the sheep replied, 'I live by my cousin's favour, my Lord, and do not trouble men at all.'

So God asked the sheep, 'Who is your cousin?' and the sheep replied, 'The ox, my lord.' 'How can the ox be your cousin?' asked

God, and the sheep answered, 'The ox's hooves are double, and so are mine. It has two horns, and so have I, haven't I, my lord?'

Then God asked again, 'I agree that it is as you say, but how does it happen that you have a short tail while the ox has a long one?'

'I get that from my mother's side, my lord,' replied the sheep.

Told by Yi Sang-Hwa; Dĕgu (1933).

15
The Pheasant, the Dove, the Magpie, and the Rat

ONCE upon a time a pheasant, a dove, and a magpie lived in a forest.

One year when the harvest was bad the pheasant went to the house of a rat who lived nearby and cackled in a most patronizing manner, 'Hey, you! You miserable fellow half eaten by the cat. Give me something to eat!' Then the rat's wife rushed out from the kitchen and slapped the pheasant's cheeks with the hot fire shovel. And to this day the pheasant's cheeks are red.

A little later the dove went to the rat's house and cooed roughly, 'Hey! You petty pilferer of the rice-chest! I want some food!' So the rat's wife came out from the kitchen and beat the dove about the head with a fire stick. And to this day the dove's head still bears the marks.

Last of all the magpie went to the rat's house and asked politely, 'Is your husband at home? Please will you give me something to eat? We have had a terrible harvest, you know.' Then the rat said to the magpie, 'Don't you live with those odious fellows, the pheasant and the dove?'

'In the same village, sir,' replied the magpie softly, 'but not in the same house.'

The rat was very pleased with this answer and gave the magpie food. And his wife praised the magpie and said, 'You have a handsome face, and you speak most charmingly.'

This is a story I heard long ago.

Told by Gim Gi-Tĕg; Tong-yŏng (1930).

16
The Ants and the Hare

IN ancient times the ant was an idle creature which led a parasitic existence on the back of the hare and sucked its blood.

One day the hare said to the crowd of ants that lived on its back, 'I've got some delicious food for you to-day, it's called cooked rice. But you'll all have to get down, and not sit idle on my back.' So all the ants got down from his back. Then the hare held out a lump of cooked rice on a big leaf and said to the ants, 'This is the food. Come and get it.' So all the ants ran towards it. But as soon as they came near the hare took a step backwards. He licked the rice himself, and again called to the ants. 'Come on, I say,' he called. The ants went forward again, and once again the hare took a step backwards just as they came near the rice.

This happened several times, and then the ants got angry with the hare for tantalizing them so. But he went on doing it, and then as he stepped backwards he tripped over a stone. He was startled, and in his alarm he ran up a tree. So the ants waited under the tree for him to come down. But the hare called to them to come up the tree. They were very hungry and thirsty, and so they chased him up the tree. As soon as they reached the top the hare leapt down and ran away.

So the ants lost their home on the hare's back, and could no longer suck his blood. They almost starved, and their waists became very thin, just as we see them to-day. Their eyes, too, almost disappeared. And it is said that it was this misfortune that forced them to work as they do now.

Told by Yi Ŭn-Sang; Masan (1930).

17
The Deer, the Hare, and the Toad

THERE were once a deer, a hare, and a toad. One day they decided that they would hold a party, and they arranged that there should be a table for each of them. According to custom the first table was allotted to the eldest, and so they told each other how old they were.

The deer spoke first. 'When the world was first created,' he said, 'I helped to nail the stars to the sky with a hammer. So I am the eldest.'

Next the hare spoke. 'I planted the tree from which was made the ladder you used when you nailed the stars to the sky,' he said. 'So I am the eldest.'

At their words the toad burst into tears. They asked him why he was so sad and he explained, 'Once I had three sons. They each planted a tree. The eldest made the handle of the hammer you used to nail the stars to the sky. The second made the handle of the plough that drove the furrow of the Milky Way. And the youngest made a pack-carrier to carry the sun and the moon. But they all died before the work was finished. When I hear you talking about it it makes me very sad, for it reminds me of my dead sons.'

The others recognized the toad as the eldest among them and conceded him the seat of honour.

Told by Zong Zin-Il; Yangsan (1920).

18

The Green Frog

ONCE upon a time there lived a green frog who would never do what his mother told him. If she told him to go to the east he would go to the west. If she asked him to go up the mountain he would run down to the river. Never, never would he obey his mother in anything.

At last his mother grew very old, still worrying about her son's future. At last she fell ill, and realized that she was about to die. So she called her son to her bedside and said to him, 'My dear son, I shall not live much longer. When I die do not bury me on the mountain. Do you hear? I want to be buried by the river.' She meant of course that she wanted to be buried on the mountain, for she well knew her son's perverse ways.

Very soon afterwards she died. Then the green frog was very sad and wept bitterly. He repented of all his misdeeds in the past, and made up his mind that now at least he would do as his mother had asked. So he buried her by the riverside. And whenever it rained he worried lest her grave should be washed away. He used to sit and lament in a mournful voice. And to this day the green frog croaks whenever the weather is wet.

Told by Zŏng Yŏng-Og; Seoul (1944).

19

The Locust, the Ant, and the Kingfisher

ONCE upon a time a locust, an ant, and a kingfisher decided to hold a party. The locust and the kingfisher were to go and get the fish, and the ant was to prepare the rice. So they went off separately to find the various foods.

The ant met a peasant woman who was carrying a basket of rice on her head. It crawled up her leg and bit her, so that she jumped and the basket of rice fell off her head. Then the ant snatched it up and carried it off.

The locust went down to the lake and sat on a leaf that was floating on the water. A fish came and swallowed it, and then the kingfisher, which had been waiting nearby, swooped down and caught the fish, and took it to the party.

The locust came out of the fish, and began to quarrel with the kingfisher over who had caught it. He insisted that he had caught it, while the kingfisher insisted that he had.

The ant burst out laughing when he saw them quarrelling. He laughed so much that his waist became thin, just as it is to-day. The locust took hold of the kingfisher by his bill and pulled, so that it became the long bill we see now. And the kingfisher bit the locust's head, so that it got its present shape.

Told by Yi Sang-Hwa; Dĕgu (1933).

35

20

The Bedbug, the Louse, and the Flea

LONG, long ago a bedbug reached the age of sixty, and to celebrate the occasion held the customary party, known as *hwangab*, that marks the completion of a whole sexagenary cycle. He invited his two closest friends, a louse and a flea.

The louse and the flea were very pleased to receive their invitations and set out together to go to the party. The sprightly flea leapt ahead without regard for the louse and before long had left him far behind. The louse too wished to hasten on his way, but he could not walk very fast, for he was a portly creature, and his legs were very short. So he shouted to the flea, 'Wait for me, my friend! Since we were invited as honoured guests we should behave with due composure. Do not hop about so impatiently.'

So the flea walked a little slower for a time, but before long he lost patience with the tardy louse, for by now he was feeling rather hungry. So he ran straight to the bedbug's house. The tables were heavily laden with delicious food and drink, so the flea said to the bedbug, 'I am very thirsty, please let me have a bowl of wine.' So the bedbug filled a bowl with wine and handed it to him. Then he went out to meet the louse on the way, for he guessed that having to carry such a plump body made walking very tiring for him.

While the flea waited for them to arrive he refilled his bowl several times from the bottles on the table, and soon got very red in the face. When the bedbug arrived at last with the louse the flea was quite drunk and was humming a tune. All the bottles were empty. The louse was already annoyed at the flea's behaviour, and now he lost his temper completely and slapped his face. Then there was a rumpus indeed. The flea and the louse came to blows and grappled fiercely with one another. Their host the bedbug tried to get between them to part them, but they fought on and in the end fell on top of him, so that he was squashed quite flat.

So to this day the bedbug is still a flat creature, the flea has a tipsy red face, and the louse has a mark on his back where the flea kicked him.

Told by Czoe Og-Hi ; Gwangzu (1943).

21

Nails

LONG ago a young man went to a temple in the mountains to study. He used to go and wash in the mountain stream which flowed before the temple, and habitually cut his nails whenever he took a bath. Then he would throw the nail-clippings away and make water on them. Each time he did this a rat used to come, and unknown to him, used to eat the clippings and drink his urine.

He studied at the temple for three years, and then returned to his home. When he arrived he was astounded to find there an exact replica of himself. The other young man wore the same clothes, and his voice and manner were identical with his own. It was absolutely impossible to tell the two men apart. The young man's parents had already welcomed his double as their son. So he stood and gaped, quite paralysed in his alarm, and shouted at the other in a shaking voice, 'Whatever has happened? And who are you?'

His wife was greatly embarrassed. So she asked several personal questions, such as the ages of the various members of the family, and things that had happened in the past. Both men, however, answered correctly. So his mother asked, 'Which of you knows how many bowls and dishes I have in my house?' The false son had been there for some time before the real one arrived, and had had time to look around. So he gave the correct answer, while the real son could not. So the false son was accepted as genuine, and the real son was driven from the house.

So he went and wandered aimlessly about the country. One night he was lost in the mountains and he found a lonely house standing in a valley. He knocked at the door, and a woman came out and welcomed him kindly. 'I knew that sooner or later you would come here,' she said. 'I am well aware of what is troubling you.' Then she gave him a bag full of medicines, and said, 'Take these medicines home with you, and then the three of you, your double, your wife, and yourself, must drink them. Then the truth will be manifest.'

So he went back home again and proposed that they should take the medicines as a last test. The real son drank without the slightest hesitation, and remained as he was. But the false son refused to take

37

it. Then the mother scolded him roundly for his refusal, and compelled him to drink it. So with the greatest reluctance he drank it, and immediately fell down dead. And his body immediately changed into the shape of a rat. Then the wife took the medicine, and at once experienced violent labour pains. In a few moments she gave birth to many dead rats.

So the truth was found. The young man's double was the rat which had eaten his nails and drunk his urine while he was living in the mountains.

So from that time it has been the custom, when cutting one's nails, to smell them and then put them in the chamber pot.

Told by Zŏng Zin-Il; Yangsan (1932).

22

The Nine-Tailed Fox

ONE day a man made water by the roadside. Then he saw that he had done it on a white bone. He asked rather pointlessly 'Is it cold?' and the bone replied, 'Yes, it is cold.' So he asked again, 'Is it warm?' And the bone replied, 'Yes it is warm.'

The man was very alarmed at this remarkable occurrence, and he ran away. Then the bone got up and ran after him. It nearly caught him up, and he was more frightened than ever. Just then he came to a wine shop. So he turned to the bone and said, 'Just wait here a moment. I'll get you some wine.' Then he went into the shop and ran away through the back door. He went on his way and saw no more of the bone.

A few years later he happened to pass by the same wine shop. He saw another one in front of it, that appeared to be newly built. There was a pretty young woman selling wine in the new shop, so he went in. As he drank he chatted to the girl. His earlier experience came to mind, and he said. 'A few years ago I outwitted a white bone on this very spot.' As he spoke the girl turned into a nine-tailed fox. 'I was that white bone,' she cried. 'I have been waiting for you to come back.' With these words she sprang on him and ate him up. And the moral is that one should not make water on white bones.

Told by Gim Yang-Ha; Zŏngpyŏng (1928).

38

23
Butterflies

LONG, long ago there lived a girl whose parents had betrothed her to a man whom she had never seen. Unfortunately her betrothed died before they could be married. When she heard of his death the girl got into a palanquin draped in the white cloth of mourning and went to the dead man's house. There she unplaited her hair and wept in mourning. Each morning and afternoon she went to his grave and walked round it, weeping bitterly and calling him by name.

In those days it was not permitted to a daughter of a *yangban*, or gentleman, to marry again when once she had been betrothed or married. And it very often happened that young widows died by poison either self-administered or given to them by their relations.

This girl used to go and lament her sad lot at her betrothed's grave, and she used to pray, 'Some day I shall meet you in the other world, and if there is truly affinity between us, may this grave break in two.'

One day she went as usual to the grave with a woman servant and the grave did suddenly burst open. The young widow immediately leaped into it. The servant was terrified, but tried to stop her mistress. She made a grab at her, but only succeeded in seizing a small piece of her skirt, which came away in her hand as the grave snapped shut.

As she held the cloth in her hand it broke into many pieces. Every piece turned into a butterfly and fluttered away.

It is said that the butterflies we see to-day are all descended from the patterns on the young widow's skirt.

Told by Bag Sŏg-Ryong; Tong-yŏng (1946).

24
The Unmarried Girl's Grave

ONE day a man made water by the roadside. It happened that at that spot there was a grave level with the ground. That night the man dreamed that a beautiful girl came to him and said, 'To-day you showed me your most precious possession, and now all my bitterness against the world has melted away. You have made it possible for me to travel to the other world, and I am deeply grateful for your kindness.'

The dead girl had never known a man in this world, and so she could not go to the other world, but was condemned to wander for ever on the earth. The man's breach of etiquette had, however, rescued her spirit from its unhappy fate. So now she wished to repay his kindness before she went to the other world.

So it happened that the man passed the Civil Examination with ease and married a beautiful wife. On his wedding night the girl appeared once more and said to him, 'I think I have repaid my debt to you. Farewell!' She vanished and never appeared again.

It is said that from that time if a woman dies before she marries she is buried in a flat inconspicuous grave, so that a man might unwittingly make water on the grave. The customary Korean grave is a circular mound of heaped-up earth.

Told by Yu Czun-Sŏb; Zŏnzu (1931).

PART TWO
LEGENDS

25

The Man Who Wanted to Bury His Son

ON the border between Ogczŏn County in the Province of North Czungczŏng and Tĕzŏn County in the Province of South Czungczŏng there stands a high mountain.

Long ago a most filial couple lived near this mountain. They had a baby son, but they also had to support the husband's mother. They were extremely dutiful toward her, and spent much of their time looking for delicacies for her.

When the baby grew a little older it often happened that the grandmother gave him the food they had prepared specially for her. Sometimes they scolded their son and told him that he must not eat his grandmother's food. But the old woman was most displeased when they scolded him, for she thought that her grandson might be hungry and need the food.

The couple began to fear that they might not be able to get enough food for the old grandmother and in the end they decided that they must take their son away and bury him. So the husband went up the mountain with a mattock. He dug the ground and found a strange bowl. Then his wife came up carrying their son on her back, and said to her husband, sobbing bitterly, 'I think it would be a terrible thing if we buried our son. So let us take him home again, and whenever mother is eating I will take him outside, and when she has finished I will bring him back. In that way mother will be able to eat all we give her, and we will not have to bury our son.' Her husband agreed with her, and went back home, taking with him the bowl he had found on the mountain.

Strange to say, as soon as they put anything in the bowl it immediately filled to overflowing with whatever they had put in. So they tried putting a penny in it, and it filled with coins. They decided that it must be a reward from Heaven for taking such great

43

care of their aged mother, and said, 'We may use this bowl while mother is alive, but when she dies we must bury it again in the place where we found it.'

The couple were enabled to feed their aged mother properly, and were not obliged to bury their son. When the grandmother at last died they took the bowl back to the mountain and buried it in the ground.

Some time afterwards a man who had heard the story of the bowl went out to the mountain to find it, but it was nowhere to be found. It is said that the bowl gave the mountain its name of 'Sigzang-San' or 'Food-storied Mountain'.

Told by Hong Og-Zŏng; Zinczŏn (1942).

26

A Dutiful Son

LONG, long ago, in Gĕsŏng, the capital of the Goryŏ dynasty, there lived a most filial man whose mother was dangerously ill. He bought all the medicines he could, but not one of them could cure her.

One day a Buddhist priest came to him and asked, 'Have you a son?' When he said he had a little boy the priest said to him, 'Put your son in a big kettle, secure the lid tightly and boil it for a whole day. Then make your sick mother drink the resulting broth, and she will be cured.'

The dutiful son found himself in a serious dilemma, and hesitated to kill his only son. Then he reasoned, 'Though I shall lose my son, I can always get another. But if I lose my mother I can never have another. Therefore I must sacrifice my son to save my mother.'

At that very moment his son came back from school so he seized him and plunged him into the boiling water in the kettle and fastened the lid securely. But a few minutes afterwards another boy came in. He was exactly like his own son whom he had just put in the kettle. He was very surprised 'and asked him who he was. He questioned him closely and found that he was without doubt his own son. So he tore the lid off the kettle, and there he saw floating in the water a big *dong-sam*, the wild ginsen root shaped like a man.

44

He gave the broth to his sick mother and she got better at once. The mysterious priest had been deeply moved by his filial piety and had given him the magical ginsen. In the neighbouring village of Gĕsŏng there stands to this day the Hyoza-mun, or the Shrine of the Dutiful Son, in memory of this man.

Told by Go Han-Sŭng; Gĕsŏng (1932).

27

The Lake of Zangžĕ

ONCE upon a time, near the castle of Zinzu, in the province of Gyŏngnam, there lived a rich man called Zangžĕ. He was an avaricious and cruel man, and never showed charity towards any man. He had, however, a daughter, who was modest and kind-hearted, in complete contrast to her father. If any of the villagers was in need she would give him rice or money, and she would give alms to beggars, unknown to her father. For if he caught her doing good works he would fly into a rage and beat her unmercifully. In spite of all, however, she was always patient, and ever anxious to do good for others.

One day an aged beggar, dragging his feet wearily and leaning on a stick, came to the gate of Zangžĕ's house. At that moment Zangžĕ happened to be outside with one of his servants, grooming his horse. When he saw the old man he snapped angrily, 'Well, what do you want?' The old man held out a bag and said, 'I have nothing to eat. I am starving. Please give me just one *mal* of rice, I beseech you.'

While the old man was speaking an evil thought came to Zangžĕ. He drew his servant aside and whispered to him to go and fill the old man's bag with horse dung. So the servant took the bag away, and filled it up with filth, and then brought it back to the old man. Deeply grateful at such apparent generosity the old man bowed so low that his nose almost touched the ground. Then he went on his way carrying the bag, and Zangžĕ and his servant burst into fits of laughter.

Zangžĕ's daughter had been watching all this, and was very sorry for the old man for the shameful trick that had been played on him.

45

So with flushed face she ran into the house, and wrapping a *mal* of rice in a silk skirt she rushed after the old man. When she caught up with him she said, 'Throw away your bag, and take this one.' The old man looked at her and asked, 'What do you mean?' She told him, 'Your bag is full of horse dung. My father is the most heartless man. I am very sorry for what he has done to you, so please accept this from me. It is a *mal* of rice.' But the old man replied, 'Oh my dear lady, I know about it already. I came to test him. But you are a most charming girl, and I appreciate your kindness very much. You had better come with me now, for if you stay here a terrible fate will overtake you.' So saying the old man took her by the hand, and led her away.

Before they had gone many yards she heard a sound like a deafening clap of thunder. When she looked round her home was no more to be seen, but a broad lake covered the spot where it had stood. At the same moment the old man disappeared. She went to the shore of the lake, and wept with grief for her poor father. And every one of her tear. as it fell in the water was changed instantly into a white lotus flower.

The next morning the villagers found a stone image of the Merciful Buddha at the spot where she had wept. They identified it as the spirit of the daughter of Zangzě, and to this day the lake is called the Lake of Zangzě.

Ondoru Yawa. From *Ŏrini.*

28
Yŏni and Her Stepmother

LONG, long ago there lived a young girl, called Yŏni, who was as beautiful as the radiant moon, with eyes like shining stars. Unfortunately her mother died and her father married again. Her stepmother treated her cruelly and used constantly to devise new ways of tormenting the poor girl. She made her do all the most menial tasks about the house, until she was quite worn out, and her hair, that had been straight and long as a tailor's work-board, became twisted and tangled like a magpie's nest.

Yŏni and Her Stepmother

One cold winter's day her stepmother sent her out into the mountains to fetch fresh vegetables. It was of course quite impossible to find fresh vegetables in the middle of winter, but her stepmother forced her to go out with a basket, clad only in a thin summer dress. So off she went, and searched in vain in the snow that lay deep on the mountain. Not a thing could she find. Before long the short winter day came to an end, and it became very dark. She could not return home now, and so she looked around for a cave or something where she might shelter for the night. She had not gone far when she found a big gate. She pushed it open and went through. Inside she found a wide field, and in the centre of the field stood a beautiful thatched house. She knocked at the door and a boy came out and asked her politely, 'Why have you come here? Is there anything I can do for you?'

She told him her sad story. The boy was very sympathetic, and went at once into the field and brought her a lot of fresh rape. She thanked him profusely for his kindness, and turned to go. But the boy restrained her. 'My name is Willow,' he said. 'Please come here again. When you do come, stand in front of the gate and call out, "Willow, Willow, Willow Leaf! Yŏni has come, please open the door." Then I will come out and welcome you.' Then he gave her three bottles, one white, one red, and one blue. 'Take great care of these bottles,' he said. 'The liquid in the white bottle can make flesh grow on the bones of the dead. Then if you sprinkle the red on it, it will produce blood. Finally the blue one will bring the body to life. Some day you may have occasion to use them.'

When Yŏni returned home in the morning her stepmother was amazed to see the fresh rape. So she sent her out again, and once more she brought it back. The third time the stepmother followed her, keeping some distance behind, so that she would not be seen. She saw Yŏni stop before a gate and call out, 'Willow, Willow, Willow Leaf! Yŏni has come, please open the door.' Then she saw a boy come out and take her inside. After a while she came out again, carrying a basketful of fresh rape. Then the stepmother hurried home by a short cut, and arrived long before her step-daughter.

When Yŏni at last arrived, her stepmother went to her and said roughly, 'You have a secret lover. I know all about it.' Yŏni said nothing, for she knew it was useless to deny anything her stepmother said. Nor would she complain to her father of her unfairness, for she was afraid of hurting his feelings.

The following morning the stepmother went out into the mountains and stood before the gate. 'Willow, Willow, Willow Leaf!' she called. 'Yŏni has come, please open the door.' The boy came at once and opened the gate. When he saw her he said, 'Who are you?' Without replying the stepmother rushed at him and killed him with one blow. Then she set fire to the house and the field and destroyed them completely.

Next day she sent Yŏni out to fetch fresh rape. She came to the gate, and called out in the usual way, but no answer came. So she pushed the gate open and went inside. There a scene of utter desolation greeted her, the house lay in charred ruins and the field was blackened by the fire. Before her lay the scattered bones of the boy.

She was overcome with grief and wept bitterly. Then she remembered the bottles he had given her. She gathered up the bones and laid them out so that they formed a complete skeleton. Then she took out the bottles and poured the white liquid on the bones. At once they were clothed in flesh. Then she sprinkled the red liquid on the body, and the hot blood began to course through his veins. Finally she sprinkled the blue liquid on him, and he opened his eyes and smiled. 'I am a servant of the Heavenly King,' he said. 'It is my duty to make the rain fall on the earth. But lately I was sent down here to help you. In the middle of winter I planted rape, and watered it with the spring showers that are at my command. Now my task is completed, and I am going back to Heaven. You are to come with me and be my bride. Let us go now.'

With these words he took her by the hand, and they rode up the rainbow into the sky.

Told by Zŏng Dŏg-Zo; Ŏnyang (1914).

29

The Geomancer's Three Sons

LONG ago there was a noted geomancer who had three sons. His fame had spread throughout the land, and many people came to him to consult him about the correct positioning and direction of graves, for if mistakes were made in these matters dire calamities would befall the families of the dead. But he never said anything about his own grave, though he was already over seventy, nor did he teach his art to his sons. Many times his sons asked him where they should bury him when he died, but he always used to put them off, saying, 'Wait a little longer. I have determined it in my own mind, but it is not yet the time for me to disclose it to you.'

As the years went by the old man came to look so weak that his sons were very worried about him, and asked him yet again what he meant them to do. Still keeping his secret their father told them, 'I cannot disclose to you the secret of my grave with my own lips. When I die you must go and ask Yi, and he will tell you everything.'

Soon afterwards the old man died, and his three sons went to Yi to ask him about their father's grave. 'Our father told us to come and consult you. Will you please give us instructions about the grave in which we are to bury him.' 'Yes, indeed,' replied Yi, 'Your father told me about it. But I think you are going to find it very hard.' The three sons were very surprised, and said, 'If it is our father's wish we will undertake any adventure whatsoever, whether in a tiger's cave, or beneath the deep pool where the wicked dragon lurks. We three brothers will together strive to fulfil his wishes.'

Yi answered very quietly, 'That is not what I mean. If you bury your father in the place he has suggested, then the very next day the eldest son will die. On the hundredth day following the second son will die, and after a year the third son too will die. So your fate is determined. That is why I have hesitated to tell you.'

This information disturbed the three sons greatly. 'If that is the case, of what use can your advice be?' asked the eldest son. But Yi went on, 'Your father knew it clearly, but he could not tell you. Yet there is one more secret. Though you three die young, there will afterwards arise three Ministers from your family.'

The three sons guessed that he was testing their sincerity, and so they answered, 'It is nothing to us whether after our deaths Ministers are born or not. Our father's will must be done. Let us do as he has commanded.'

So the funeral took place, and they buried their father in the grave he had indicated. The very next day the eldest son died, though touched by no illness, leaving behind his wife and only son. His mother was deeply grieved, but the other sons were very alarmed, for they knew that the time for their own deaths was fixed. How terrible it must have been for them, as their fate crept inexorably upon them!

On the hundredth day after the eldest brother had died the family busied themselves with the memorial service. Then suddenly the second son fell down in a swoon, and died. He too left a widow and only son. Their mother was stricken with grief, for her sons had never told her the secret of their father's grave. But now the youngest son disclosed the truth to her, weeping for fear of his own death, for both his brothers had died exactly as foretold. When the second son's funeral was over the three widows were alarmed that the youngest son, who was not married yet, might die within nine months.

One day the youngest son said to his mother, 'Mother, the day of my death is foretold, and I cannot sit idly at home. Let me set out on a journey so that I may forget my anxieties. I will try to return in time for the anniversary of my father's death, but if I do not, you must think of it as the day of my death too.' His mother and the other members of the family were very sad, but there was nothing that they could do about it. He was in all probability going to his death, and as he left the house he stopped many times to look back.

He was passing along a mountain road one day at nightfall. He looked for somewhere to pass the night, but there was no house in sight. He walked on, tired and hungry, and at last he saw the light of a house. He knocked on the door, and he was admitted by an old woman of about fifty, who received him kindly. She was very good-natured and obliging, always ready to help the children of the village. She gave him food and said he might stay there and rest.

After a while the old woman got up and went out. She was going to the next village to call on a girl who was to be married next day. Before she left she said to the youngest son, 'I am just going along to the next village. There are blankets and pillow for you. I will be back before long. Good night.'

Now this girl in the next village was very fond of the old woman, and very much wanted to see her once again before she was married. But she had been kept very busy with preparations for the wedding, and had had no opportunity to leave the house until nightfall. At last, after dark she left to go and call on the old woman. And so in the darkness they missed each other on the road. When the girl arrived the old woman was not at home, but she did not realize this, and opened the door and went inside into the room where the young traveller was sleeping. He woke up and struck a light, and so they met. They introduced themselves, and soon made friends. The girl was deeply moved by the young man's story, and felt very sorry for him, and her heart was filled with true affection. She told him of her marriage, and that it had been arranged against her will, so that he took pity on her too. And so they fell in love.

In the morning the young man was dead, for it was the appointed day. The girl was very sad, and, ignoring her father's anger, determined to sacrifice herself for her dead lover. She took his body back to his mother. When his mother and his brothers' widows heard her story they admired her sincerity greatly, and recognized her as the youngest son's wife.

In due course she became the mother of a son. Now there was one son for each of the three dead brothers. From their earliest days they were outstanding among the boys of the village, and when they grew up all three became Ministers of the Government, just as the prophecy had foretold.

Told by Zŏng Tĕg-Ha; Ŏnyang (1936).

30
The Curse on the Only Son

LONG, long ago there lived a boy who was an only son. His ancestors for nine generations had likewise been only sons. They were cursed with the doom of *ho-sig*, which meant that they were fated to be eaten by tigers, and his father, grandfather, and all their predecessors going back to the ninth generation, had all been seized by tigers. This doom had befallen them all at the same hour of the same day of the same month when they were twelve years of age. So one day this boy went to consult a fortune-teller, who told him that he too was fated to suffer the same doom of *ho-sig*, and that he would die when he was twelve years of age.

He could not bear to stay idly at home waiting for his fate to come upon him. So, being now twelve years of age, he left his home and his weeping mother, and set out to travel about the country. He wandered aimlessly from one place to another, and at last he came to Seoul. Here he found a famous fortune-teller. He counted what money he had in his purse, and found it was one hundred *yang*. Half of this sum he set aside, and offered the rest to the fortune-teller, if he would tell him his fate. The fortune-teller agreed, but when he looked into the matter he was astounded to find how evil a fate was in store for the boy. He considered deeply for a few minutes, and then said, 'There is but one way for you to avoid your destiny. There is in Seoul a Minister called Gim. If on the day appointed for your death you can take refuge in his daughter's room, then you will escape. Only thus can you be saved.'

So the boy went to the Minister's residence, and lingered in front of it, but he was at a loss to find a way of entering. By good fortune he found a small house nearby, where an old woman lived. He offered her some of his money, and she agreed to let him lodge in her house. He told her the secret of his evil destiny, and how each of his ancestors for nine generations had suffered the same fate. The old woman was greatly touched by his unhappy story, and promised to do all she could to help him. As it happened the Minister's daughter was her niece.

In the evening of the appointed day the old woman prepared delicious food and drink, and entertained the guards on the twelve gates of the Minister's residence. Then, when they were drowsy from the effects of the wine, she took the boy into the house and led him to the inner room where the Minister's daughter lived. She was not there at the time, for she was at supper, and the old woman hid the boy behind the screen. When at last the girl appeared her aunt gave her some sweetmeats which she had specially prepared for her, and said, 'My dear niece, I have brought you something nice to eat. You had better have it later when you are hungry. I will leave it behind the screen here for you.' With these words she put the food behind the screen and went home again. The daughter's room was in a building apart from the main house, and so no one saw her come or go.

After a while the Minister's daughter began to feel hungry, and so she went to the screen to get the sweetmeats her aunt had put there. When she folded the screen back she found the boy hiding there. She thought he must be a ghost, and at once began to recite the *Zu-Yŏg* (Book of Changes). The boy did not vanish, but sat before her with a mournful expression on his face. Recovering from her surprise the Minister's daughter asked him, 'What are you, a ghost or a human being? Why are you sitting there?' He answered her and told her his whole story. She was deeply moved, and hid him in the wall closet, that he might be saved from his miserable destiny.

Then one of her friends came in, a girl who lived not far away, and was also the daughter of a Minister, Yi. They passed the time pleasantly, talking of one trifle or another, and then the daughter of the house asked her friend, 'If someone were to come here who desperately needed help, what would you do?' And her friend replied, 'Why, I would do all I could to help, of course.' So Gim's daughter went to the wall closet and brought the boy out. 'He is in deadly peril,' she said. 'We must do all we can to save his life.' Then she shut him in the closet again, and the two girls sat up watching.

In the dead of night a big tiger broke into the house. It came and squatted before the daughter's room, and humbly begged her, 'Please give me the boy you have hidden.' The two girls remonstrated with it sternly but quietly, 'What a bloodthirsty creature you are,' they said. 'And no one is allowed into the Minister's residence without permission. We cannot let you come in here, and the most unpardonable crime of all is to kill and eat a man.' The tiger replied, 'I have eaten ninety-nine only sons. If I eat that boy to-night I will became a man. Please give him to me.'

But the two girls were unmoved by the tiger's pleas, and began to recite the Book of Changes. The tiger prowled around the house snarling furiously, but at the sound of the first cockcrow it went away. The girls went to take the boy from the closet, and found him almost fainting in his agony. They gave thin rice gruel to eat, and he soon recovered completely. He was very relieved to hear that the tiger had gone, and thanked them profusely for their kind protection. They talked to him for a while, and found he had some talent for composing verses, so they advised him to enter for the examination for the Imperial Civil Service, which was to be held the following day. They found out what form and subject were to be set, and together composed a poem, which he learned by heart.

The examiners were the Ministers Gim and Yi, and when they read the boy's poem they were both struck with its brilliance. So he passed the examination with the highest marks and each Minister offered him his daughter in marriage. He could refuse neither offer, for he was equally indebted to both girls. So he married them both, and took them to his home, where they all lived in harmony with his mother and had many children.

Told by Zŏng Bog-Sul; Ŏnyang (1915).

31

The Secret Royal Inspector, Bag Mun-Su

IN the days of King Yŏngzo the Secret Royal Inspector, Bag Mun-Su, travelled alone through all the eight provinces of Korea to investigate the administration of justice by local magistrates and Provincial Governors. He carried out his duties with great success for the most part, but sometimes he found himself at a loss to deal with a problem.

One day he was travelling along a lonely mountain road when suddenly a man came running towards him and begged him breathlessly, 'Save me! Please save me! I am being chased by a man who means to kill me. Don't tell him where I am hidden!' With these words he crawled under a nearby bush to hide. Then a villainous looking man came up to the Inspector, and threatening him with a knife demanded, 'A man came running past here just now. You must have seen him. Tell me where he is, or I shall kill you.' In the circumstances there was nothing the Inspector could do but give the fugitive away. The villainous looking man seized him and took him away.

The Royal Inspector went on his way, very uneasy in his mind at what he had done. In the afternoon he came to a village and found a crowd of boys playing at being magistrates. He stoppped to watch them. He saw two boys come before the magistrate and appeal to him to settle their case. 'Honourable Magistrate! Please divide these three pennies equally between us, so that we may both be satisfied.' The boy-magistrate found the case insoluble. Then another boy came forward and said, 'It's quite easy, you know. Just give me those pennies.' He took the money, and handed one penny to each boy. The other penny he put in his pocket and said, 'That's for my fee. You should be satisfied now.'

The Royal Inspector was very impressed by the boy's shrewdness. So he went to him and asked him how he should have solved the problem that had confronted him in the morning. 'How could I have saved both the fugitive and myself?' he asked. Without a moment's hesitation the boy replied, 'That's very simple. When the man had hidden under the bush, you should have pretended to be blind.' The Royal Inspector was quite taken aback at the boy's ready wit.

Another day he came to a school where again a large crowd of boys was playing at being magistrates. The boy who was acting as magistrate sat solemnly in a chair, and another boy came before him and said, 'My pheasant has just escaped. How can I get it back?' It seemed a rather difficult problem, so the Royal Inspector awaited the decision with great curiosity. The boy magistrate said, 'The bird has in all probability escaped to the mountain. The mountain is doubtless hiding it, and is therefore an accomplice. Let the mountain be summoned to appear before me. Then I will order it to return your bird to you.'

The Royal Inspector was greatly amused to hear this answer, and went up to the boy to praise his wise judgment. But the boy-magistrate said with a serious expression, 'Who is this impudent fellow, coming into the Court and insulting the Magistrate? Arrest him at once, and put him in jail.' So the boys who were acting as Court officials seized the Royal Inspector and bound him, and shut him in a shed which they used as their jail. He made no protest, for he was very interested in the boys' innocent game.

Very soon the boy who had played the part of the magistrate came to him and apologized to him, saying, 'I am very sorry we have treated you so rudely. But even a game has its dignity, and the Court insists on its authority. So I had to do it.' The Royal Inspector was very pleased by the boy's serious attitude. So he took him to Seoul, and sent him to the Higher Academy for his education. And when he grew up, it is said, he became a Minister.

Told by Zŏng Sun-Czŏl; Seoul (1930).

32

The Legend of Marshal Gang Gam-Czan

THE father of Gang Gam-Czan once went far into the mountains and at nightfall found that he was lost. He wandered about for a while, and at last he found a cottage. He knocked on the door, and a beautiful girl came and welcomed him most kindly. She invited him to stay, and he remained with her three days. A few days after he had returned home he thought he would like to visit the girl again, but when he came to the place where the house had stood, he could find no trace of it.

Several years passed and then a woman came to him, accompanied by a young boy. She said to him, 'I have brought you your son. The cottage you visited in the mountains was no human habitation, but the house of a fox. I am the girl who welcomed you and entertained you. This is our son, and he will grow up to be a great hero, and will perform mighty exploits for his country.' With these words the woman disappeared.

True to her prophecy Gang Gam-Czan grew up to become Marshal of the Korean armies in war against China, and won many brilliant victories. And many stories are told of his supernatural powers.

While he was yet a boy he was present with his father at a wedding in the house of a Minister. The very moment he entered the house the bridegroom died suddenly. The gathering was thrown into confusion, and he went out again. Then strange to say the bridegroom came to life again. So Gang Gam-Czan went back into the house, and glared fiercely at the bridegroom. The bridegroom at once fell dead, and turned into a big fox. So Gang Gam-Czan turned to the bearers of the palanquin who had brought the bridegroom thither. 'Where did you stop on the way?' he asked them. One of the carriers answered, 'We stopped for a few minutes at the foot of a big hollow tree, and the bridegroom got down from the palanquin and relieved himself.' So Gang Gam-Czan said, 'We must go and look at that hollow tree, for it may be that on smelling his urine the fox was enabled to change into the form of the bridegroom.' The carriers hastened back to the tree, and inside it they found the real bridegroom, where he had been thrown by the fox.

After this incident the fame of Gang Gam-Czan spread among the villagers. It is said that his face was ugly and pock-marked. One day he summoned the goddess of smallpox, and with fierce threats demanded that she make his face as ugly as she possibly could. She hesitated at first, but in the end was obliged to do as he wished. So she scratched his face with her fingers, so that she made him three times as ugly as he had been before.

When he was twelve years of age he passed the Civil Examination, and applied to be appointed Magistrate of Yangzu, because in that district there were many tigers, and he wished to clear them from the place. On his appointment he summoned an old Buddhist priest to appear before him, who had been living on the highest peak of Mount Samgag, and said to him, 'You must leave my district at once, and never return.' Now this old Buddhist priest was the incarnation in human form of the King of the Tigers. From that day to this no tiger has been seen anywhere in the vicinity of Seoul.

Later on he was appointed to be Magistrate of the town of Gyŏngzu. Now this town had long been infested with frogs, which had made the air hideous by croaking ceaselessly day and night, so that all the people complained bitterly about them. So he summoned before him the biggest frog in the castle moat, and ordered, 'There shall be no more croaking by the frogs in this town.' And from that day to this no frog has ever been heard in the town of Gyŏngzu.

When he was appointed governor of Zŏlla Province a leading merchant came to him and reported that his three sons had all died suddenly at the same time. So he summoned Yama, the King of the Underworld, and asked him, 'Why did you take away this man's three sons?' Then Yama answered, 'This merchant murdered three wealthy men, and took all that they possessed for himself. Their bodies he buried under the floor of his house. To punish this crime I took away his three sons.' Gang Gam-Czan found the three corpses where Yama had told him, and punished the wicked merchant as he deserved.

One day he went to Gurye in the Province of Zŏlla with his mother. The roaring of the River Zansu kept her awake at night. So he wrote a charm on a piece of paper and threw it into the river. And from that day to this the river has flowed without a sound.

At the village of Doczǒng he was greatly troubled by the mosquitoes. So again he wrote a charm on a piece of paper and threw it in the air, and from that day to this no one has been bitten by a mosquito anywhere in that district.

Told by Gim Gi-Hwan ; Tong-yǒng (1932).

33
The Story of General Gim Dǒg-Nyǒng

GENERAL Gim Dǒg-Nyǒng was a warrior of renown who achieved great fame for his redoubtable exploits in the Battle of Imzin against the Japanese. He studied the science of war and learnt the art of swordsmanship at Mount Mudǔng, in Gwangzu, in the province of Zǒlla. Tradition says that he was born with the blessing of the spirit of the mountain upon him, and there are countless miraculous stories told of his birth and his life.

An evil curse had been laid on his mother that she should be seized by a tiger and killed. It happened that one day when she was working in the fields a Buddhist monk appeared and stood watching her. He told a passer-by, 'I am not really a monk, but a tiger. I have come here to eat that woman so that I can become a man. Just watch me and you will see.' The monk then jumped three times in the air, and was instantly transformed into a big tiger. Then he went and prowled around the woman as she worked. But a little later the tiger jumped three times in the air, and once more became a Buddhist monk. 'I tried hard to kill and eat her,' he said, 'but each time I tried to approach her countless flaming swords appeared around the field, and I could not get near her. I can never kill her now, for to-day is the appointed day. And so I can never become a man.' With these words the monk disappeared. Despite the evil curse laid upon her all the gods of Heaven and Earth joined together to protect the child she carried in her womb. This child was the great Gim Dǒg-Nyǒng.

It is related that his grandfather had been executed on a false charge brought by a wicked Minister in Seoul. His father therefore prayed for twenty years to all the gods and the Buddha that a son might be born to him, who should avenge his grandfather's death.

When he had prayed for ten years a daughter was born, and in anger and disappointment he stabbed her to death. After ten more years of prayer, however, Gim Dŏg-Nyong was born.

As a boy he was unusually courageous, and exceedingly gifted in the art of strategy. He was extremely skilful in the game of checkers, and used to play with an Elder in Seoul. But never for one moment did he forget the duty laid upon him to avenge his dead grandfather.

One day he went to a noted swordsmith who lived in his native village, and asked him to make him a sword. He requested that various secret and magical methods be used in its manufacture, and so the smith guessed that he was dealing with no ordinary man. When he handed the finished sword to Gim Dog-Nyŏng the smith said, 'I know that I must die to-day, and that I will do without the slightest regret. I am content that you should sever my neck in twain at once.' Gim replied, 'You know something of the secret of my sword. It is better that your life should be sacrificed, so that it may not be betrayed to the world.' So he lifted the sword and lunged at the smith, but only cut his sleeve off. So he spared him, and advised him to say nothing to anyone about the matter.

Gim then went to Seoul with his magic sword, and took his revenge on the Minister who had been his grandfather's enemy. Then his sword, which had the power of destroying distance, returned him instantly to Gwangzu. There he at once began a game of checkers. The Minister's death was reported to the authorities, and orders were given that Gim should be punished for the deed. But when they found that he could travel every day from Gwangzu to Seoul, covering the distance of two hundred and fifty miles as if it were nothing, they cancelled the judgment upon him.

Told by Gim Gi-Hwan; Tong-Yŏng (1932).

34

The Blind Man and the Devils

IT is traditional for blind men to be fortune-tellers in Korea. They wander through the streets carrying sticks and crying out in strange voices. So people go up to them, and ask them what they should do

59

to solve their worries, or what the future has in store for them, when they should hold marriage ceremonies or funerals, to find things they have lost, or when they should move to a new house.

In the distant past there lived in Seoul a most renowned fortune-teller. He was blind, but he had some supernatural power whereby he was enabled to see evil spirits and chase them away. One day, as he walked through the streets, he met an errand boy who was carrying a large box filled with cakes of many colours, the sort of thing that might be set before guests at a feast or a funeral. Then he saw a crowd of devils, in many coloured clothes, red, green, and purple, hovering over the cakes. He was most alarmed to think of the malign influence that these evil-tempered devils would exert in the house to which the cakes were being taken, so he followed the errand boy, keeping a discreet distance behind him, for he was rather suspicious to see a blind man following him.

Before long the errand boy came to a prosperous-looking house and went in, while the blind man waited outside. Very soon he heard loud cries of alarm from within the house, and on asking the reason for the uproar was told that the daughter of the house had suddenly died. So at once he determined to save the girl, for he knew the cause of her illness, which must have been brought upon her by the evil demons he had been following. He went to the master of the house and said, 'I am a blind fortune-teller, and I think I can save your daughter.' He then told him what he had seen on the way to the house.

The master of the house accepted his offer, and at once he set about working his magic. First he had the daughter's body taken into a small room, and closed all the doors and windows tightly. Then he pasted paper over every crack and crevice in the room, so that there was no place where even a needle might pass. Then sitting by the body he began to recite a magical sutra. He was alone in the room, and concentrating all his energies on the work of exorcism, and then the sound of groaning could be heard from within. The blind man still sat quietly reciting, and the room was filled with an ever-growing volume of noise, for the devils that haunted the body of the girl were screaming in their agony, and striving to escape. Then a servant girl, alarmed by the tumult from within, went to the window, and pierced a hole in the paper covering it with the tip of her little finger moistened in her mouth, so that she might be able to peep inside. Then all the devils immediately escaped through the hole she had so thoughtlessly made, and thus evaded capture by the blind man. Now they were free, and there was nothing he could do about it. Then the dead girl at once opened her eyes, and was restored to her parents, but the blind man said, 'I shall not live long now, for the devils that have escaped will certainly take their revenge on me.' With that he left the house, and refused to accept any of the presents the girl's father offered him.

The fame of the blind fortune-teller now spread among the people, and at last came to the ears of the King. The King was a cautious man, and inclined to be sceptical of such an extraordinary story. He felt that there was a grave danger that the blind man might be an impostor who would cheat the ignorant people, and so decided that he should be punished unless his claims could be proved. He therefore summoned him to the Court, and tested him to find out his real capacity. He had a rat killed, and ordered it to be placed before the blind man. Then he asked, 'What is that in front of you?' The blind man answered without delay, 'It is a rat, Your Majesty.' The King was a little startled, and asked again, 'How many rats are there? Can you tell me that too?' 'There are three rats, Your Majesty,' replied the blind man. Thereupon the King burst out laughing, and then began to reprimand the blind man in a stern voice, 'You are a liar and an impostor. There is only one rat, yet you have answered, "Three." So now we know how a blind fortune-teller deceives people. You are nothing but a charlatan. You are a public menace, and I sentence you to be hanged immediately.'

The blind man protested against this severe sentence, and insisted that he was right. 'Your Majesty. I have a clear impression of three rats. There can be no mistake about that.' Despite his protests, however, he was led away outside the East Gate of the castle to be executed. Then some of the courtiers examined the rat with some curiosity, and found to their amazement that there were two perfectly formed baby rats inside it. They told the King, who was deeply impressed by the blind man's uncanny insight. He gave orders that he should be released immediately.

Now, it was the custom, that when urgent messages were to be sent to the prison authorities a man was sent up the watchtower at the eastern corner of the palace to signal with a flag. If the flag was waved to the right it meant that the prisoner was to be reprieved, but if it was waved to the left it meant that the execution was to be carried out. So a man was sent up the tower to send a message that the blind man should be spared. But when he tried to wave the flag to the right an evil wind sprang up suddenly and pushed the flag over to the left. However hard he tried to push it to the right, it always swung over to the left.

So the blind man was executed, and immediately the evil wind died away. The mocking laughter of devils echoed round the castle, and voices saying, 'Now we have our revenge! We can now go away.'

Told by Zŏng Tĕg-Ha; Ŏnyang (1936).

35
Young Gim and the Robbers

LONG ago there lived two Ministers, Gim and Yi by name, who were very close friends. Minister Gim had a son and Minister Yi had a daughter. When the two children were four or five years old their fathers agreed that they should be betrothed.

Some years later, when young Gim was eight years old, the Minister Yi invited him to his daughter's birthday celebrations. His father was away from home at the time, and so young Gim set out accompanied by a large retinue of servants. It was quite a long way to Minister Yi's house.

While the two children were sitting at the feast a messenger came rushing in from Minister Gim's house. He reported that no sooner had his master returned home than a band of robbers had attacked the house. They had killed the minister and carried off his wife, and stolen all the treasure they could lay hands on.

Young Gim hastened home in great alarm, and found that the messenger's report was indeed true. No one, however, could tell him who the leader of the robber band was. Despite his tender years young Gim made up his mind on the spot to track him down and take his revenge. So he set out at once along the mountain roads to look for his mother.

As he was passing over a hill he heard frantic shouts from the valley. He looked down and saw a boy fighting desperately with a bear. So he rushed down and saved the boy, who told him that he too had been bereaved in the same way by the same robber band, and his home had been burnt to the ground. So he had built a cottage in the valley where he lived now, hoping that the day would come when he could take his revenge on the robbers. Young Gim proposed to him that they should swear to be brothers, and the other agreed. So they became sworn brothers.

The two boys set out together, and one day they came to a broad river. When they were in midstream a terrible storm suddenly sprang up and the ferry capsized. As the boat sank young Gim fainted. When he came to he was lying on the river bank and another boy of his own age was tending him. There was no sign of his first friend. The second boy told him that he had found him floating on the river while he was fishing. Gim thanked his new friend for saving him and asked him who he was. He replied that the robber band had swooped on his household and killed his father and mother. They had carried off his sister. So young Gim proposed that they should swear to be brothers, and told him of the sworn-brother whom he had lost in the storm.

The two boys set out together to seek their revenge on the robbers, and before long they came to another big river. This time too the ferry they were crossing by sank in a storm. Gim's second companion was drowned, and Gim himself was rescued by an old woman who lived on an island. She told him that the island was ruled by the chief of the robbers who had killed his father and the parents of his friends, and had plundered much property from the people. He felt a wave of fury rise in him and burned to take his revenge, but he could do nothing for he was lying in bed helpless as a result of his injuries.

One day the robber chief sent a messenger to the old woman's house to bid her send away the strange boy she had found. He warned her that if she disobeyed this command she would be put to death. But she was unwilling to send him right away, and so she led him to a small thatched hut by the riverside and left him there. One day a ship came and anchored in the stream before the hut. There was a venerable old man standing on the deck. He called to young Gim, 'You are the son of the Minister Gim, are you not? I have come to rescue you.' So young Gim went with the strange old man and followed him to his retreat deep in the mountains. There he lived with him and studied the arts of magic.

When young Gim was sixteen years old the old man said to him, 'You must go back to your own country without delay. The robber chief has taken up arms against the King and a great war is raging. The King is in great danger. You must go to his rescue, and then in three years' time I shall meet you on the same day of the same month.'

So young Gim set out for home. On the way he saw a wild horse rushing toward him. It was plunging madly, but when Gim came near it calmed down and stood still. Gim guessed that it must be a dragon horse and mounted on its back. It leapt up immediately and rushed forward neighing gently. Before long it stopped and pawed the ground as if to tell him to dig there. So he dismounted and dug, and found a set of magic armour with spears and swords. He put on the armour and mounted the dragon horse once more. As he rode along he looked like some majestic general.

When he came to the royal castle he found it on the point of surrender. With his magic he transformed his horse and himself into birds and flew over the enemy army. Then he returned to his proper form and stood before the King. Bowing low he said, 'Your majesty, I am the son of the Minister Gim. I shall lay the enemy low without fail. Let Your Majesty's mind be set at rest.' The King was delighted to hear him, and conferred on him the rank of Great Marshal.

So young Gim turned himself into a dog and went to spy out the enemy camp. At the entrance to the camp was a fearsome black face, the incarnation of a bear a thousand years old, belching hot flames from its mouth, that scorched the castle of the King. There was also a genii with a slender body, the incarnation of a fox a thousand years old, assiduously studying a book of astrology. Beside him stood a dwarf, the incarnation of a rat ten thousand years old, swinging his long tail like lightning, whence flowed a mighty flood that threatened to submerge the castle. A furious giant, the incarnation of a tiger one hundred years old, was hurling daggers of flame against the King's camp.

Marshal Gim by his magic poured water on the scorched walls of the castle and blocked the flood with a mountain. He called up a downpour of rain to quench the fiery daggers. But in the end he was overwhelmed by the enemy's superior numbers, after a desperate battle. In the enemy's camp he found the son of Minister Yi and his daughter, his betrothed. But she was killed in the battle.

Marshal Gim fled with the King to an island. But with the skill in astrology, the slender genii, the incarnation of a fox, was able to find out where they had gone. The dwarf, the incarnation of a rat, tried to submerge them with an even greater flood which it pumped from its tail. Gim fell asleep, and in a dream saw a butterfly which seemed to invite him to follow it. So he turned himself into a swallow and flew off with it. They flew thousands of miles and in the end they came to a cavern in a great mountain. They went inside and the butterfly vanished. There Gim found the boy who had fought with the bear and had been lost in the storm. He was studying a book of strategy. Gim told him of the perils he had undergone and of the great danger threatening the King. His friend answered, 'I have been waiting for you to come. I sent the butterfly as my messenger to summon you. Now let us join together to seek revenge on our foe!'

With their magic they reached the island where the King was in the twinkling of an eye. Then they joined battle in earnest. But great misfortunes befell them. Marshal Gim's friend was slain in the fighting and at last the island vanished from sight, completely submerged by the flood that the dwarf had pumped from its tail.

So Gim and the King took refuge on another island, but before long this one too was almost submerged. Once more Gim had a dream and saw a crow flying in front of his eyes. Again he turned himself into a swallow and followed it. It led him far away to a cavern in another mountain. There he found his friend who had been fishing and had afterwards been lost in the storm. He was practising the arts of war. He proposed that they should go and take revenge on their enemy together, and went to the island with Gim. But he too was killed in the battle. So Gim and the King fled to yet another island, but this one too was soon threatened by the rising flood.

So Gim and the King embarked on a ship and set sail for the open sea. Then the venerable old man came down out of the sky and alighted on their ship. It was the very day when he had promised that he would meet Gim. The old man said to him, 'Though your training was not complete I sent you to aid your King. Now that you are in such a desperate situation I am obliged to come to your rescue myself.' Then he recited a magical hymn and at once the sky grew dark. Lightning flashed through the air, and a mighty rain of thunderbolts fell on the enemy. Before long not one of the enemy army was left alive.

Then all became quiet once more and Marshal Gim and the old man went to the enemy island. There Gim found his mother and the sister of his second friend, who had been a fisherman and had been killed in the second battle. Then he returned home with the King accompanied by his mother and the girl, whom he married soon afterwards.

Told by Zŏng Zin-Il; Yangsan (1932).

36

General Pumpkin

LONG, long ago there lived a rich man who had an only son. This boy had an enormous appetite and was particularly fond of pumpkins. His parents got all the pumpkins they could for him. They sowed all their fields with pumpkins, and bought them in vast quantities from the neighbours and in the market. They made pumpkin cakes, pumpkin puddings, pumpkin soup, pumpkin porridge for their son, and he ate nothing else. He would eat a big straw bagful at a sitting, and yet he always complained that he was hungry.

His parents spent so much money to feed him that in the end they were ruined. And to make matters worse the gluttonous eater of pumpkins used to break wind so often and so violently that in the end the villagers refused to put up with him any longer, so fed up were they with the smell and thunderous rumblings. Finally they drove him away from the village.

So he wandered from village to village begging pumpkins. People who had not heard of him often gave him work, for he looked very big and strong, and he did not ask for money, but only pumpkins as reward for his labour. But he lost every job in a few days when his employers found what an extraordinarily filthy glutton he was.

One day he came to a big Buddhist temple in the mountains. It was a very rich and famous temple, with many priests, but often fell victim to a band of robbers, under their chief, Hairy Zang. Zang used to disguise himself as an ordinary wayfarer and go to the temple to spy out the land. Then at night he would lead his band against it and carry off all the valuables they could lay hands on.

When the Abbot saw the enormous frame of the pumpkin eater standing before the gate of the temple he went and welcomed him warmly, for he thought that this gigantic stranger would be a match for the robbers. He led him into the temple and bowing humbly before him asked him what his favourite food was. 'You do look a strong man indeed, sir,' he said. 'What do you like to eat, and how much?'

'I eat nothing but pumpkins,' answered the glutton. 'You had better cook as many as you can for me, say a whole kettle full.'

So the priests of the temple entertained him with a whole kettleful of pumpkin porridge, and then brought him another kettleful of pumpkin cakes. Then they asked him to help them if the robbers should attack the temple.

That evening the robber chief came to the temple. When he saw the feast of pumpkins being made ready he asked a priest 'Have you a party to-night?'

'Yes, General Pumpkin is here,' was the answer.

'How many soldiers has he?'

'He has come alone, and will eat them all himself.'

The robber chief was astounded to hear this, and decided to stay the night in the temple so that he might take a closer look at the terrible general. Some of the priests recognized him and went and told the Abbot. Then the Abbot went and told General Pumpkin that the robber chief was staying in the next room. So General Pumpkin told the priests to take drums and hide in every corner of the temple at midnight, and put out all the lights. Meanwhile all the followers of the robber chief gathered outside the temple and tried to break in. Suddenly in the stillness of the night there came a deafening rumble like thunder, and the air was filled with an unbearable stench. General Pumpkin had broken wind. Then a violent gale blew down the high brick wall surrounding the temple. The robber chief tried to run away in his alarm, but whichever way he turned he was confronted with the roll of drums from every dark corner. In the end he was killed, and all his men were crushed under the falling bricks of the wall.

The Abbot thanked General Pumpkin for his services, and invited him to stay in the temple as long as he lived. He lived there for many years, and had all the pumpkins he wanted. To supply him the priests planted a large area of the temple fields with pumpkins every year.

When he grew old the three sons of a rich family that lived near the temple came to him and asked him to help them fight a white tiger which had killed their father. He went to their house one day and they entertained him with pumpkin delicacies of every kind. All they wanted him to do was to break wind just once.

So in the afternoon the three sons of the family donned their armour and shouted, 'Come out and fight, white-tiger.' Immediately there appeared a tiny tiger, no bigger than a rat, and completely white. They all leapt in the air to fight.

General Pumpkin peeped through a chink in the window-paper to see what was going on, and, horrified by what he saw, fell down in a faint. As he fell he broke wind violently, and a deafening roar filled the air. The white tiger was paralysed with terror at this sudden explosion and the evil stench that followed. Then a bamboo stake from the fence pierced its body and it fell down dead.

When the three young men came inside again they found the old man lying dead in the room surrounded with excrement. They were very sorry to see it, and provided him with a fitting funeral. And for three years they mourned for him as they did for their father.

Ondoru Yawa, told by Bang Zŏng-Hwan; Seoul (1925).

37
The Castle of Seoul

IN the middle years of the Goryŏ dynasty there lived a man called Yun Gwŏn. The Government sent him to select a field to the south of Mount Bĕg Ag, which is the high rocky mountain near

Seoul, now known as Mount Bug Han, and to plant plum trees there. But when they began to grow large he was ordered to prune them ruthlessly so that their branches should not grow thick, for Do Sŏn, the famous Buddhist of the Kingdom of Silla, had inscribed on a stone on one of the peaks of Mount Bĕg Ag, 'The next King shall be Yi (which means plum), and the capital shall be transferred to Han Yang (the old name of Seoul).'

As thus predicted a General named Yi deposed the King, and reigned in his stead. But there were many who remained loyal to the former King, and they compelled Yi to move his capital from Gĕsŏng. So he summoned a noted Buddhist, by name Muhag, who lived in a small temple of Mount Godal, and bade him select a site for a new capital.

Muhag set out, and crossing over Mount Bĕg Ag, he came to Dong-Ya, 'Eastern Field,' just south of the mountain. He stood there pondering where he should go, when he heard a farmer ploughing. He was shouting at his ox and saying, 'You are as stupid as Muhag (which means illiterate), always going the wrong way!' The Buddhist Muhag pricked up his ears when he heard this, for it sounded as if it referred to him. So he said to the farmer, 'You just said your ox was as stupid as Muhag. My name is Muhag. Perhaps you can help me. I am looking for a site for a new capital, and this seems a likely place. What do you think about it?' The farmer then advised him to go ten *ni* (2½ miles) to the northwards. The field where they met is now called Wang Sim Nyi, which means 'Go ten ni', and it is said that a stone inscribed with these words was found buried in the field.

Muhag followed the farmer's advice, and found a suitable site at Han Yang, surrounded by steep mountains on three sides and the deep river Han on the fourth. It was decided that the new capital should be built here, and a castle with walls surrounding it. They could not make up their minds, however, about the location of this wall. One night it snowed, and in the morning they found a circle of snow around the site. They decided therefore to build the wall along this circle of snow. And they called the capital Seoul, which is said to be derived from sŏl-ul, a Chinese word meaning snow, and a Korean word meaning fence.

Told by Czoe Gyu-Dong; Seoul (1936).

38

Rival Magicians

THREE hundred and fifty years ago, in a temple on Mount Myohyang, there lived a practitioner of magic, by name Samyŏng-Dang. It was his firm belief that he was the greatest magician in Korea. One day it came to his ears that a certain noted Buddhist, Sŏsan-Děsa by name, who lived in the Zang-An Temple on the Diamond Mountain, excelled greatly in the art. Thereupon he set out for the Diamond Mountain to meet this Sŏsan-Děsa, and prove his own superiority.

Now Sŏsan-Děsa knew he was on the way, and summoned one of his disciples. 'I shall be receiving a guest to-day, from a temple on Mount Myohyang,' he told him. 'I want you to go and meet him.' The disciple looked at him doubtfully, and said, 'I have never met him, so how shall I recognize him?' The master answered, 'You will have no difficulty, for as he comes he will make the water in the river flow back upstream.'

The young disciple walked along by the river to meet the guest as his master had ordered, though he still doubted very much what he had been told. Before long, however, he saw the water in the river turn and flow back upstream, and then a Buddhist came towards him. Guessing that he must be the guest from Mount Myohyang he bowed and said, 'I am from the Zang-An Temple on the Diamond Mountain. I have come to meet you.'

Samyŏng-Dang was astonished to be so unexpectedly greeted, but he concealed his surprise so that his dignity might not be impaired and calmly replied in a soft voice, 'I am much obliged to you for your kindness in coming to meet me.' Then they went together to Zang-An Temple.

The moment Samyŏng-Dang saw Sŏsan-Děsa he stretched out his hand and caught a bird that was flying by. Enclosing it in his hand he asked, 'Is this bird alive or dead?' Sŏsan-Děsa had his foot across the threshold as he came to greet Samyŏng-Dang, and immediately countered with another question, 'Am I coming out of the room, or going in?' So they greeted one another smilingly.

When they sat down, Sŏsan-Dĕsa had a bowl of water brought in, with fish swimming in it. He said to Samyŏng-Dang, 'We are both Buddhists, and it is not lawful for us to eat fish. We may, however, swallow them once, providing we immediately vomit them out again alive.' He immediately began to eat the fish, and Samyŏng-Dang followed his example. Then Sŏsan-Dĕsa vomited the fish out and placed them in the bowl, where they immediately revived. But the fish eaten by Samyŏng-Dang all died, despite all his efforts not to be worsted in the trial.

Then they began to pile up heaps of eggs. Samyŏng-Dang began piling the eggs up from the ground, while Sŏsan-Dĕsa began his pile in mid-air, and built it down to the ground. For lunch he offered his guest a bowl of needles, saying 'Do have some of my delicious noodle soup.' Then he began eating ravenously, but Samyŏng-Dang could not eat it at all.

So Samyŏng-Dang was defeated by Sŏsan-Dĕsa, and conceded that he was the greatest magician in the land. Moreover he enrolled himself among the disciples of Sŏsan-Dĕsa.

Zosŏn Gubi Zŏnsŏl Zi.

39
The Governor and the Buddhist

MANY years ago a son was born to the head-man of Hyŏb Czŏn, in the province of Gyŏng Nam, when he was nearly sixty years of age. He doted on his son to such an exaggerated extent that he would not even send him to a teacher to be educated. The boy was still utterly ignorant when he attained the age of thirteen.

There was a famous Buddhist who lived in the Hĕ-In Temple, which was in the same district, and renowned as one of the biggest in Korea. Hearing of the head-man's idle son, he called one day on his father and said to him, 'You are already very old, and your son and heir is completely illiterate. Your family may suffer for this in the future. Will you entrust your son to me that I may give him the education which he needs?' The head-man was persuaded by the Buddhist's words, and entrusted his son's education to him. He promised that he would not interfere in any way, and gave the Buddhist a document to that effect.

The Buddhist then took the head-man's son to the temple, and subjected him to the customary stern discipline. The boy was often harshly scolded, and soon began to feel that the restrictions imposed upon him were intolerable. So one day he tried to escape from the temple, but the Buddhist restrained him. He explained the real purpose of his education to the boy, and showed him the document that his father had written. So he devoted himself to his studies, and in a few years he had mastered all the classics, for he was a very talented boy. He was well advanced in his preparation for the High Civil Examination, but he still bore a deep grudge in his heart towards the monks in the temple, who treated him so harshly. At last he passed the Government examination, and was appointed governor of his own province of Gyŏng Nam.

Now that he was powerful he determined to get his revenge on the monks for the harsh treatment they had meted out to him. So he went out to the temple with an imposing train of attendants. His former master, the chief Buddhist of the temple, and all the monks met him courteously at the gate. When the Governor saw his former master all his resentment melted away, and in its place came a feeling of deep gratitude, so touched was he by the venerable character of the Buddhist.

The two men talked far into the night of their association in the past, and then the Buddhist went to his library and brought out a strange paper. On it the Governor's future was described in great detail, with all the ranks to which he would be promoted, that he would be appointed Governor of Pyŏng-An Province, and the age at which he would die. As he rolled the document up again the Buddhist said, 'I will see you again at Pyŏngyang, when you have been appointed Governor of Pyŏng-An Province.'

A few years later they were very pleased to meet again at Pyŏng-yang, when the former pupil was appointed governor there. They talked together till far into the night, and went to bed in the same room. But the fire beneath the floor made the room so uncomfortably hot that the governor could not sleep. So he got up and took his bed to the next room.

In the morning he found the Buddhist dead in the room he had been forced to leave. He had been murdered, and so the Governor ordered a strict investigation into his death. It was found that he had been killed by one of the official dancing girls who had mistaken him for the Governor.

The Governor was overcome with gratitude for the Buddhist's noble self-sacrifice, for there could be no doubt that he had foreseen what would happen, and had given his life to save his friend.

Told by Czoe Gyu-Dong; Seoul (1940).

40

The Young Man and the Priest

LONG ago a rich man had an only son, on whom he lavished the greatest care and affection. While the boy was still young his father found a wife for him and he was married. One day a travelling Buddhist priest came to the house, and reading the young man's destiny in his face, said, 'I see in this boy's face that he is fated to lose his wife, and that great misfortune will come upon the family.' His father asked the priest, 'Is there no way in which such dire misfortune may be avoided?' The priest replied, 'Let him come with me to the temple in the mountains, and there study Buddhism for three years. If he does this he will acquire the Buddhist virtues, and he will be absolved from this doom.'

The young man went with the priest and devoted himself to the study of the Scriptures. One night, when the three years were almost completed, he had a dream in which he saw a beautiful girl. The priest knew of the dream, but said nothing to the boy. Next morning, however, he told the priest, who then advised him strongly, 'Do not let yourself be led astray by the passions. Rather devote yourself more faithfully to your studies.'

Try as he might, however, the face of the girl he had seen in his dream still haunted him, and he desired ardently to see her once again. One day a fit of deep depression seized him, and he wandered aimlessly out through the San-mun, or 'Mountain Gate,' which divided the temple from the everyday world. He went down into the village, where he found a wine-shop, and he rashly drank a cup of wine. He forgot his Buddhist vows, and went back to the temple just

73

a little drunk. The priest rebuked him sternly for his lapse, and he apologized most humbly for his mistake.

But that night he dreamed of the beautiful girl again, and she tempted him with fair words. 'I am living at the top of the hill behind this temple,' she said. 'I should be very happy to meet you there.'

'What excuse can I make to my teacher?' asked the young man.

'Tell him that you have lost your appetite lately, and so you are going to pick fruit on the mountain,' she replied.

So next day he took a basket and a knife and went to the priest to tell him he was going up the mountain to pick fruit. The priest answered, with an innocent look on his face, 'Don't be too long.'

When he came to a clump of bamboos near the summit of the mountain the young man saw the beautiful girl waving to him. So he put the basket and the knife down, and followed her in among the bamboos.

The priest came up the hill behind him, and found the basket. He made certain cuts in it with the knife, and then went down to await the young man's return.

The girl took her guest into her house amid the bamboos and they lay down together in the room. He fell asleep, and when he woke he saw that he was lying in a cave with the body of a dead woman. The body was wearing a jacket, but no skirt. Terror stricken he ran out of the cave, grabbed the basket and the knife, and rushed down the hill to the temple. He told the priest everything that had happened to him up on the mountain.

The priest then led him up the mountain again and, when they came to the clump of bamboo, said, 'You have twice been haunted by evil spirits. Tell me, what do you see over there?' Following his gaze the boy looked reluctantly at the cave, and saw that it was not the body of a woman, but of a female tiger wearing a woman's jacket.

The priest then explained to him what had happened. 'Your wife was fated to be eaten by a tiger,' he said. So the male tiger went to seize her, but only succeeded in getting her jacket, because Buddha had determined to punish it. It died soon afterwards, and then its mate put on the jacket and tried to kill you in the bamboos. But Buddha slew the evilly disposed female too, as you see her lying yonder. Now all your enemies are dead, so that you can safely return home.'

So the young man went home to his wife, who was no longer in any danger, and they lived happily together.

Told by Yi Sang-Hwa; Dĕgu (1926).

41

Zo Han-Zun who became a Stone Buddha

LONG, long ago in Sinan-myŏn, in the district of Zŏng-zu, there lived a poor man called Zo Han-Zun. He was honest and hard working, and always ready to do good turns for others. There was a river, called Dal-Czŏn, which flowed between Sinan-Myŏn and the town of Zŏngzu. This river used to flood every year, and cause great inconvenience to the people, for it was then quite impassable. Zo therefore decided that it was absolutely necessary to build a bridge, and, turning over various ideas in his mind, he thought that the best thing would be to ask people to contribute money for its construction. So every day he went round all the neighbouring villages to make the collection, and all the villagers were greatly moved by his enthusiasm, and contributed generously towards the cost.

When enough money had been collected Zo called a large number of stonemasons to help him and set about building the bridge. All went well for a while, but one of the stones they were to use was so big and heavy that they could not get it to the site, however much they tried. Zo was very worried about it, and stayed awake at night thinking about it. One night, however, when he had at last fallen asleep, he had a dream. A spirit appeared and said to him, 'You are worried about that big stone. I will set your mind at rest.' With those words the spirit summoned a crowd of his friends and they rounded up a great team of cattle. They harnessed them to the stone, and dragged it to the riverside without difficulty. Zo was overjoyed to see it, but then he woke up and realised it was only a dream.

In the morning he walked despondently to the river. To his great

75

surprise he saw the stone set in position, and all the cattle nearby dripping with sweat and looking utterly exhausted.

So he built the bridge successfully, and his neighbours benefited greatly from his generosity. To reward him the Heavenly King determined that when he died he should be reborn as the son of the Emperor of China. But on looking more closely into the matter the Heavenly King found that owing to his poverty Zo had only contributed two pennies towards the cost of building the bridge. And moreover he had bought himself a pair of straw sandals out of the money he had collected. Such a misdemeanor deserved punishment, and so the Heavenly King decided that he should be reborn instead as a Princess, and not as a Prince as he otherwise would have been.

Some time later Zo died, and the Empress of China gave birth to a Princess, in accordance with the will of the Heavenly King. Strange to say there was found tattooed on the baby's back the phrase 'Reincarnation of a Korean, Zo Han-Zun.' The Emperor was most astonished, and at once dispatched a messenger to Korea to inquire what manner of man this Zo might be.

The Emperor's envoy came to the court of the King of Korea and asked, 'Is there anyone in this land named Zo Han-Zun? If there is, may I ask what sort of person he or she may be?' The King of Korea replied, 'No, there is no such person in my Kingdom.'

When the envoy reported the King's answer to the Emperor he had the princess killed, for he was afraid that she might be the incarnation of some evil monster. And from the very night when she died so wretchedly her spirit began to haunt Zo's descendants in Korea. After a while it appeared in a dream to a member of the family, and said, 'I am your ancestor Zo Han-Zun. I was reborn as the daughter of the Emperor of China, but very soon I was cruelly killed. So now I have returned to protect my descendants, and I shall become a stone Buddha on the mountain behind the house.'

When they awoke in the morning the members of Zo's family climbed the mountain and there they found a strange statue they had never seen before, just as the dream had foretold. They were very glad to find the stone Buddha, for they could worship it to bring prosperity to the family. So they held a joyful festival there, and invited all their neighbours to a feast before the new altar.

Afterwards they built a small temple over the statue. Strange to say the statue began to grow daily bigger, and in a few months the temple was too small for it. So they rebuilt it on a larger scale, and this they had to do several times again. When people prayed there it performed many miracles, curing sickness, averting calamities, and the like.

Told by Czoe Gyu-Dong; Seoul (1942).

42

The Story of Admiral Yi

ADMIRAL YI SUN-SIN invented the Turtle-boat, the world's first submarine, and won many victories in the war against Japan in 1592–1598. He was noted for his cleverness from his earliest years.

One day, when he was very young, his father said to him, 'You see me sitting here in the room. Can you think of any way of forcing me to come out?'

Young Yi Sun-Sin pondered a moment and then replied, 'No, Father, that is quite impossible. But if you were outside, I'm sure I could make you go in.'

So his father got up and went out of the room. Then Yi Sun-Sin shouted gleefully, 'That's right, Father! You have come out of the room, haven't you? See, I've won.'

His father smiled and praised his son for his cleverness.

Told by Zŏng Hě-Ryong; Seoul (1950).

43

The Mast of Sand

LONG, long ago the Emperor of China sent an embassy to Korea with a most unreasonable request. 'You are to load all the waters of the Han River on a ship and send them to China,' it ran.

The King of Korea and his Ministers were most perplexed at this request, and could not think what to do. Then the Prime Minister, Hwang Hŭi, spoke up. 'You should reply to the Emperor of China in these terms, Your Majesty,' he said. ' The King of Korea will be delighted to transport all the waters of the Han River to China. The ship will, however, need a mast made of sand. As you know, there is very little sand in Korea, but I am told that in the North of China there is a vast desert. I should be very grateful if you would have a three hundred foot mast of sand delivered to me as soon as possible.'

It is related that after this the Emperor of China never again sent any unreasonable request to the King of Korea.

Told by Yi Ŭn-Sang; Masan (1930).

44

The Tiger and the Dwarf

IN the days of old there lived a famous hunter who was such a skilful marksman that he could shoot down a bird on the wing. One day he set out to go hunting on the Diamond Mountain in the Province of Gangwŏn. He spent a night in the house of an old woman at the foot of the mountain. In the morning she gave him a bag of singed cooked rice sufficient to last a week, and he set out, despite the old woman's earnest warning. 'You should go home at once,' she said. 'I have seen many hunters go up into the mountain, but none of them ever came back.' But he ignored her advice and went off, and he too was never seen again.

After he had gone on this expedition a son was born to his wife. As it happened he grew up to be a dwarf. The other children often teased him because he had no father. So when he was eight years old he asked his mother for a gun, so that he might go out and avenge his father's death. She gave him a gun, and for three years he practised day and night.

One day his mother said, 'Your father could shoot the left ear off my water-jar from the distance of a quarter of a mile when I was carrying it on my head. And yet the tiger killed him. So you must practise a lot more yet.'

78

So he practised assiduously for three more years, until he could shoot the left ear off his mother's water-jar from the distance of a quarter of a mile. Then his mother said to him, 'Your father could shoot the eye off a needle from the distance of a quarter of a mile while I was holding it in my fingers. You must practise a lot more yet.' Then after three more years he became so skilful that he could shoot the eye off a needle from the distance of a quarter of a mile. But he still practised for a few months more.

Then one day he bade farewell to his mother and left home with his gun. He came to the house of the old woman who lived at the foot of the Diamond Mountain. 'Your father was an excellent marksman,' she said. 'He could shoot an ant off a rock at the distance of a quarter of a mile without touching the rock at all. Can you do that?'

He tried to do it, but without success. So he stayed with the old woman for three years, practising ceaselessly night and day, neglecting even to eat and sleep. Then the old woman gave him a bag of singed cooked rice sufficient to last for several months, and he went off up the mountain to look for tigers.

One day as he sat on a rock smoking his pipe a Buddhist priest came up and asked him for a light. The dwarf gave it to him readily, but as the priest was lighting his pipe noticed tiger's fangs in his mouth. So he immediately shot him in the breast, and he fell to the ground, transformed into a tiger.

Then the dwarf went on his way. He had not gone very far when he came across an old woman digging sweet potatoes in a mountain field. He went up to her and asked her to give him some. 'I am very hungry,' he said. 'Would you be so kind as to give me some sweet potatoes?' Without turning round the woman answered, 'I'm too busy just now. My husband was shot a little while ago and his spirit has just appeared to me. I must have sweet potatoes to bring him back to life.' The dwarf noticed that instead of hands she had tiger's claws, and so he shot her in the breast. She fell down dead and was transformed into a female tiger.

Next he came to a spring where a girl was drawing water. 'I am very thirsty,' he said, 'Please give me a drink of water.' 'I cannot,' she replied. 'The spirits of my father-in-law and my mother-in-law have just appeared to me. Someone has killed them. I must take this healing water to them and restore them to life. I have no time to waste.' From the front she appeared to be a beautiful young girl, but her back was the back of a tiger, and so the dwarf shot her too.

A little further on he met a young man. He went up to him and asked him the way. But the man merely told him that the spirits of his parents and his wife had just appeared to him and told him that someone had killed them. So he was on his way to hold a memorial service to bring them back to life. He was in a hurry and would not tell the dwarf the way. The dwarf noticed that between his legs he had a tiger's tail, and shot him at once. He fell down dead, and was transformed into a young tiger.

In this way the dwarf killed a whole family of tigers, but he was not yet satisfied, for he did not know which tiger had killed his father. So he searched here and there and at last he came upon a great crowd of tigers assembled in a valley. He looked down on them from the top of a hill, and realised that they were holding a feast. There were hundreds of them making merry, eating, drinking, and dancing. He levelled his gun at them from his vantage point and began to shoot. He killed scores of them, but he ran out of ammunition long before he had killed them all. So the tigers came and took him prisoner. They took away his bag of food and led him before an enormous old tiger, who seemed to be the leader of the band.

The leader glared at him and said, 'This dwarf has killed many of my dear comrades and has ruined my birthday. And I have heard that a whole family of my relations was shot down on their way here. He is probably the one that did it. He is a menace with his gun. He even seems to surpass the other one we caught about twenty years ago. What shall I do with him?'

The dwarf guessed that this must be the tiger that had killed his father, and seethed with impotent rage. Then one of the tiger elders said, 'He would make a tasty dish for your birthday. I suggest you eat him up at once.' All the other tigers agreed with this suggestion, so the leader seized the dwarf with his forepaws and swallowed him, gun and all, at one gulp. He said with a smile, 'This dwarf is too small to chew.'

The dwarf came to the tiger's stomach, which was as big inside as a village. There were human bones scattered here and there, and in one corner he found a gun with his father's name engraved on it. Beside the gun was a set of bones that were most probably his father's. So he gathered them up and put them in his bag. In another corner he found a girl lying senseless. He tended her carefully, and she recovered consciousness. Then they looked round for something sharp they might use to cut a hole in the tiger and get away.

Fortunately the dwarf found a knife in his pocket, and with it he cut a hole in the tiger's skin from inside. They looked through it and could see the sky. The girl looked out to see whether the tiger was in a field, or on the seashore, or on a cliff, or in the mountains. Meanwhile the dwarf began to cut along the tiger's side. He and the girl were very hungry, so he looked around for something they could eat. He saw the tiger's liver hanging overhead, and cut a piece off it. Unfortunately they found it unfit to eat.

By now the tigers' leader was in terrible pain, and groaning aloud in his agony. The other tigers could not understand why this should be so, and could do nothing to help him. Then one of them suggested that perhaps an apple or a pear might relieve his sickness, so he went and gobbled up all the fruit he could. The dwarf and the girl inside ate all the fruit he swallowed, and when he went and drank at a spring they were able to slake their thirst.

The tiger's pains grew steadily worse, until he could stand them no more. He went quite mad, and rushed around roaring, leaping in the air, and attacking the other tigers. At last it sank down and lay still. The dwarf was still not quite sure that it was dead, so he took his knife and cut the various organs of its body. But it did not move, and so he was convinced that it must be dead. So he came out of the belly of the tiger with the girl and saw all the other tigers lying dead, slain by their leader in his frenzy.

They skinned the big tiger and set out for home carrying the skin. On the way they called on the old woman. Her hair had turned completely white from worrying for the dwarf. Then she too went with him. At last the three of them reached the dwarf's home. His mother was overjoyed to see him safe and sound. He told the villagers of all the tigers lying dead on the mountain. They went out and skinned them, and made a great profit by selling the skins.

The dwarf buried his father's bones in a fitting grave, and then went up to Seoul with the girl to visit her parents. She had been carried off by a tiger one evening and given up for dead. They were overjoyed to see her return unharmed. Her father was a Minister, and he readily agreed to accept the dwarf as his son-in-law. So the dwarf and the Minister's daughter were married.

Ondoru Yawa, told by Zŏng Bog-Sul; Ŏnyang (1915).

45
The Tiger's Grave

LONG ago a son was born to a rich man. He grew up in comfortable circumstances, but when his father died the family fell on evil times, and they gradually declined into poverty. As a result of this he reached the age of thirty still unmarried. He was most diligent and honest, and dutiful to his mother, so that he was held in high repute among the villagers.

When he came home from work one evening he found his mother seriously ill. He stayed at home to nurse her, and gave her all the medicines he could get, but none of them had any effect. Then one day he heard from the villagers that there was a famous doctor living in Unbong. Unfortunately he had no relatives whom he could send for the doctor, nor could he leave his sick mother to go and consult him himself. He did not have enough money, in any case, to pay the expenses that would be incurred, and so in despair he wept by his mother's sickbed.

One day his mother said with a sigh, 'I would very much like to be treated by the noted doctor in Unbong once at least before I die.' Her unhappy son decided at once that he must go and consult the doctor. He borrowed money from one of the neighbours, pledging his wages in advance, and left his home, first asking one of the villagers to do him the favour of looking after his mother while he was away. He crossed over the steep pass of Zi Ze, and reached Unbong just as night was falling. He went at once to the doctor, and was given some medicine. Without stopping to rest he turned and set out for home, carrying the box of medicine on his back.

When he reached the pass he found a merchant struggling with a big tiger. He was grappling with it and when he saw the young man he shouted to him for help. With his concern for his mother uppermost in his mind he at first thought of passing by and ignoring the merchant. But on reflection he felt that he must help the unfortunate man who was fighting for his life. So he went up to the tiger from behind and tried to kill it. Then the man said, 'You hold the tiger, and I will tear its eyes out.' So he put his bag on the ground, and gripped the tiger tightly with his arms. Thereupon the man let go of the tiger and ran away, taking the poor son's medicine bag, which he had put by the roadside, and made no attempt to tear out the tiger's eyes.

Thus the merchant cheated him, and even robbed him of the medicine that might have cured his mother's illness. He had to keep his grip on the tiger, for if he had relaxed it even for a moment he would have been eaten. When he thought of his mother sick in bed and waiting anxiously for his return he went almost mad in his despair. His bones grew cold, and his hair stood stiff on end. Chills ran up and down his spine, and his body was covered in goose flesh. In the end he fell down in a faint.

When he came to his senses he was lying on the ground, and the tiger was nowhere to be seen. He hastened homeward through the mountains oppressed with anxiety for his sick mother. As he came near his village he found something white lying in the road. It was his own medicine bag, for which he had felt such concern. The smell of fresh human blood assailed his nostrils, and he found nearby a man, torn to pieces—it was the merchant who had cheated him and run off with his bag. He had clearly been killed by the tiger as a punishment for his crime.

When he got home the son boiled the medicine and gave it to his mother, and in a few days she recovered. The story spread among the villagers, and they praised him as a model of what a filial son should be.

He was cutting firewood in the mountains one day, when he heard the sound of a gun and saw a tiger coming towards him. He recognised it at once as the very same tiger that he had met, and which had got back his bag for him. So he hastily hid it under a pile of firewood. A few minutes later a hunter came up and asked him if he had seen a tiger pass that way, but he pretended he had seen no such thing. So the hunter went away and the tiger was saved. When the tiger left it expressed great gratitude with its eyes, and nodded its head several times. When he came home in the evening the young man told his mother what had happened, and the story gave her great pleasure.

One moonlight night mother and son were talking together in their room when they heard the tread of a strange animal outside. They looked out and saw the tiger carrying a girl on its back. It jumped into the garden, placed the girl gently on the ground and went away. They went out and found her lying unconscious, so they carried her into the house and tended her. They forced hot water into her mouth and massaged her limbs, so that she recovered completely in a very short time. She was very pretty, and she told them what had happened to her. 'My home is in Gŭmsan, in the province of Zŏlla,' she told them. 'I was combing my hair after supper when a tiger suddenly appeared and kidnapped me. What happened after that I cannot remember. I am very grateful indeed to you for saving me.'

Next morning they reported the matter to her parents. They were very relieved to hear that she was safe, and it was arranged that the young man and the girl should marry. The marriage took place soon afterwards.

One evening the tiger appeared again, and took the young man to the corner of the back garden. It scratched the ground with its paws, and waved its tail violently. It seemed to be trying to tell him something, but he could not understand what it meant. Next morning it was found dead on the same spot, so he buried it there. From that time the family became more prosperous, and three years afterwards a persimmon tree suddenly appeared on the grave with ripe fruit on it. It is said that the tree is still growing in Zangsu.

Ondoru Yawa, told by Gim Du-Hŏn; Zanghŭng (1921).

46

Hong Do-Ryŏng, the Filial Tiger

IN·the district of Masan, in the province of Gyŏng-Nam, there once lived a tiger called Hong Do-Ryŏng. This tiger had the strange habit of killing any woman it saw wearing a blue skirt. The tiger had actually been a man, and this is the story of his transformation.

Hong Do-Ryŏng was a most filial son, devoted to his mother. One day she fell ill, and lay for a long time in a most critical condition. Hong gave her all the medicine he could get, and called in all the most famous doctors, but all in vain, she got no better. All his money went, and he fell into dire poverty. At last he decided that the only way to cure his mother was by prayer. So he went deep into the mountains, and, after performing the correct purification ceremony, sat in quiet meditation, praying to the gods day and night. At last a mysterious being appeared and said, 'You must take one hundred dogs, and prepare medicine from them for your mother and she will be cured.'

At these words Hong became even more unhappy. Where was he to get a hundred dogs? He did not have enough money to buy even one dog, let alone a hundred. In his perplexity he sat and wept, sighing deeply with distress and anxiety. At last he said, 'If only I could be a tiger! Then I could easily get a hundred dogs.' He stayed on the mountain and continued to pray. After a few weeks the same mysterious being appeared before him, and gave him a piece of paper on which was written a spell which would turn him into a tiger and back again.

He took the paper home with him, and then got up every night at midnight when everyone was asleep. He would read the spell and turn into a tiger. Then the tiger Hong would creep round the village and catch and kill a dog. He would take it home, and then read the spell again and be transformed into his proper shape. And every morning his wife would find a dog on the doorstep which she would use to prepare medicine for her mother-in-law, or perhaps make soup from it for her. Ninety-nine nights passed in this way, and ninety-nine dogs had been killed to cure Hong's mother, who seemed indeed to be very much better.

Hong's wife, however, had come to suspect her husband's nightly absences, and on the hundredth night determined to find out his secret. She pretended to sleep, and when her husband went out at midnight she peeped through the window to see what he would do. She saw him take a piece of paper from under the thatch of the eaves and read it, whereupon he was transformed into a tiger. Then she saw him put the paper back and run from the house. Horrified by what she had seen, she went and took the paper and burnt it in the kitchen fireplace.

Tiger Hong brought the last dog to the house, and looked for the spell paper, but in vain. So he could not turn himself into a man again. The hundredth dog cured his mother completely but her son remained a tiger. The infuriated Hong killed his wife for her folly. She was wearing a blue skirt at the time, and thereafter the tiger

Hong killed every woman he saw wearing a blue skirt. He went and lived in the mountains, though he would often come back and prowl around his house in tears. And from that time the young women of the village used to go to fetch water at night wearing white skirts, as they could not go in the daytime wearing blue skirts.

Ondoru Yawa, told by Zo Zĕ-Ho; Saczŏn (1925).

47
The White-eared Tiger

LONG ago there stood a house on the lofty Pass of Czŏl-Lyŏng in the district of Yu-Yang, in the province of Gang-Wŏn. The owner of this house was forty years of age, but childless. He used to make a living by gathering the magic herb of wild ginsen in the mountains, leaving his wife alone in the house.

One day a certain Gim Hyŏng-Man, who had heard about this man who dwelt on the remote mountain pass, came to the village at the foot of the pass. He wanted some mountain ginsen, and hoped to be able to buy some from this man. He asked the villagers to direct him to the house, and they pointed to the dense forest that covered the mountain and said, 'That is the only way. If you go up there you will find the house, though none of us has ever been up there.'

Gim pushed on into the forest as they had told him. The mountain path was rough and dangerous, and many times he thought of giving up his quest. But he persevered, and in the end found a small house right at the top. He called for the master of the house, and was surprised to see a woman come out, about forty years of age. 'My husband went to the market on the other side of the hill,' she told him. 'He left early this morning, and he is not back yet, though he has usually returned by this time in the evening. You had better wait. He won't be long.'

Gim sat down outside and waited, while the woman went on cooking the evening meal. It got very dark, but at a late hour the husband had not returned.

The woman was very alarmed, and said, 'Something must have
86

Tigeress Being Killed (p. 88)

Mudang, a Shaman Witch
(p. 169)

Commanding Spirits, Goblins
(pp. 126, 143, 149, 152)

Wedding Procession (pp. 106, 110)

happened to him. I must go and look for him, but it is very dark. Would you mind coming with me, please?'

Gim could not refuse. The woman took a torch in her hand and led the way, and Gim followed with another torch. They had walked quite a considerable distance down the path when the woman suddenly stopped. She picked up a white handkerchief and said, 'This is my husband's handkerchief. 'It's horrible! He must have been killed.'

They looked around and saw spots of fresh blood on the ground. The woman rushed into the bushes in great alarm, following the trail of bloodstains. In a few minutes they were startled by the roaring of a tiger. The woman rushed towards it holding her torch aloft, and found a big tiger sitting on a rock eating a dead man. It was her husband! She rushed at it and thrust her blazing torch in its face. Frightened by the fire it ran away, dragging the body with it. She pursued it vigorously, having no intention of letting it take her husband's body from her. In the end it dropped the body and sat a little way off, licking its lips.

The woman handed her torch to Gim, and embraced the bleeding body of her husband. It was already cold and stiff. She turned to go home, carrying the body on her back, and asked Gim to follow her with the two torches. When they got back she put the body in a storeroom, and invited Gim to rest in the house. He had never experienced such a dreadful adventure, and was almost fainting in his fear. He lay down in the room, still trembling and gasping. After a short time he heard a roar, and then a loud crash echoed in the stillness of the night. Then the woman shouted, 'I have killed the tiger! Come out and see.'

A great yellow tiger lay at the entrance of the storeroom with its throat cut, and the woman stood beside it with an axe in her hand. She told him how she had killed it, 'I was sure it would come down to the house to look for its prey, and sure enough it came. It smelt blood and came to the storeroom. I was hiding behind the door, and I killed it with this axe.' With these words she hacked the tiger to pieces, that she might savour her revenge to the full. Then she went on, 'This is the notorious White-eared Tiger. You can see its white ears, can't you? The villagers have been trying to catch it for years, and now I have killed it.'

Gim asked her to tell him about it. So she told him its history. 'Some years ago the villagers down the hill gathered outdoors in the cool of a summer evening. One man went away for a moment, and did not come back. So they all went to look for him, and found him lying grievously hurt in a cornfield. He died almost at once and they buried him. A few days later they found the dead man standing by a tree near the grave. When they touched him he fell to the ground. The tiger had dug the body up and had leant it against the tree. Then the villagers saw a big tiger with white ears squatting on a nearby rock. One of the village elders then said that when the white-eared tiger was deprived of its prey it would come back to play with it. He therefore advised them to throw it a coat belonging to the dead man. So they threw it one, and it took it in its fore-paws and ran happily away. That tiger was yellowish brown in colour, and had white ears. It is the very tiger we caught to-night, isn't it?'

Day broke as she finished her story. She served breakfast to her guest, and then offered him some roots of mountain ginsen, saying, 'This must be what you came for. Please accept these few roots.' She refused to let him pay for them, saying that they were a small return for the valuable help he had given her in the night.

The same evening he went back to the house with some of the villagers, to attend to the funeral. But he found she had followed her husband in death, for she had set fire to the house, and burnt her husband's body and herself in it.

Ondoru Yawa, told by Czoe Zin-Sŭn; Gosŏng (1926).

48

The Tiger-Girl

IN the capital of Silla, one of the ancient kingdoms of Korea, it was customary for all the people, men and women, young and old, to gather once a year in the Buddhist temple of Hŭng-Yun Sa, and pray for happiness and prosperity. According to various reports the gathering took place on or about the twelfth of February, or during the fifteen days following the eighth of August. In the evenings the people used to sing and dance in the temple precincts by moonlight until far into the night.

One year a very beautiful girl went to the temple. She prayed every night before the altar, and mingled with the happy crowds. She met a young man, Gim Hyŏn, and they soon became intimate, spending every night together. When the festival came to an end he set out to accompany her to her home. She implored him not to go with her, but he would not listen to her entreaties. She ran off, and came at last to a poor thatched cottage on the slopes of a mountain. Gim had chased her all the way, and went into the room after her. When she saw him she told him to hide behind a screen which stood in a corner of the room. This he did without delay.

Then suddenly he heard two tigers roaring outside. 'Sister,' they roared, 'We smell a man. We are very hungry, sister. Give him to us, please.' Gim trembled in terror behind the screen, but the girl answered, 'Brothers, you show an unpardonable lack of courtesy. He is my guest. Now please go away.'

Her two tiger-brothers went away, and the girl went to Gim and said with a sigh, 'Please do not be afraid of me. I am not a woman, but a tiger. You have loved me sincerely, and I am deeply grateful to you. But a tiger once loved by a man may not live, and so I must die soon.' Gim looked at her incredulously; she stood before him as beautiful and fair as any woman. 'No, no,' he said, 'That cannot be true. You must not die. I will stay with you and protect you.'

Thereupon she turned herself into a tiger, and back again into a woman. 'Now will you do as I ask?' she said. 'I wish to die at your hand. To-morrow morning I shall come into the market place, and throw the people into confusion. Then I will go and seize the King's daughter. You must come out here to find me, and kill me with your sword. You will be able to save the princess, and you shall have good fortune for ever.'

The next day things turned out as she had said. A tiger rushed through the streets of the capital, and carried off the King's daughter. Gim went to the King, and was given authority to go and kill the tiger. He went out to the mountain, killed the tiger, and rescued the Princess. The King was deeply grateful and gave her to him in marriage. And he built a temple by the So-Czon River, in memory of the tiger, and called it Ho Wŏn Sa, the Temple of the Tiger's Wish.

Ondoru Yawa, told by Song Sŏg-Ha; Ŏnyang (1926).

49

The Tiger Priest

A TRAVELLER once lost his way among the hills. At nightfall he found he could neither go forward nor return the way he had come. At last he found a narrow path, and followed it. After he had walked along it for a considerable distance he came out into a valley where there stood a large house. He went up to it and knocked at the outer gate, but there was no reply from within. So he went in and called the master of the house at the second gate, but again got no reply. Again he passed through and tried all the gates in turn, up to the eleventh, but received no reply. Then he opened the twelfth gate, and found a beautiful girl in tears in the house.

'Please pardon my intrusion,' he said to her, 'but I am a traveller, and I lost my way in the mountains. Why are you so sad?'

The girl looked up and said, 'Stranger, if you value your life you had better escape while there is yet time. If you stay, you will assuredly be killed.'

But the traveller would not go. He asked her to tell him what had made her so unhappy, and she told him the secret of the house, sobbing bitterly. 'My father was a rich and influential man, and I had several brothers. One day a Buddhist priest who lived in a temple in the mountains came to my father and asked him to give me to him in marriage. My father refused, and my brothers too. So in a rage the priest murdered all my family, and I am the only one left alive. The priest will be here to-night, and if he finds you here he will kill you too.'

On hearing her unhappy tale the traveller determined to help her. With a drawn sword he concealed himself in the wall-closet, and awaited the murderous priest's return. About midnight he came into the room. The girl smiled innocently at him as if nothing had happened, and gave him a cup of potent wine to drink. He suddenly became very red in the face, and lay down and fell asleep immediately. The traveller came out of his hiding place, stabbed out the priest's eyes, and tried to cut his throat. Aroused by this onslaught the wicked priest let out a mighty roar of pain, and lashed out wildly in all directions. He could not catch his assailant, for he was already blind. The traveller struck at him again and again, and at last he fell dead. They took the body outside to bury it in the garden behind the house, and then they saw that it was not a priest but the body of a great yellow tiger spotted with brown.

The girl thanked the traveller profusely for the service he had rendered her. He was very hungry, and so she cooked rice for him, and hot soup. Then at dawn he began to make preparations to go on his way. The girl implored him not to leave her there alone. 'I shall never forget how much I owe to you,' she said. 'Please stay and live with me in this house. I cannot leave for three years, for I must stay to tend my father's grave for at least that time.'

The traveller refused, however, for he was filled with horror at what he had seen, and had no desire to remain in that accursed house. So he went off through the twelve gates. The girl came with him to the outer gate to see him on his way, and then committed suicide, hanging herself from the beam over the gate. Her broken heart was more than she could endure.

In after years the traveller became a famous general, Osŏng Buwŏn-Gun. A great war broke out, and he was appointed to the command of all the armies. He was opposed by a powerful enemy force of two hundred thousand men. A desperate battle took place, and seemed likely to prove decisive. In the midst of the fighting the General found a yellow silk handkerchief clinging to his sword as he brandished it, and hindering his actions. He was defeated in the battle, and fell down on the field in a faint. Then it seemed to him that the handkerchief dissolved before his eyes, and in its place there appeared the girl whom he had met within the twelve gates. She spoke to him reproachfully and then changed back into the handkerchief, which then vanished in the air. So he cried aloud, 'Dear young lady, I did you a grievous wrong. I was far too heartless towards you. Please forgive me.'

So he hastened to the house in the mountains, and found the girl's body intact with the eyes still open, though the tiger-priest had rotted away long ago. He took the body on his knees and stroked it fondly with his hands. Then it closed its eyes. He buried the girl in her father's grave, and once more left the house.

Then he led his men into battle a second time. The tide of battle turned against him and he was hard pressed. In the final assault the enemy commander rushed at him, and was on the point of killing him. Then all of a sudden the yellow silk handkerchief appeared again, trailing on the enemy general's sword. It wrapped itself around the blade, and the general could not move his arm freely. So Osŏng had no difficulty in cutting off his adversary's head.

The handkerchief vanished into the sky, and never appeared again. Osŏng never forgot his debt to the girl, but went every year to mourn at her grave.

Ondoru Yawa, told by Song Sŏg-Ha; Ŏnyang (1926).

50

The Grave of a Faithful Dog

IN the district of Gyŏngzu, in the Province of North Gyŏngsang of the Kingdom of Silla, there once lived a widow who had a son and a daughter. She was so poor that she could never go and see the famous sights, but worked hard all day long for her children, so that they might be strong and healthy. They grew up and married, and soon afterwards their mother died.

The King of the Underworld, Yama, asked her when she came before him, 'How often did you visit the temples? Did you see all the famous sights?' She answered, 'I was fully occupied with bringing up my son and daughter, and I never had any time to go out.'

So King Yama declared, 'You are accustomed to staying in the house. So you had better be a dog, and go back to your son, and guard his house for him.' And she was sent back to the world as a dog.

In time the dog gave birth to pups, and they gradually grew up. Then the master of the house, her son, decided to kill and eat the mother dog. That night she disappeared, and ran off to her daughter's house. She sat on the doorstep weeping. The mistress of the house, her daughter, was surprised to find her brother's dog in such a state, and giving it a bowl of rice, stroked its back in the kitchen.

Then a Buddhist priest came to the son's house, and asked him,

92

'Have you a dog?' He answered, 'Yes, I did have one, but it has disappeared. Why do you ask?' The priest replied, 'That dog is the reincarnation of your mother. She worked so hard to bring up her son and daughter that she had never been able to go and see the famous sights. So the King of the Underworld arranged for her to come back to her son's house as a dog, to protect him from thieves. But it is afraid now that you will kill it, and so it has probably gone now to your sister's house. So don't kill her, but let her see as much of the world as you can.'

So the son went to his sister's house, and told her what the priest had said to him. Then he took the dog on his back, and carried it around to see as many beautiful mountains and famous temples as he could.

When they were on their way home the dog got down from his back, and digging a hole in the ground, lay down and died. So he buried the dog there, and from that day the family became very rich and prosperous.

From *Zosŏn Gubi Zŏnsŏl Zi.*

5 1

The Stone Memorial to a Dog

IN the village of Sillim, in the district of Sŏnsan, in North Gyŏngsan Province, there can be seen the grave and stone memorial of a dog.

About a hundred years ago there lived in the district of Sŏnsan a certain Gim Sŏng-Bal. He went one day to the market that was held in the town on the fifth day of every month. He met many friends there and drank much wine with them in the wineshops of the town. Then he set out for home much the worse for drink, and on the way fell asleep in a field, known as Wŏlmol-Zŏng.

Suddenly a grass fire broke out, and the dry autumn grass of the field began to blaze. In his drunken stupor Gim was unaware of his danger. Fortunately he had a dog, and it happened to come along on its way to meet him as he returned. It saw the dangerous position its master was in, and ran to him and tugged at his clothes with its teeth. But try as it might it could not wake its master.

93

So it ran to the nearby river, dipped its tail in the water, and ran back and damped the grass around its sleeping master. This it did many times over, and kept the fire from reaching its master. At last the fire went out, but the faithful dog fell dead from its burns and exhaustion.

When Gim awoke and realized what had happened, he was deeply touched by the death of his faithful dog. He buried it where it lay, and never forgot its devotion. The story spread among the people of the district and they too were greatly impressed by the dog's noble behaviour. So they erected a stone monument in front of the grave, to commemorate the dog's heroism. And on the monument they inscribed the words Ŭigu-Czong, meaning 'The grave of the Faithful Dog', and the magistrate in office at the time actually wrote the words himself.

From *Zosŏn Gubi Zŏnsŏl Zi.*

52

The Deer and the Snake

LONG long ago there was a great deluge, such as had never been seen before. The River Dědong overflowed its banks and washed away many houses. All the fields became a vast lake, and all the inhabitants and their animals were drowned.

An old man in Pyŏngyang went rowing on the flood in a boat. He found a deer almost exhausted and drowning, and he rescued it. Then he found a snake floating on the waters, and he rescued it too. Before long a boy came floating by, and the old man saved him also. He carried them to the shore in his boat. There he released the deer and the snake. The boy however would not leave the old man, since both his parents had been drowned and his home destroyed by the flood. So the old man gave him food to eat and adopted him as his son.

One day the deer came back and tugged at the old man's sleeve, swinging his tail from side to side. The old man guessed that it was trying to tell him something and so he followed it. Before long they came to a rock in the mountains. The deer pawed the ground near by and the old man guessed that something must lie hidden there. He began to dig, and lo and behold, he found a jar buried there full of gold and silver. He took the treasure home with him and was now a rich man.

His foster-son became very conceited and began to spend money extravagantly. His father would chide him for his recklessness, but he often answered him rudely and took no notice of his admonitions. In the end he decided that he would go away and live by himself, but his father refused to let him go. So the boy became angry and abusive, and brought a false charge against him. He went secretly to the local authorities and said, 'My foster-father stole a lot of money, and he has some story that he got it from a deer.' The official who was responsible for such matters went and arrested the old man, and would not listen to him when he told the true explanation of his wealth. He was cast into prison, but confidently expected that some day he would be released, for he was indeed innocent of any crime.

One night the snake came to him in his cell. It bit him on the arm and went away. His arm immediately swelled up from the effects of the poison and the pain became unbearable. 'The snake returns evil for good,' he said to himself, 'How absurd that is!' But a little later the snake came back holding a small glass bottle in its mouth. It applied the bottle to the painful swelling on his arm, and at once the swelling subsided and the pain ceased, so that he was completely cured. Then the snake disappeared once more.

In the morning he heard a great commotion outside. He heard that the magistrate's wife had been bitten by a snake during the night and seemed likely to die from the poison. He guessed that it must have been the same snake as had bitten him, and so he had word taken to the magistrate that he could cure his wife's hurt. The magistrate sent for him immediately and he took the rest of the magic ointment the snake had brought him and applied it to the lady's wound. At once she was cured completely.

The magistrate was at last convinced of his innocence, and he was released at once. Then his wicked foster-son was arrested and punished for his crime.

Told by Gim Gi-Hwan; Tong-yŏng (1935).

53
The Pheasants and the Bell

ONCE upon a time there lived a woodcutter. One day he went into the mountains to cut firewood, and there he saw two pheasants flying up and down in a distracted manner. When he came nearer he saw a snake on the point of devouring their eggs, which were lying under a bush. So he took the stick that supported his pack-carrier and beat the snake to death with it.

Some ten years afterwards he went on a journey to Yŏngwŏl in the Province of Gangwŏn. One night he lost his way in a forest and at last came upon a house with a light in the window. He thought that perhaps he might stay the night there, and so he went and knocked at the door. A young girl came out and received him kindly, and took him in and gave him a good supper.

After a little while the woodcutter asked, 'Are you living here alone, or are you expecting the rest of your family to return?' As he said this the girl changed colour and snarled viciously at him, 'Ten years ago you killed a snake with your stick. I am that snake. I bid you welcome, my enemy! Now I shall savour my revenge to the full. I am going to eat you up!'

The woodcutter was very frightened at her menacing words, and begged her to spare his life. 'You were trying to eat the pheasants' eggs,' he pleaded, 'I took pity on them and so I made up my mind to save them. So I beat you with my stick, but I did not mean to kill you. If I did kill you, it was quite by accident, and I apologize most humbly for my deed. Do spare my life, I beseech you!'

The girl considered for a momentand replied, 'If you wish to live, there is one thing you must do for me. Near the summit of this mountain there stands an old deserted temple, and in it hangs a great bell. If you can sit here in this room and make that bell ring, then I shall let you go free and unharmed. Can you do that for me?'

The woodcutter answered in great embarrassment, 'How can I ring that bell if I am sitting here? It is quite impossible. You are just toying with me, are you not?'

'You mean you cannot do it?' said the girl. 'Then you shall die this very minute.'

So the girl transformed herself into a big snake to kill him, but no sooner had she done so than the solemn boom of the bell came clearly to their ears through the night. The snake immediately became a girl again, and sighed, 'You must be under Heaven's protection. I cannot hurt you now.' With these words she vanished.

In the morning the woodcutter climbed to the top of the mountain. There he found the temple standing desolate. Under the great bell he found two pheasants lying dead, their heads battered and their wings broken, and on the surface of the bell itself were great dark stains of blood. He realized then that the two pheasants he had helped so long ago had sacrificed their lives to repay his kindness. They had dashed their heads against the bell, so that its sound might save their benefactor.

Ondoru Yawa, told by Yi Hŏn-Gu; Myŏngczŏn (1925).

54
The Centipede Girl

THERE was once a poor man who lived on the outskirts of Seoul. He was so poor that he could neither provide food for his family, nor keep a roof over their heads. His dire poverty reduced him to the uttermost depths of despair, and at last in the extremity of his misery he resolved to put an end to his life.

One day he left his wife without telling her where he was going. He went down to the banks of the Han River, and walked along until he came to a towering rocky cliff. He climbed to the top, closed his eyes, and hurled himself over the precipice into the deep water below. He imagined that he must be killed instantly. Half an hour later, however, a beautiful woman who was washing clothes by the riverside found him lying on a sandbank. He was unconscious, but otherwise completely unhurt. Before long he came to his senses, and she asked him what had happened. He told her of his poverty, and his resolve to end his life. So she said to him, 'Happily you are safe. I hope you will never try to do such a terrible thing again. You are still young, and sometime Fortune will smile on

97

you. If you like you can come home with me and rest a while at my house.'

Thereupon she led him away, and soon they came to her house. It was very large and built of brick, and stood alone in the valley. Altogether it gave an impression of great wealth. The man stayed there as a guest, and very soon fell in love with the girl. He forgot his family completely. In any case he was sure he must be dead, for had he not thrown himself in the river to put an end to his life? Never in his wildest dreams had he imagined that any such delights could exist in the world as the life he was now leading with this mysterious girl. She was of the most ethereal beauty, and gave him the finest clothes to wear, and the richest food to eat. Moreover the house itself was luxurious beyond his wildest imaginings, and he was completely overwhelmed by it all.

They lived together happily for a few months. Then, however, his new life began to pall a little, and he thought wistfully of his helpless family in Seoul. So he told his mistress that he would like to go away for a while, though he did not tell her that he wanted to visit his family. But she had already guessed his intention, and said, 'If you leave me now, I am afraid that you will forget me and never come back.'

The man too thought that it was quite possible that he might stay with his family and not return to her, but he answered vehemently, 'How could I ever forget you? Have no fear. I will come back to you without fail.'

'On your way back, then,' said the girl, 'take no notice of anyone who may try to deter you. Come straight back, and I shall be waiting for you.'

So he left her, and set out for his own house, where he had left his own family. When he reached the village he was astounded to see a magnificent new house built where his old home had stood. When he came closer he saw his own name on the gate. A sudden suspicion flashed into his mind that his wife might have been unfaithful in his absence. This thought made him rather angry, but then he reflected that he had no right to blame her, for he had neglected her for a long time.

He knocked at the gate, and his son came and opened it. He looked at his long-lost father with joyous tears in his eyes. 'Welcome home, Father,' he cried, and then called to his mother, 'Mother,

98

Father is home!' She immediately rushed out into the garden, wearing the most beautiful clothes.

Her husband looked sternly at her and asked, 'Who built this house? Where did you get the money?'

His wife looked at him questioningly. 'Wasn't it you who sent me money every day? I thought it was you who sent us all these wonderful presents. Am I mistaken, then?'

The truth slowly dawned on her husband. It must have been none other than the rich woman he had stayed with, for there could be no one else who would help his family. So he pretended he had just been joking, and changed the subject. He said nothing of his suicide, nor of the mysterious woman he had met.

He was very happy to be reunited with his family after his long absence, but as the months went by he began to think longingly of the beautiful woman he had left in the country. At last his desire to see her once again became so strong that he could bear to wait no longer. Once again he left his wife and family and set out for his mistress's house.

On the way he had to pass by a big hollow tree. Just as he came to it he was surprised to hear a voice calling him by name. 'My dear grandson,' it said, 'I am the spirit of your grandfather. Listen to me. You must not visit that woman again. I give you this warning for your own good. She is no woman, but a centipede a thousand years old.'

It certainly sounded like his grandfather's voice, but he refused to believe what it had told him, for he trusted the woman implicitly. He would not have been deterred even if the warning had been true, for having once attempted suicide he was no longer afraid of death. So he answered, 'Grandfather, I must see her again. I promised her I would return, and nothing will prevent me from keeping my promise. Death is nothing to me, for I believe that I have died once already. And even though it meant death I would see her, for it was she who saved my family when starvation stared them in the face.'

The disembodied voice spoke solemnly to him. 'I see that you are determined to go,' it said. 'There is one way for you to escape death. Go and buy the strongest tobacco you can, smoke it, and keep the juices in your mouth. As soon as you see her, spit them in her face. If you fail to do this you will surely die. Poor man, she has cast a spell on you with her beauty.'

So he went to the market and bought the strongest tobacco he could find. Then he set out again, and smoked hard all the way to his mistress's house. He carefully stored the tobacco juices in his mouth. When he got to her house he peeped in through a crack in the gate, and there he saw the tail of a great centipede in the house. Nothing daunted he determined to see her once again, whatever the outcome. So he boldly knocked at the door. His mistress came out and opened the gate and received him gladly. But he spoke not a word, for he was still holding the poisonous tobacco juices in his mouth. Seeing his clenched mouth and the strange expression of his eyes, she guessed that something must have happened, and she turned pale in her alarm.

He came into the room and gazed at her. She was as beautiful as ever, just as he remembered her. Her raven hair, her eyes clear as crystal, the curve of her brow, her nose and mouth—all were just as they had been before. He was torn between his love for her and the dire warning his grandfather's spirit had given him. He was on the point of spitting the poisonous tobacco juice in her face, when she suddenly gave a sob. She bowed her head and wept. He stared at her, undecided, and it seemed that she became twice as beautiful as before. As he looked he relented and turning to the window spat out the tobacco juices.

Her anxiety passed and she smiled. 'Thank you for sparing me,' she said. 'The voice that you heard is not your grandfather's. It was the accursed snake that lives in the hollow tree. I am a daughter of the Heavenly King, and the snake was one of the servants in the palace. He fell in love with me and seduced me. The matter came to the ears of my Heavenly Father and he punished us both. Me he ordered to live for three years in the world of men as a centipede, and my seducer he condemned to live eternally as a snake. Ever resentful of his fate he has always tried to do me further harm. To-day is the last day of my sentence, and to-morrow I return to my father. Had you spat in my face I should have had to suffer three long years more.'

So they had just one more day of happiness together, and that night they dreamed the sweetest of dreams. When the man awoke in the morning he found himself lying on a rock. There was no sign of the house, and he was quite alone.

Ondoru Yawa, told by Yun Bĕg-Nam; Seoul (1925).

55

The Two Brothers and the Magistrate

THERE once lived two brothers who understood the language of the birds. Moreover they were very clever at drawing deductions from the smallest signs. One day they went walking along a narrow path through the rice-fields. The path was bordered by luxuriant green grass. Suddenly the younger brother stopped and said, 'Brother! Look at the grass. It has been eaten on the left side of the path, but not on the right. Doesn't that suggest that a cow has just been along here that was blind in its right eye?' 'Yes,' replied his brother, 'It must have seen the grass on the left of the path with its left eye.'

They walked on, and then a man ran up to them and asked them if they had seen a cow wandering unattended. 'You would easily recognize it,' he said, 'it is blind in its right eye.' They had not seen it and told him so, but they were very gratified to have their deduction confirmed in this way.

Later in the day they went into the mountains. As they walked along they heard a magpie crying in the distance from a tall pine tree. It seemed to be calling them. 'Come here, young men. Come here. I cannot go away until you come.' So they went over to see what it was about, and found a man lying murdered under the pine tree. He could hardly have been dead an hour. There was a sword stuck in his chest, and blood was trickling from the wound. They had never seen such a sight before in their lives, and it filled them with horror. They turned and fled from the spot. Then a villainous-looking man appeared and seized them, and said threateningly, 'You are the murderers, aren't you. You plotted together to kill him, didn't you? I shall take you to the authorities and report the matter.'

So the two brothers were hauled before the magistrate and thrown into prison. They protested their innocence, and to prove it told the magistrate about the magpie, and explained that they could understand the language of birds. The magistrate seemed unimpressed, however, and ordered them to be locked up.

In the morning they were taken from the prison to appear before the magistrate. He pointed to the top of a tall maiden-hair tree and said, 'You hear the crane crying on the tree over there? Can you tell

101

me what it is saying?' So the brothers interpreted its cries and said, 'Your Honour! Give me back my eggs! I know you stole them from my nest while I was away. You have them there in your sleeves, wrapped in silk.'

The magistrate was most impressed by this demonstration of the brothers' unusual knowledge. He took the eggs from his sleeve and told his attendants to return them to the crane. Then he released the brothers from prison, and moreover invited them to dinner at his residence. He served them the finest food and drink, but when they had tasted the beef and the wine, they would not eat them, but sat staring at each other. Then they thanked the magistrate for his hospitality and left the house. The magistrate was curious to know why they had refused the beef and the wine, and sent one of his servants to follow them and hear what they might say.

Before they had gone very far the servant overheard them talking. The younger said, 'Brother, would you have wanted me to eat the beef? It was human flesh, wasn't it? And the wine—didn't it smell of human blood?'

The other answered, 'I didn't realize it at first, but it soon dawned upon me. It was a good dinner, of course, except for the beef and the wine. The magistrate is very clever for the son of a wandering monk, isn't he?'

So the servant rushed back to the magistrate and told him what he had heard about the beef and the wine, and the disparaging remarks about him being the son of a wandering monk. The magistrate was furious, and had the brothers arrested again. He asked them, 'What did you mean by saying that the beef was human flesh and the wine smelt of human blood? That was certainly not true. Tell me why you said it.'

The younger brother answered, 'Go and ask the butcher and the owner of the wine shop, Your Honour.' So the magistrate sent for them. The butcher confessed that he had fed the calf with his wife's milk for a few days, as the cow had died immediately after giving birth to it. The owner of the wine shop asked that the farmer from whom he bought wheat for making yeast should be sent for. So the farmer was summoned and he explained that that particular wheat had been grown in the field beside the graveyard. This information satisfied the magistrate, and he released the brothers with many apologies for the inconvenience he had caused them.

He said nothing about their remark that he was the son of a
wandering monk. He was afraid that it might be true, since they
were right in everything else. So he went and asked his old widowed
mother about the circumstances of his birth. 'Mother,' he said,
'What is my true surname? Tell me the truth about my birth, or I
will confine myself in my room and fast to death.'

His mother answered, 'That is a very strange question, isn't it?
You have the same surname as your father, of course.' But the
magistrate suspected that she was not telling the truth, and locked
himself in a room and fasted, until such time as his mother might
give him the true answer.

At last she came to him and said, 'My dear son, open the door,
and I will tell you the truth.' He opened the door, and she came in
and said timidly in a low voice, 'Your father went up to Seoul for
the Civil Examination, and stayed away a whole year. While he was
gone I made friends with a Buddhist monk who came to the door
to beg alms. Now do you understand?'

The magistrate then resigned his post, and retired to a temple in
the mountains. He became a priest and devoted himself to prayer
and meditation for the rest of his life.

Told by Zŏng In-Mog; Ŏnyang (1915).

56

The Story of Zibong

LONG ago there lived a gentleman who had a servant called Zibong.
Wherever his master might go, Zibong used to accompany him.
One day he went to Seoul to take the Civil Examination. He left his
family behind, and set out on a horse, which Zibong led. Two of his
daughters were married, but Zibong had been crossed in love by
the third, who was the youngest and most beautiful. In his pique he
became most mischievous.

On the way to Seoul his master sent him to a wine shop one day
to buy him a bowl of wine. Zibong bought the wine, and carried the
bowl out to his master. But on the way he stopped and started to
scoop something out of the bowl with his fingers. His master

shouted, 'Zibong! What are you doing there? Hurry up! I'm dying of thirst.' Then Zibong answered with a lie, 'I spat carelessly in the wine, so I'm trying to scoop it out with my fingers.' So his master decided to do without the wine and let Zibong drink it.

He made trouble of one sort or another for his master all the way to Seoul. When they arrived there they stayed at an inn. The gentleman took the examination, but had the ill-luck to fail. Moreover Zibong was constantly playing all sorts of pranks, so that his master was disgraced in the eyes of the people of Seoul. He spent all his money, and could not feed Zibong. So in exasperation he said to Zibong, 'You must leave Seoul, go back home at once. I will follow later.' Then he wrote a letter to his wife, in which he asked her to have Zibong put to death, because he was the cause of all his misfortunes.

Zibong set out for home with the letter. He suspected that the contents of the letter might not be altogether to his advantage, so he got an old man to read it for him, for he could not read himself. The old man read the letter and told him that it directed his mistress to have him put to death. So Zibong got the old man to write another letter, directing that when he arrived he should marry his master's youngest daughter, as a reward for his inestimable help to his master, without which he could not have passed the examination. He put the new letter in the original envelope, and carried it to his mistress. She read it, and at once arranged for her youngest daughter to be married to Zibong. They then moved into the house next door.

A few weeks later the gentleman himself arrived back, and was quite astounded to see what had happened, for it was quite the reverse of what he had intended. 'How did this happen?' he roared, 'My orders were quite different.' Then he said to the other servants, 'He won't get away with this. Tie him up in a bag and throw him in the sea.'

The servants seized Zibong and tied him up in a bag as their master had ordered. Then they set out for the sea carrying the bag. On the way, however, they began to feel thirsty, and so they went into a wine shop for a drink. They left the bag on the road outside. Zibong had been waiting for a chance to escape, and now he heard a blind man go by, tapping the road with his stick. So he called to him, 'Come here, blind man. I was blind too before I got into this magic bag. A famous doctor of magic told me to try it. I did, and now I can see, but I cannot get out of the bag. Come and untie me, and then I will lend it to you, so that you will be cured as well.'

The blind man was delighted to hear this, and untied the bag with alacrity. Then Zibong got out, and thrusting the blind man in his place, tied the bag up securely. Having done this, he walked off, tapping with the blind man's stick.

The servants came out of the wine shop, and carried the bag to the sea. Then the blind man shouted, 'Stop! Stop! I am a blind man, and I am trying to get my sight back.' But the servants replied, 'None of your tricks, Zibong. Be quiet!' They threw the bag in the sea, and the unfortunate blind man was drowned.

A month later, to everyone's surprise, Zibong reappeared at his old home. He carried a fan in each hand, and said, 'How are you all? I have been to the Dragon Kingdom under the sea. I dived right down to the bottom of the sea, where I found a most magnificent palace. I was welcomed and taken to the King. He entertained me right royally, and gave me a most sumptuous repast. The food and drink were incredibly delicious, and I ate and drank till I could take no more. I am sure that it must be the happiest possible place to live. Now let us all go down there and live in happiness for ever. We must each take two fans, to use when we dive into the sea.'

They were all taken in by his specious words, and, taking two fans each, they all went with him to the seashore. Zibong said, 'Father must go first, and the rest of us will follow.' So the gentleman plunged into the sea, but found himself spluttering and choking. He found that he was drowning, and waved his fans violently, to tell the others that he had been tricked again. But Zibong merely hurried the others into the water, saying, 'Look at Father! He's waving his fans to get us to hurry up and follow him.'

So they all followed him one after the other, but when the youngest daughter was about to plunge in Zibong took her by the hand and said, 'Don't jump! Can't you see? They will all be drowned.'

But for all his guile the malicious Zibong did not find happiness. He could not win the youngest daughter's love. One night she leaped into the sea to follow her parents, who had been so shamefully tricked by her husband.

Told by O Zin-Yŏng; Ŏnyang (1916).

57

The Three Unmarried Ministers

LONG ago there were three ministers, the Prime Minister, the Minister of Home Affairs, and the Minister of Education, who were not married. One day the King asked them the reasons why they did not marry.

The Prime Minister told his story first. 'When I was very young,' he said, 'I did marry. At the time I was still at school studying for the High Civil Examination, and even after I was married I went on with my studies. I was very poor, and so my wife had to take in sewing for the neighbours to earn enough to give us a bare living. One day I came back from school and saw my wife eating something. When she saw me she hastily hid it under her knees on the floor and went on with her sewing. I was feeling very hungry, and upbraided her for her selfishness. "What are you hiding there under your knees?" I asked her. "I would not have thought you would eat without me." She replied with an innocent air, "I have hidden no food at all." At this I lost my temper, and accused her of trying to deceive me. "I saw you with my own eyes," I shouted. "You were eating something and hid it hastily when I walked into the garden. You must not try to deceive me in this way."

'She was very embarrassed, and drew out a lump of yellow clay from under her knees. "It is only clay," she said apologetically. "I must finish these clothes to-night so that I can be paid for them, and so be able to buy rice for supper. I was so hungry and thirsty that my mouth was quite dry and my throat utterly parched. Because I had nothing else I licked this lump of clay. You are quite mistaken if you think I would eat when you were not here. I am very sorry I have annoyed you so much, for I should not have given you the impression that I would."

'When she had given me this explanation I was ashamed that I had been so foolish as to chide her, and told her how much I appreciated her sincerity and the devotion with which she worked. We were living in abject poverty and it was entirely due to her unceasing toil that I was able to continue my studies.

'A few years later I passed the High Civil examination, and was appointed Governor of Zezu, the biggest of the islands in the Southern Sea. I set out to take up my post accompanied by my wife and many attendants. We boarded a ship at the port of Mog-Po. Unfortunately the sea was very rough, and our ship was tossed on the tempestuous waves of the strait. We were in grave danger of sinking, and the captain came to me and said, "There must be someone on board who ought not to be here, so that the gods of the sea are angry with us." To this I replied, "Then we must find him at once if we are to reach the island in safety. How are we to find out who it is?" The captain answered, "Let everyone take off his coat, and throw it in the sea. If it floats, that person is acceptable to the gods, but if it sinks then he is the cause of our distress." So I took off my coat and threw it overboard first, and it floated. All the others did likewise, and their coats floated too. Then my wife's turn came. She threw her coat over the side and it sank at once. Without the slightest hesitation she plunged into the sea and vanished from our sight. At that very moment the wind dropped and the fury of the waves abated, and in a dead calm we came safely to the island. My wife had sacrificed her own life to save me and my companions. And I was enabled to fulfil my mission on the island, and thereafter I won steady promotion. Everything I have I owe to my wife. How then could I marry again, and be unfaithful to her memory?'

The Prime Minister told his story with tears in his eyes and the King was deeply touched by the sincerity of his affection for his wife. He nodded gravely and said, 'I appreciate how you feel. You are quite right not to marry again.'

The King then turned to the Minister of Home Affairs and asked him in his turn to tell the reason why he did not marry. So the Minister of Home Affairs told the following story:

'I too married when I was very young. One day, however, a dire misfortune befell me. My political rivals brought a false charge against me. I was found guilty, and exiled to a distant place. When I took my farewell of my wife, she asked in tears, "When will you come back?" No limit had been set to my period of exile, so I answered evasively, "I shall return when one egg stands upright upon another." I meant of course that I did not expect ever to return, and that my exile would be for the term of my natural life.

'My wife, however, took my words seriously, and from the very moment I went away tried day and night, all the year round, to make one egg stand upright upon another. She neglected all her normal occupations, and gave no attention to dressing beautifully, or cooking herself delicious food, or keeping the house clean and comfortable. Before long her friends and relations and all the neighbours despaired of her and left her alone. She was utterly distracted, and almost crazy from despair, and so no one would have anything to do with her.

'Five years passed in this way, and then one moonlight night it happened that a secret Royal commissioner was making the rounds of the city of Seoul. He passed along the street in front of my house, by now half-ruined, and with its thatch rotting away. He was surprised to hear a woman cry out. He thought there was something strange about her cry, and so he went up to the house and peeped stealthily in through the torn paper of one of the windows. He saw my wife clapping her hands and laughing happily, her eyes fixed on two eggs on the floor. He opened the door and chided her. "You must not laugh riotously at this late hour," he said. "Why are you clapping your hands like that? You do seem remarkably happy to-night. What are those two eggs for?"

'My wife looked at him and replied, radiantly happy, "A minute ago, Sir, two eggs stood upright, one upon the other. I have been trying to make them do that in vain these five years. To-night I succeeded. And now my husband will come back."

'The commissioner was rather puzzled by her words, and asked her for an explanation. So she told him about her husband, his name, his exile on a false charge, and his parting words to her. He was greatly moved by her indefatigable industry and devotion, and her extreme misery in her unhappy lot. So he went to the late King and told him about her, and recommended that I be released from exile.

'The King was pleased to grant my release, and very soon I returned home. My wife was waiting for me at the gate, overcome with happiness at meeting me again. But the moment she saw me, she fell down in a faint, and did not revive again. Oh, poor woman! She had devoted herself heart and soul to the working of a miracle, and had worn herself out. She had become so weak that she died at the very instant of my return.

'So you can see that I owe her an enormous debt. How could

I ever forget her enough to marry some other woman, Your Majesty?'

The Minister of Home Affairs wept, as the Prime Minister had done, and the King approved his story also.

Now it was the turn of the Minister of Education, and he began, 'I also married when I was very young. After the wedding ceremony at the house of my bride's parents I went to my room and waited for her to be brought to me. I was very young and shy, and so I sat in a corner of the room with my back to the door. After a little while her mother brought her in, but I was too shy to turn and look at her, or to say anything to her.

'We sat like that for some time, and then my bride came over and plucked my sleeve. I was appalled at her boldness in daring to take the initiative, which no innocent bride would ever do. So I jumped up and rushed out of the house and ran barefooted all the way to my parents' house.

'After that I went to a temple far away in the mountains and devoted myself to the study of the classics, forgetting all else. I stayed there for several years, and then passed the High Civil Examination. I was then appointed magistrate of Namyang, in the Province of Gyŏng-gi.

'I set out in a palanquin to go to my post, accompanied by many attendants and a band. On the way from Suwŏn to Namyang we passed through a large village. One of my attendants asked me to get down from the palanquin and pay my respects at a haunted house that stood in ruins in the centre of the village. He told me that misfortune would befall any traveller who failed to do so. Many years previously, he explained, the daughter of the house was married to a young man, who ran away and left her on the wedding night. She still lay in the same room, with her eyes open.

'So I got down and walked to the house. As I approached I saw the name plate by the door, and suddenly remembered that this was not the first time I had been there. I realized that it was the house where I had been married. I went in through the gate, and found the place deserted. My bride was dead, and her parents had died of their grief. No one had entered the house for years. I went to the room where I had awaited my bride and found her body lying there, with no signs of decomposition, and with her eyes wide open and full of resentment. It dawned on me that I might have been mistaken about her. I went and sat in the same place as on my wedding night, and suddenly I thought I felt her plucking my sleeve. It seemed impossible that a dead body could do such a thing, so I turned and looked at her. She was still lying there. So I looked down and found that a brass ornamental plate on a wooden chest was catching in my sleeve when I moved. I moved again and again it pulled my sleeve.

'I realized now that I had been mistaken on my wedding night, and repented bitterly of my hasty action. So I reached out my hand and gently closed her eyes. No sooner had I done so than her body melted away like ashes.

'She was of a rare beauty, chaste and honest, and yet I lost her because of my hasty temper. So I resolved to control my rash impulses in future, and was thus enabled to reach the position I hold now. So I too really owe my success to my wife. How can I forget her purity and innocence? Can you understand now, Your Majesty, why I do not marry again?'

The King approved his story too, and said, 'You three Ministers have undergone rare and wonderful experiences, and they have made you the great men that you are. I am proud to have such noble and capable men as my ministers, so loyal and faithful in the service of my country.'

Told by Song Ssi; Seoul (1948).

58

The Young Widow

LONG ago there lived a famous minister whose name was Yi. He lived in a big house in Gahwoe-Dong, in Seoul. He had a married daughter, but three months after her wedding her husband died and she was left a widow, at fifteen. Her father was very anxious that she should be happy, and worried greatly about what he could do for her. Custom forbade the remarriage of the widowed daughter of a leading family, and to marry again brought great dishonour upon the house. Yi felt that this was very hard on his daughter, for she was still very young. So he was most perplexed as to what he should do.

The Young Widow

The young widow lived in a separate house in the grounds of his mansion. Every night her father used to walk round her house until she put out her light and went to bed, so that no accident should befall her. One moonlight night he was strolling round the garden smoking his long slender pipe when he was astounded to see the shadow of a man on the paper window of her house. It was very late, and she should have gone to bed long before. There was apparently someone in the room with her, and they were whispering together. He was very alarmed, and crept stealthily over to the window. He stood still and listened. His daughter was talking. 'My dear bridegroom,' she said, 'Would you like a cup of wine? Let me have one with you.'

Yi's hair stood on end, for he was convinced that the worst had happened. He drew his sword, and peeped into the room through a chink in the window paper to see who this intruder might be. Fortunately there was no one there but his daughter. She had stood up the bolster against the wall on the folded blankets, and was talking to it. She was holding the brass lid of a tea bowl in her hand, filled with rice tea, and pretending to serve a cup of wine to her bridegroom. Then she threw the tea in the brass chamber pot, and filled the lid again. This time she drank it herself, as if her bridegroom had handed it to her.

Her father's fears were somewhat relieved, but he was even more surprised by what she did next. She laid out the blankets and made her bed in the warmest part of the room, which was heated by a fire underneath the floor. Then she undressed, and taking the bolster in her arms, embracing it as if it were her husband. 'My dearest bridegroom,' she said. 'Let us go to bed now.' Thereupon she blew out the light.

Her father was very troubled by what he had seen, and that night he could not sleep, but lay awake wondering what he could do for his daughter. He felt that no good could come to her, or himself even, if she were to be left as she was. He would have to do something for her, though it seemed unlikely that he would be able to arrange a formal remarriage. He pondered the problem for hours, and at last an idea came to him.

The next morning he called his most faithful servant secretly to his room. 'You are the most reliable man I have,' he said. 'I have a special favour to ask of you. Will you do as I wish?'

The servant answered humbly, 'Your Excellency, I am always ready to carry out any order you may give me.'

The Minister went on, 'I shall honour you with a surname, to which, as a slave, you have not been entitled. You will be a free man, and I will grant you enough land to support you and your family as long as you live. The matter in which I require your help is a highly confidential one.'

His servant wept tears of gratitude. 'Your Excellency,' he said, 'the gift of a surname alone, and my freedom, would be the greatest of gifts, and yet Your Excellency is so kind as to grant me life-long prosperity as well. How shall I ever repay my debt to you? Though my life were taken from me now I would die happy.'

The Minister then said, 'Before I tell you what I want you to do I would like you to send all your family away immediately, as far away as possible, to some island, or Zŏlla Province, where they must stay, and never return to Seoul. Then come back to me. I will be waiting for you.'

The Minister gave his servant money to meet the expense of sending his family away. He went and sent them off without delay, and in the afternoon came back to the Minister for his instructions. The Minister said to him in a low voice, 'The thing I require of you is a very simple matter. I want you to go outside the South Castle Gate to-night before the curfew, and to stay the night there. In the morning, when the Great Bell of Zongno Street tolls and the gate is opened again you are to seize the first bachelor who comes out of the gate. You will bind him and put him in a sack, which you will bring back here and hang on a beam in the storeroom in the corner. You understand what I mean? You must do this before dawn, and no one must see you doing it.'

The servant memorized every detail of his master's instructions, and said, 'Your humble servant will carry out your orders without fail. And then what am I to do afterwards?'

'Then,' the Minister went on, 'your duty is completed. You must go and join your family, and never come back to Seoul, or see me again. Farewell forever, my good and trusty servant. Here is your surname and the deeds to your property, in token of your loyal service.'

The servant took his master's gifts and went out of the South Castle Gate. He lodged in a nearby inn, and in the morning he got up early and went and waited just outside the gate. He took with him a big sack and some stout ropes. Before long the Great Bell boomed and the gate was opened. A few people came out. Before long a young bachelor came out of the gate, and in an instant he caught him. At this time bachelors wore their hair in a long braid behind. The man protested loudly, but the servant took no notice. He bound his arms behind his back, and thrust him into the sack. He hastened back to the Minister's house, and hung the sack on a beam in the storeroom. Then he reported to his master. 'Your Excellency,' he said, 'I have done as you ordered, and the bag is in the storeroom. Farewell forever, Your Excellency.' And he left the house.

The Minister went to the storeroom and found the man weeping in the sack. He untied him and took him into the reception room and asked him who he was. The young man said, 'My name is Czoe. My home is in the village of Gĕmudŏm, by the town of Gyŏngzu, in the Province of Yŏngnam. I live there with my mother. Three years ago I was taken from my home and put in the army by the Government. I was sent to join the garrison on the Duman River, on the north-eastern border of the Province of Hamgyŏng. When I left home my aged mother was very ill, and I am afraid she may be dead now. I have completed my three years of service, and I arrived at Seoul last night on my way home. Then this morning a stranger seized me without reason outside the South Castle Gate. Please let me go. I have done no wrong. I am in a hurry to see my mother again; I have missed her very much.'

The Minister spoke soothingly to him. 'I understand very well how you feel,' he said. 'But now you are my guest, and I would like you to rest here a while. Your mother will be all right. You have been away for three years, so what difference will a few days make?'

His host invited the young man to take a bath, and gave him new clothes to wear. He was indeed a handsome and well proportioned man. The Minister entertained him lavishly, giving him the best food to eat, and the most comfortable bed to sleep in. But unfortunately he could not read or write. So the Minister set about teaching him to read, and showing him the Thousand Character Classic. He said, 'You were born as a man, so you must be able to read. I will not let you go until you have mastered this book.'

The Minister took great pains in teaching him, and the young man worked very hard. One evening, when they had finished the daily lesson the Minister said to him, 'You have made remarkable progress. In a week's time you may go home. But I have one special request to make of you when you go. Do not forget it.'

The young man was very anxious to know what this request might be. He had been treated very kindly by the Minister, and educated by him, and he was anxious to do all he could to repay his generosity. So he asked the Minister to tell him his wishes at once. But he refused. 'I will tell you before you go,' he repeated. And every night when they finished the lesson the Minister reminded him of his request, but he would not tell him what it was.

The night before he was due to leave the young man slept fitfully, dreaming of his aged mother. He had missed her terribly for three years while he had been serving in the garrison, and now he had been obliged to stay in the Minister's house for nearly a month. Now all he wanted to do was to go home as soon as he could. So in the morning he got up before the dawn, while everyone else was still asleep. When the first light of the coming day appeared he could bear to wait no longer, and left the house alone. He hastened to the South Castle Gate, and reached it just as it was opened. He went through and hastened southwards, almost running in his eagerness.

In a few hours he was half-way to Suwŏn. He felt rather tired, and sat by the roadside to rest. Suddenly he remembered the Minister's request. He was very sorry that he had forgotten to ask what it was before he left, and was ashamed of himself for his thoughtless ingratitude. So he sat and pondered what he ought to do, whether he should go back to Seoul and ask what it was, or whether it might not be better to forget the whole thing. While he was still sitting there he saw a train of horses and palanquins hastening down from Seoul. He thought it must be the wedding procession of a wealthy family, so rich and luxurious it was. Then when it reached him one of the drivers ran to him and bowing deeply said, 'Excuse me, Sir, but are you not Czoe who stayed at the residence of Yi the Minister?' 'Yes I am,' replied Czoe. 'What can I do for you?' The driver made no reply, and went back to his companions. All the drivers and carriers immediately went away, and left the horses and palanquins on the road. Not one of them remained.

Czoe went over to the palanquins in great curiosity. He found that the horses were loaded with wooden chests full of money and precious stones, and the palanquins filled with silk and rich garments. There was one palanquin more richly decorated than the rest, and bigger and loftier. He looked into it, and saw a beautiful girl sitting there, her eyes shyly averted, but half smiling. At last Czoe could guess the Minister's unknown request. He had given him his daughter.

He engaged new drivers and carriers from the nearest village and went straight to his native village near Gyŏngzu, the ancient capital of the Silla Dynasty, in South-East Korea. His mother had died long ago, and his old home was almost in ruins. So he built himself a great and beautiful mansion, such as the leading families had in Seoul. He lived in the greatest happiness with his bride, attended by many servants. But the leading men of the village would not associate with him, because he was of humble birth, and had been illiterate when he went away. They thought that he must have picked up some unknown girl in Seoul on his way back from the frontier garrison. They viewed him and his fortune with suspicion, and resented his living in the manner of a noble family. So they treated him with scorn. This was the one flaw in his happiness, and the only thing which caused him to be dissatisfied.

Fifteen years passed, and now Minister Yi's son had grown up. He had been only five years old when his sister had gone away, and now he was twenty. He had passed the customary examinations and attained high literary honours, and by his father's influence had been appointed to the rank of 'Ŏsa', or Secret Royal Inspector. He was now waiting to be dispatched on a mission to the provinces.

His father spent a week training him for his mission. One night when he had finished his work his father said to him, 'My dear son, the Royal order telling you your destination will be handed to you outside the Castle gate when you set out. It must be kept secret because if it were known beforehand certain of the noble families of Seoul might communicate with their relatives in the place you are going to and make things difficult for you. So it must be confidential, and moreover I have a special request to make of you when you receive your orders outside the Castle Gate.'

Yi's son asked his father to tell him at once, but he refused, and reminded him of his request every night.

On the day appointed for his departure he disguised himself as a beggar, as was the custom for Secret Royal Inspectors. He put on a battered hat and dirty clothes and straw sandals. On his back he carried a bundle tied in cloth, and in his hand a staff. He went outside the gate, and there found his father waiting for him. His father handed him his badge which authorized him to use garrison horses and troops, and said, 'You are to go and inspect the Province of Yŏngnam. If you should go to Gyŏngzu I would like you to call on a certain Czoe, in the village of Gĕmudŏm. That is all I have to ask. Now be on your way!'

The Royal Inspector set out on his travels, and went from one place to another to observe conditions among the people. He felt that the first thing he should do was to go and see the man his father had mentioned, for his father had advised the King to give him the honourable appointment he held, and had arranged that he should visit this part of the country. So he went to Yŏngczon, which was the nearest town to Gyŏngzu. Since his father had mentioned him specially he felt sure that this man Czoe must be of some importance, either a most respectable leading citizen, or a villain of the worst kind. He found out all he could about him, and found that he had been a poor illiterate bachelor of humble birth, that he had once served in a border garrison, had married a girl from Seoul, and was now living in lordly state. All in all, there seemed to be something strange about him.

So one day in his disguise as a beggar the Royal Inspector went to Gĕmudŏm. He came to Czoe's house, and was astonished to find that it was an exact copy of his own house in Seoul. He went to the door and begged to be allowed to spend the night there. He was taken to a guest room, and saw that there too everything was the same as in his home in Seoul. The food he was given was the same, and served in the same way. He felt that all this certainly called for some investigation. And in the morning when he left the house he was given a sum of money and a full set of new clothes, which was also the custom of his family with passing travellers.

So when he left, after thanking his host for his hospitality he thought the matter over deeply. He came to the conclusion that the only thing to do was to arrest Czoe. He went and got a company of garrison troops, and stationed them in hiding around the house. Then dressed in his beggars rags he went up to the door. The servant who answered his knock asked him what he had done with his new clothes. 'Another beggar took them,' he said, 'and I would like to stay here another night.' He was admitted and taken to the same room.

Before long a wine-table was brought to him. On it he saw a golden bottle and a golden cup, both of which, when wine was poured or drunk, made a sound like the singing of nightingales. He was utterly amazed, for at home his father had an exactly similar set. He remembered that long ago, when he was about five years old, there had been two sets, but one had disappeared, and had never been seen again. The two sets had been a gift from the Emperor of China to his father, when he had been sent as a Royal Commissioner to Peking long ago. It was most unlikely that there should be anything similar in Korea. And yet, here was another set exactly like the other. It could only have come from his father's house. So he concluded that this man Czoe must be condemned as a thief.

So, still disguised as a beggar, he went to Czoe and said, 'This golden bottle and this golden cup are the most wonderful things I have ever seen. Where and when did you get them? They must have cost a lot of money.'

Czoe was rather displeased by his question and said, 'It is no concern of yours where I got them. You are not trying to suggest that I stole them, are you?'

Then a woman's voice was heard outside, 'My dear husband,' she said. 'I know that a woman should not speak to a strange man, but I have good reasons for wanting to have a few minutes private conversation with your guest. Would you mind leaving the room for a moment, please?'

Her husband was accustomed to doing as his wife wished, and replied, 'Oh yes, if you wish it. I will go for a walk in the garden.'

Czoe left the room, but the woman did not come in. She said from outside, 'I would like to know why you speak so seriously about the golden bottle and cup.'

The Royal Commissioner answered, 'I am now a poor beggar, accursed and despised. But my family was once very rich and influential. But now my parents have disappeared, and I do not know whether they are alive or dead. This bottle and cup remind me of my old home. We had two sets, just like these.'

Then the woman swept the door aside and rushed into the room. She was weeping and tried to take the guest by the hand. 'Oh my poor dear brother,' she cried, 'You are a beggar, reduced to this miserable state! Let us go and find our parents together. Don't you recognize me? I am your sister.'

The Royal Commissioner was completely taken aback at the woman's words and her familiar approach. He pushed her hand aside and upbraided her severely. 'Lady of the house,' he said. 'You must be mistaken. My only sister died many years ago, when I was five years old. I followed her funeral procession to the grave, and every year my parents used to take me to her grave on the anniversary of her death and we all wept in the mountain graveyard. This is the truth, and I have no sister living. You are quite mistaken to think that I am your brother.'

Then the woman cried more loudly. 'My dear brother, you do not know the real story. I married at fifteen, but three months after the wedding my husband died. I missed him very much indeed, and was most unhappy. Father realized how I felt, and gave me to Czoe to be his wife. So that the family should not be disgraced by my remarriage it was all arranged secretly. Then Father pretended that I had died, and held a funeral for me. That grave is not a real grave, but I can believe that my parents wept before it as you said. They must have missed me very much. Dear Brother! let us search through the whole country and try to find our parents. If they are dead, we must find their remains and bury them with due reverence.'

Now the Secret Royal Inspector understood what his father had done so that his young widowed daughter might be happy, and at the same time avoid dishonour by keeping her second marriage secret. But there was still one thing that worried him, and that was how she had recognized him as her brother. So he said, 'Lady of the house, there is still one thing that I do not understand. However did you recognize me as your brother?'

'I will tell you,' the woman went on. 'Under the circumstances I could not write to my family in Seoul as a daughter should. So whenever anyone from Seoul was a guest here I always used to go into the next room and listen to hear if he had any news of my family. When you came here yesterday I thought that your profile was rather like my brother's, but I could not be sure. When I heard that you had come back to-day I decided to test you with the golden bottle and cup. And you recognized them. Now do you understand, dear brother? If our family has fallen into poverty it does not matter if people come to hear that I am alive and married a second time. Now let us travel to all the mountains and rivers of the Eight Provinces to find what has become of our poor parents. You shall be a beggar no longer.'

Now at last the Secret Royal Inspector understood everything, and told his sister the truth about himself and their family. 'My dear sister,' he said, 'Now I see everything clearly. Our family has not fallen into poverty, and our parents are in the best of health. I am a Secret Royal Inspector. When I left Seoul Father just suggested that I call upon a certain Czoe in the village of Gĕmudŏm. He did not tell me who he was. To tell you the truth, I thought he was a thief, and planned to arrest him this very day. I have already stationed soldiers round the house. But for you I might have made a very serious mistake.'

Thereupon his sister called her husband in from the garden and introduced him to her brother. They were all very happy at the reunion, and talked much to one another, for there should be no secrets among relations. The Secret Royal Inspector asked his brother-in-law if there was anything that he desired. Czoe replied that he would like to be accepted into the ranks of 'Yang-ban', or the leading men of the village, but that so far they had refused to have anything to do with him. The Inspector promised that he would arrange everything for him. He would go at once to the Court House and open an inquiry. He told Czoe not to come when the court officials came to call him, nor when the Governor himself came. But when the group of Scholars came to call him he was to attend the court. He then consulted Czoe as to which of his neighbours had earned the right to be rewarded for their good works, and which deserved to be punished as wrong-doers.

At last the Inspector bade farewell to his sister, and left the house, still disguised as a beggar. He stood in the street and publicly announced his presence, shouting, 'The Royal Inspector is here!' Hundreds of soldiers suddenly appeared and gathered around him, brandishing their spears in threatening fashion and shouting the same words. They say that 'the very grass by the roadside trembled in fear'. The Royal Inspector was carried to the court house, and immediately opened his inquiry. All the local officials and the group of Scholars attended, and all bowed low in obeisance before him. All the villagers watched the impressive scene from outside the wall.

Before he opened his inquiry the Inspector slapped his thigh and cried, 'I am very sorry that I did not invite noble Czoe to attend here.' When they heard this all the leading men of the village began to regret that they had treated Czoe in such an off-hand and arrogant way. So they all sent valuable presents to his house in an endeavour to placate him.

Then the Inspector sent the officials to bring Czoe to the court, but he refused to come. Then he sent the local Governor to fetch him, and again he refused to come. Then the Royal Inspector said, 'Twice I have sent the wrong people. Now the group of Scholars shall go to summon this gentleman to the court.'

So the group who had been most scornful of Czoe were obliged to go and invite him to attend the court to advise the Inspector. This time Czoe came to the court, walking with the Scholars who now had to count him as one of their number. When they came to the court Czoe walked alone through the high central gate that was reserved for dignitaries of the highest rank. The Royal Inspector went barefooted to receive him at the gate. All the people were astounded, and imagined that Czoe must be a man of the very highest rank, superior to the Royal Inspector, and perhaps only slightly inferior to the King. They did not of course know anything of the relationship between Czoe and the Royal Inspector.

Czoe sat beside the Royal Inspector for some time, and when he rose to go the Inspector accompanied him to the door, barefoot as before, to see him on his way. Once again the group of Scholars escorted him to his home.

Thus, in fulfilment of his father's wishes the Secret Royal Inspector accorded the highest honour to Czoe. Then he completed his mission and returned to Seoul. He brought valuable information to the King, and to his father he reported that his sister and her husband were living happily together.

Told by Bag Gwan-Su; Ulsan (1943).

59
The Legend of the Virgin Arang

ON the high bank of the River Nagdong in the district of Miryang, in the province of South Gyŏngsang, there stands a lofty tower, called Yŏngnam-Nu. Just below this tower along the steep cliffs that border the river there is a dense grove of bamboos. In this grove there once stood a small memorial shrine, but to-day nothing remains but a tiny stone monument to commemorate the sad story of the virgin named Arang.

Her surname was Yun, and her personal name in childhood Zŏng-Og, or 'Chaste Jade'. Her father was a nobleman of Seoul who was appointed magistrate in Miryang, where these sad events took place. She came there with her father when she was eighteen years of age. She was very pretty, and advanced in the study of the classics, so that many suitors came to woo her. In her father's opinion, however, none of them was a suitable match for her, and she remained unmarried.

Among the officials of low rank there was a young bachelor named Bĕg Ga, whose duty it was to carry the magistrate's seal. Attracted by the beauty of the magistrate's daughter he devised a plan to win her love, for humble man as he was he could not speak directly to her, and marriage with her was out of the question. He therefore became friendly with her nurse and disclosed his secret to her.

One evening when Arang was reading in her room her nurse came to her and said with a smile, 'To-night the moon is full. Wouldn't you like to go for a stroll outside? The view from the tower of the river and the wide expanse of reeds would be delightful. Come with me and see it.'

Arang went out into the garden with her nurse. They stood for a while by the lotus pond admiring the pale moonlight shining through the stillness of the night. Anxious not to be too long because she had not asked her father's permission to go out, Arang said, 'It is very late, Nurse, I must be going back.' But her nurse paid no attention to her and insisted that she come and see the view from the Yŏngnam tower. Somewhat reluctantly Arang followed her to the top of the tower. There she sat on the balcony and looked down on the beauty of the night.

The young official Bĕg was already hiding behind one of the thick wooden pillars awaiting her arrival. The nurse now made some excuse to leave the lady, and as soon as she had gone the young man stepped out and whispered to Arang. 'Do not be afraid. You do not know me, but I love you to distraction.' Arang was terrified at this unexpected intrusion, and screaming loudly tried to run away. But there was no one there except the young man who rushed at her and tried to take her in his arms. She resisted strongly, and the young man drew his dagger to threaten her. Arang resisted him to the last, when he stabbed her and she fell dead on the floor. Her body he threw into the bamboo grove below the tower.

Next morning, when it was discovered that Arang was missing, the magistrate her father ordered the most careful investigation. Not the slightest clue could be found, for the nurse and the young official Bĕg contrived to keep their connection with the affair quite secret. Because of the shame of this incident, which should not have happened in a noble family, the magistrate himself resigned and returned to Seoul.

Thereafter, when any new magistrate took up his post in Miryang he was found dead the very next morning. There was never any trace of his having been murdered, however, and the mysterious death of every new magistrate on the night of his arrival greatly perplexed the Government in Seoul. Thenceforth no one was willing to be appointed magistrate of Miryang.

One day an official named Yi Sang-Sa applied for this post, for he had in mind a scheme to clear up the mystery of his predecessors' deaths. On being appointed by the government he came to Miryang. The officials there made preparations for the funeral which they thought would take place on the following morning.

On the night of his arrival the new magistrate Yi lit as many candles as he could to illuminate every corner of his residence, and sitting in the centre of the hall began to read in a loud voice. Suddenly a strange wind sprang up, the door opened of its own accord, and there appeared the ghost of a girl, with her hair in disorder, one arm and one breast cut off, and a dagger piercing her throat.

Not in the least horrified by the terrible apparition the magistrate shouted boldly, 'Are you a ghost or a living creature?' The ghost replied, 'I am the spirit of Arang lingering in this world because my revenge is not yet accomplished. Whenever I have come to a new magistrate on his first night here he has been horrified by my appearance and has died of fright, but you are the boldest and bravest magistrate I have ever seen. My murderer goes to your office every day. At roll-call on the third day from now a yellow moth will flutter round him. By this sign you shall know him and you will be able to punish him on my behalf.'

Next morning the officials who had prepared a funeral for the new magistrate were greatly surprised to find him alive. At roll-call on the third day he saw a yellow moth flying to and fro over the back of a young official named Bĕg Ga. He summoned this fellow to appear before him, and confronted with his crime he confessed everything. He was found guilty and executed at once. They found the girl's body in the grove, and buried it where it lay. After this the ghost appeared no more. A shrine was built beside her grave where people came to pray, and even to hold an annual festival to avert calamities and ensure the safety of the town.

Ondoru Yawa, told by Hwang Hag-Su; Mityang (1925).

60

The Story of a Gentleman

LONG ago there lived a *Yangban* or gentleman, who had a wife and a seven-year-old son. One day he went up to Seoul to take the Civil Examination, leaving his family behind at home.

While her husband was away on this long journey his wife found a lover. Her young son then chided her for her unbecoming behaviour. She was ashamed at her son's reproaches, and for a while she was faithful to her husband. But before long her lover returned. Again she was tempted and fell, and their relationship became extremely intimate. Once more her son spoke to her sever.ly about her conduct. Then, crazed with fear that her husband might come to hear of it, poisoned her son, and let it out that he had died of a sudden illness.

123

After the lapse of several months her husband returned. He had had the misfortune to fail in the examination. He asked his wife what had happened to his son, and she told him that he had died of a sudden illness. His old maid-servant, however, knew what had really happened, and told him that his wife had poisoned their son. He was appalled at this revelation, but he could find it in him neither to accuse his wife nor to appeal to the court, for it was such a shameful affair that if it became widely known the whole family would suffer the gravest dishonour.

He decided that the only thing for him to do was to leave his home forever, and wander aimlessly around the country, like any vagrant. One day he met a boy on his wanderings, and they travelled along together. They had gone only a little way when the boy cried out as if he had suddenly remembered something. 'I've got it!' he said. 'I've just remembered that I didn't pay enough at the inn where I stayed last night. I'm sure I gave them a penny short. I must go back at once and pay them the extra penny.'

The gentleman was rather surprised at such extraordinary honesty. He told the boy that it hardly seemed necessary to walk back all that distance just to pay one penny. 'It is too late now, anyway,' he said. 'They won't bother about a little thing like that. I don't think you need go back just for one penny.'

The boy flushed slightly with anger and replied, 'I don't think you're a very honest man. If you mean to be a true companion you must not say things like that.' With these words he turned and hastened back to the inn.

The gentleman was rather ashamed of his own careless attitude, and deeply impressed by the boy's unshakeable honesty. He walked slowly on his way alone, and before long the boy caught up with him again. At nightfall they came to a village, and lodged in the same inn. In fact, they shared the same room. The gentleman was very tired from his exertions, and went to bed straight after supper, and fell asleep at once.

When he awoke next morning the boy had already gone. After breakfast when he felt in his purse for money to pay the bill he found there was nothing there. He realized that the boy must have stolen all his money. Now he had been twice deceived, once by his wife, and once by this cunning lad.

A little later on, as he was crossing a hill, he saw a magpie flying around near the top of a pine tree. He stood and watched, and noticed that there was a brood of young magpies in a nest near the top of the tree. They seemed to be very hungry, and yet the mother bird would not leave them to hunt for food. She seemed to be afraid that something might happen to them in her absence. Then a crane in a neighbouring tree turned to the magpie as if to say, 'Don't worry about your babies, I will look after them while you are away.' The magpie seemed to answer, 'Thank you, Crane. I will leave them in your care.' Then it flew off to find food for its brood. The gentleman was deeply moved by this display of motherly affection and neighbourly friendship among birds.

But no sooner was the magpie out of sight than the crane swooped down on the nest and ate all five of the baby magpies. When he saw this the gentleman was all the more convinced that to trust is to be deceived.

When he came to the next village he went into a wine-shop to rest. He drank a few cups of milky rice-wine. While he was sitting there a group of young men came into the shop. They were carrying a crane they had shot. They said jokingly to the proprietress, 'Cook this for us, if you please. We know that people do not usually eat cranes, but we are going to try to-day.'

Thereupon they skinned the crane and cut it open, and inside it they found five magpie chicks. The gentleman realized that it must be the very crane he had seen eat the magpie's brood, reflected on the just retribution of fate, and the almost incredible ways in which it might come about, as was shown by the wicked crane being shot and cut open.

After a while the young men began to get a little drunk, and started to make fun of the proprietress. 'You have been a widow long enough,' they said, 'Why don't you marry again? That rich old widower Hong will be out to-night to kidnap you. That's just as it ought to be. Girls shouldn't be left unmarried. That's the traditional custom, you know. But we can't let you stay as you are. You had better marry a young man. What about one of us?'

The proprietress of the wine-shop was quite a good-looking widow, and it seemed that the high-spirited young men of the village made a habit of dropping in and making fun of her. To judge from appearances, she seemed to be of noble birth. The gentleman was sorry to see her present unfortunate state. He decided that he would try to protect her in case Hong should try to kidnap her that night.

In the evening he changed clothes with the proprietress, and slept in her room in her place. About midnight the servants of the widower Hong, who was the most influential man in the village, rushed into the room. They seized the gentleman and carried him off, for they thought he was the widow. They put him in the room where Hong's only daughter was sleeping, for they thought that the presence of his daughter might soothe the 'widow's' alarm at being kidnapped.

In the morning Hong opened the door of his daughter's room, and was greatly astonished to find there a man dressed in woman's clothes. His daughter seemed to be very pleased with this unexpected guest, and so he consented to their marriage. And, ashamed at his first ignominious failure, Hong gave up all idea of trying to kidnap the widow. Then the gentleman told his father-in-law, Hong, and his wife, that he would like to take the widow as his second wife. This was allowed, and so the gentleman won two wives from his adventure.

A few years later he attempted the Civil Examination again, and this time he passed. Before long he was appointed Minister of Justice. Among the cases which came before him were two of the most serious on record. One was a thief and swindler of the worst type, and the other a woman accused of adultery with ninety-nine lovers.

The thief was the boy who had stolen his money at the inn, and the woman was his own first wife, who had murdered his son. Thus in the end it was proved to him that crime earned its own just retribution.

Ondoru Yawa, told by Bang Zŏng-Hwan; Seoul (1925).

61

The Goblin Bridge

LONG ago there reigned in Korea a King called Zin-Zi, the twenty-fifth King of the Silla Dynasty. One day it came to his ears that in his realm there lived a lady of surpassing beauty, by name Do-Hwa. So he sent a messenger to her to invite her to attend at the Court. The lady, however, would not come, and sent a message to the King in these terms, 'I am married, and I live with my husband. Therefore I cannot accept Your Majesty's invitation.'

The King then sent her another message. This time he asked whether she would have accepted his invitation if she had not had a husband. She thought that the King was joking, and replied, 'Certainly if that were the case I should be delighted to come to the Court.'

Soon afterwards the King died, and two year's later the lady's husband died too. Now that she was alone she found life very dull and wearisome, and often recalled the King's pleasantry. Then one night the King appeared to her in a dream and said, 'You once promised me that if you had no husband you would come to me. Now your husband has left you, and so there is no reason why you should not welcome me.' The King stayed with her for some days and then went away. And she awoke, and found that it was just a dream. Yet, strange to say, she soon found herself with child. In due course she gave birth to a strong and healthy boy. She called him Bi-Hyŏng, and lavished all her care upon him.

The old King's successor, Zin-Pyŏng, heard of the miraculous birth of the boy, and had him brought to the Palace. The King took him under his personal protection, and provided the best possible education for him. As he grew up it became apparent that he was the possessor of magical powers. When he was fourteen he took to leaving the Palace every night by jumping right over the Crescent Tower and landing on the banks of the River Mun-Czŏn. There he used to play with a crowd of goblins. But he always came back when the Great Bell boomed at daybreak.

The King was rather alarmed at the boy's strange behaviour. One day he decided to test him to see what he could do. So he summoned him to appear before him and said, 'I want a bridge just to the north of the Sin-Wŏn Temple. Can you and your goblins build one there?'

Bi-Hyŏng gladly complied with the King's request, and every night called up a crowd of his goblin friends. They set to work, and in a very short time they had built a great stone bridge. The King was very pleased, and named it the Goblin Bridge.

The Goblin Bridge

For a while all went well, but then crowds of goblins began to come out on to the bridge at night and threaten the passers-by. Things got so bad that in the end no one dared to cross the bridge at night. This caused great discontent among the people, for they were greatly inconvenienced by being unable to cross the bridge. So the King ordered that a great ceremony of exorcism be held beneath the bridge. After that the goblins appeared no more, and people could cross the bridge in safety day and night.

In later times it became the custom for young men to gather on the bridge, and, wearing goblin masks, dance to the accompaniment of music, and run races from the bridge to the town of Gyŏngzu.

One day the King asked Bi-Hyŏng if there was any among his goblins capable of controlling the administrators of the country. 'There are many,' he replied, 'For example, there is Gil-Dal. I think he would be quite capable of doing it for you. Thereupon the King bade him bring Gil-Dal to him. So he went and brought him into the presence of the King.

When he saw Gil-Dal the King was pleased with him and bestowed high rank and a title of honour upon him. The goblin served the King loyally and strove nobly to see that justice was done. A nobleman, Im-Zong, came to the King and asked that he be permitted to adopt Gil-Dal as his son, because he had no children of his own. This request the King was pleased to grant.

Im-Zong had Gil-Dal build the Tower Gate of the Hŭng-Yung Temple. It is known as the Gil-Dal Gate to this day, after its builder.

After serving loyally for many years Gil-Dal at last grew weary of his office. So he turned himself into a fox and ran away. When Bi-Hyŏng heard that he was missing he organized a search. When he was found Bi-Hyŏng had the other goblins kill him for his cowardly betrayal of his trust.

Bi-Hyŏng steadily became more powerful and influential, so that in the end the mere mention of his name struck fear into the people. To this day the inhabitants of that part of the country paste on the gateposts of their houses inscriptions praising the merits of Bi-Hyŏng to protect them against goblins and imps.

Told by Song Sŏg-Ha; Ŏnyang (1930).

128

62

The Police Marshal

NEAR the East Gate in Seoul there once lived a strong and coura-geous man, by name Bag. Being of a most adventurous nature he was in the habit of travelling far and wide throughout Korea.

One day he was travelling along a mountain road. He had walked a very long way, and was feeling extremely weary. So he lay down on a rock to rest by the roadside. He was very drowsy, and as he was dropping off he half saw a crowd of tiny men creeping up on him from all sides. So, overcome with curiosity at what they would do, he lay quiet and waited. He heard them whispering among themselves, and then one of them said, 'I think it must be a dead body. Let us take it down to the riverside and bury it.'

Bag was sure that such tiny creatures could not move a big man like him, but such a crowd of them came up that they managed it without difficulty. Some grasped his ears and some his fingers, others spread themselves out along his body in an unbroken line. Slowly they dragged him down from the rock, and down into the valley. He was greatly amused by the dignified and solemn way they went about their task, for all the world just like a funeral procession. At last they reached the river, and put him down on the sandy bank while they dug a grave. Suddenly one of them cried, 'If it rains the body will float away. We had better weight it down with a big rock.' They went off and fetched a rock from the mountain and tried to put it on him. This time Bag was really alarmed and sprang up. All the tiny men scattered and ran away, and as they ran Bag heard them say, 'We thought he would be a real hero, but we were wrong. However great he becomes he can never be more than a police marshal.'

Bag sat up on the rock, and realized that he must have been dreaming. It was a strange dream indeed, and he sat for some time pondering on what it might mean. Then he got up and set off to continue his journey through the mountains. At dusk he came to a river where he saw a beautiful girl washing clothes, beating them with a mallet. He stood a little way off and gazed at her as the dusk deepened and the moon began to shine. Then she gathered up all the clothes into a bundle and set out for the nearby village, carrying them on her head.

Bag followed her and saw her go into a big house. He waited a little while and then went up to the gate himself and knocked. He knocked several times, but no reply came from within. So he opened the gate and entered. It appeared to be the home of a well-to-do family, for it was large and had a tiled roof. There was no sound to be heard, all was still and seemingly deserted. Dauntless man that he was he looked into the living room with great interest. and to his horror saw there several corpses pale in the moonlight. At the same time the stench of rotting flesh assailed his nostrils.

Though horrified by what he saw he could not leave the house immediately. It was the traditional belief that if anyone found a dead body he must bury it at once, or he would be haunted by the spirit. So Bag went out into the garden and dug a grave deep and wide enough to hold all the bodies in the house. Starting from the one nearest the door he tied the bodies up with ropes. At last, in the farthest corner of the room he came upon the girl he had followed. She, too, was dead, though she looked calm and peaceful as if she were asleep. Her body was still not quite cold, and there was some colour left in her cheeks, so that she was as beautiful as she had been when he had seen her first by the river side. At first he could not believe that she was really dead, and as he looked at her affection grew in his heart. With heavy heart he at last convinced himself that she was dead, and must indeed have died only a few minutes previously.

Reluctantly he tied up her body too, and then carried all the bodies outside one by one and buried them in the grave he had dug. His task completed he left the house, and hastened on his way towards the next village. He found an empty house, and decided to spend the night there, for it was nearly midnight, and he was tired and covered in sweat from his exertions. It was an isolated house, far from any village. Dust lay thick on the floor, but he lay down at once and rested. Before long he fell asleep.

He had not been asleep long when he was roused by soft footsteps approaching the house. They sounded like those of a woman wearing leather shoes. Nearer and nearer they came, and Bag began to feel alarmed. He got up and stood by the door, ready to meet any danger that might threaten him. Then he heard a woman's voice calling softly, 'Good evening, Sir. May I come in?' Bag made no reply, and then the window opened slowly. He saw the girl he had first seen by the river, and had afterwards found dead in the first house, and whom he had buried only a few hours before. He was most astonished, and thought he must be dreaming. She came into the room smiling, and bowed to him most politely. 'I have come to thank you, Mr. Bag,' she said. 'I am very grateful to you for burying us all this evening.'

'What does all this mean?' asked Bag. 'Are you dead or alive? Please tell me the truth.'

'I was alive when you saw me washing clothes at the river side,' she replied, 'but dead when you found me in the room. My grandfather fell ill of a mysterious fever, and died almost at once. The disease proved to be contagious, and before long grandmother followed him. Then in turn my father and mother passed away, and after them my brothers and sisters. The doctors could find no cure, and the neighbours were afraid to come near us. Though we had been well off we were ruined by our efforts to find a cure for this malevolent plague, and in the end I was left penniless and alone. When you saw me by the river I was the last survivor of my family, but the symptoms of the disease had already appeared on me, and very soon after I returned to the house I died. That is the whole sad history of my family, and I am deeply grateful to you for your goodwill towards us.'

Bag now realized why she had come and appeared to him, but he could hardly believe that the beautiful girl who sat before him was not a living woman. So, deeply moved, he tried to take her by the hand, but she drew back slightly, and would not let him. 'I am sorry, Mr. Bag, but I am dead, you know. There is however something I want to tell you, that I may repay you for your kindness. All I ask of you is that you should follow my advice exactly.'

She told him to go to the market place of a certain town at noon the following day. In the market place was a stone monument, and before it he would see an old bachelor with his hair hanging in a long pigtail down his back. This man he should arrest without delay.

Next day Bag followed her instructions and went to the market place. There he saw the stone monument standing among the stalls of several cloth merchants. The old man was standing in front of it, just as the girl had said. For a moment he hesitated, lest he should be mistaken, but, believing that she had been sincere in her advice, he stepped forward boldly and arrested him. He found that he was a thief who had stolen large sums of money from the open shops in the market place. The news of the arrest soon spread, and Bag gained a high reputation among the townsmen for his alertness.

From that day the spirit of the girl visited him each night that he was alone, and each time she brought him valuable information. On her advice he once stopped a nobleman who was riding through the streets of a neighbouring town and found that he was a notorious gambler. His reputation grew steadily, and people began to come to him with any problem concerning property lost or stolen. He had no difficulty in solving them all satisfactorily, for the spirit gave him infallible advice on everything that puzzled him. He won steady promotion, from being a local police chief he became the superintendent of a town police force, and then supervisor of a whole province.

One night the girl visited him much later than usual, and when she did finally arrive she came wearily with dragging steps. She came into the room listless and sad, with tears glistening in her eyes. Bag found her even more beautiful than before. But he was puzzled by her manner, and asked her what had happened. Sobbing gently she answered, 'This is the last time that I can see you. I am going away to the other world where my parents are waiting for me. I have come to bid you farewell.'

At her words Bag was overcome with regret. For one thing he would no longer be able to gaze on her beauty, and even more important, he would no longer get from her the information on which his reputation was built. 'What shall I do when you are gone?' he cried. 'Not only will I miss you terribly, but I shall be ruined. With you there is nothing I cannot do, without you I am nothing.' He tried to take her in his arms, but she drew back swiftly. 'Do not touch me,' she cried, 'I am dead, you must remember. You need have no fears for your reputation, for I bring you the most sensational information yet as my parting gift. You will gain success beyond your wildest dreams.'

'What have you for me to-night, then? I am sure you would never let me down,' said Bag.

'To-morrow is the birthday of the wife of a Minister. Her daughter is the wife of another Minister, and she will go to her mother's house with a great retinue of attendants, and with many presents. Her home is some distance from her mother's house, and the procession will have to cross a mountain pass. You will see them leave in the morning. There will be a great feast, and everyone will be invited to join in. You may attend if you wish, and you may eat anything you like, but you must drink nothing. Afterwards there will be a contest of archery up on the hill, but however much you may be pressed to take part you must on no account do so. You must take your leave and return and call out your troops, and conceal about a hundred men on the mountain side. Then you must wait for the procession to return, which will be a little before sunset. When it reaches you you must order your men to stop it.'

Bag was somewhat taken aback by this. 'How can I stop such an important procession?' he protested. 'Why should I do such a thing? The Ministers will be furious with me. You are not trying to deceive me, are you?'

She shook her head and continued. 'How can you think such a thing of me? You are my benefactor, and I must discharge my debt to you. I would never tell you to do anything that would cause you trouble. You must drag the daughter from her palanquin, and strip her naked. That is all I have to tell you, and I hope you will not fail.'

Bag hardly knew what to say, and answered in an embarrassed tone, 'I can't do that. It would be an outrageous insult to a noble lady. And if I do, what then? They will hang me, surely.'

The girl however taunted Bag with cowardice, and demanded that he act with his customary resolve. 'This is my last chance to see you,' she said. 'And it is your last chance, too. You will see what will happen. Farewell, my friend, for ever.'

She vanished, and left Bag sorrowing at his loss. He was very nervous at the prospect of carrying out her advice, but he really had no alternative. Win or lose, it was his last chance. Even if he ignored her advice, it would avail him nothing, for he would no longer have her to give him guidance. There was nothing for it, and he determined to carry out the dreadful plan.

In the morning he went to the Minister's daughter's house and saw a long procession coming out of the gate. In front attendants were leading horses heavily laden with boxes, and in the rear were women-servants bearing packages on their heads. In the centre was a lofty palanquin borne on the shoulders of many attendants, in which, no doubt, the Minister's daughter was riding. The procession turned and went along the road across the pass. Bag followed, and in due course they came to the village on the other side of the pass. Here a great feast was held. The villagers came crowding to it, and Bag himself attended and paid his regards. When the meal was over, he declined an invitation to take part in the archery contest on the hill and hastened back across the pass.

Everything had turned out as the girl had foretold. Bag summoned his men, and stationed them in the pass to await the return of the procession. As the sun sank in the west it appeared. It came down the narrow mountain road, and when it drew near Bag ordered his men to block its path. They rushed out and arrested the whole retinue. Then Bag gave orders that the Minister's daughter should be dragged from her palanquin. This was done, and the beautiful young woman stood in the road, her hands bound behind her back. She had turned very pale, her jaw set in defiance, and stood with eyes downcast in shame at the intolerable insult she had suffered. All her servants and attendants stood around, trembling with impotent rage.

Then Bag hesitated and wondered what he ought to do next, but it seemed that there was nothing for it but to have her stripped naked. So he ordered his men to take off all her clothes. They hesitated in their turn, but at last one of the older men plucked up courage to take off her outer jacket. Bag repeated the order again and again, and another man took off her outer skirt. One by one they took off her garments until only the last remained.

The woman writhed in desperation, and her attendants glared furiously at Bag, but they could do nothing but await his next order. Bag himself was in a very tense state of mind. He still could not imagine what would happen, and was very alarmed at the possibility of finding nothing untoward, for in that case he would be quite at a loss what to do next. There was nothing he could do but repeat the order to strip her completely naked.

One of his men standing behind her stripped her to the waist. Her swelling breasts made her more beautiful than ever, but she was still not quite naked. Her fate and Bag's hung on the final removal

134

of her remaining garment. The strain was beginning to tell on everyone. Finally Bag shouted with all his strength, 'Take it right off,' and immediately fainted, overcome with the suspense.

None of Bag's men was willing to subject her to this last indignity, but at last his deputy, with eyes averted, finally stripped her naked.

Now there was a deathly hush in the mountain pass, and the whole assemblage wondered whether some miracle might happen, and, turning their heads away, stood in silence. It was already past sunset, and in the stillness of the twilight Bag recovered consciousness and looked around.

What did he see? Surely there was something wrong. Yes, indeed! The Minister's daughter was no woman, but a man! A miracle had certainly happened, and no trivial one at that. The mystery was solved, and Bag shouted, 'So that is what she meant!' Then he ordered his men to examine all the attendants, and they found that all the women servants were really men, with not a single woman among them.

Now that their imposture was so clearly exposed they made a full confession. They were a gang of bandits, and the supposed Minister's daughter was their leader, young, handsome, and clever. Bag hastened to the Minister's mansion where the birthday feast had been held, and found that all the noble ladies and their guests had been murdered and their fine dresses and jewels stolen. The lady of the house and her daughter were among the dead. On the hill behind the house he found all the men lying dead.

The procession Bag had seen in the morning had been genuine enough. The real daughter had come to her mother's birthday feast. But the bandits too had come to the feast, pretending to be ordinary guests. They suggested the archery contest, and when the men went up the hill to hold it they fell upon the women and killed them all, weak and unprotected as they were. Then they made a surprise attack on the men too, and left not one of them alive.

Afterwards they stripped all the clothes from their victims both men and women, and dressed themselves in them. Thus disguised they made a passable imitation of the morning's procession, and set out across the mountain pass. They planned to carry off all the jewels and finery they had plundered from their victims far into the mountains to their remote hiding place, but in this they were thwarted by Bag's prompt action.

This was indeed the most serious case in all the annals of crime. In recognition of his services the King raised Bag to the rank of Police Marshal, the most honourable rank in the Police service of the country. Bag, however, retired almost at once, on the plea that he was exhausted by the strenuous services he had performed.

Bag often remembered the tiny men who had predicted his rise to the rank. Nor did he ever forget the girl to whom he owed so much, and of whom he cherished many fond memories.

Ondoru Yawa, told by Bang Zŏng-Hwan; Seoul (1925).

63

The Wife from Heaven

IN Andong, in the province of Gyŏngsang, there lived long ago a certain Sŏn-Gŏn, the son of a nobleman. He grew up to be a very studious young man. One day, as he sat reading, a mood of drowsiness crept over him and he fell into a doze. He began to dream, and he saw a pretty maiden who seemed to have something she wished to say to him. As he gazed entranced at her wondrous beauty and the etherial robe she wore, she addressed him in these words, 'I am a Heavenly Maiden, and the Heavenly King has sent me down from Heaven to be your wife.' Thereupon she vanished, and he awoke. He closed his eyes again, and the fair beauty seemed to linger before him. In the days that followed he often recalled her beautiful countenance, and prayed in secret that his imaginary love should come back to him.

One day the Heavenly Maiden came to him again in a dream and said, 'I, too, long to come to you, but the Heavenly King has not yet given me full permission to live with you as your wife. You must wait patiently a little longer. I have asked the finest artist to paint my portrait, and I have had the most beautiful frame possible designed for it, and I have brought it to you here to-day. You may keep it beside you always. Until I can come to be your wife you may take as your mistress your maid-servant Mĕwŏl.' With these words she vanished. Sŏn-Gŏn woke up, and there beside him he saw the

Heavenly Maiden's portrait in a golden frame. It was the most beautiful portrait imaginable, and he cherished it most dearly.

The maid Mĕwŏl he took as his mistress, as the Heavenly Maiden had authorized him to do. But he could not forget her, for she was beautiful beyond all imagination. Then one day he fell grievously ill. As he lay on his sick-bed the Maiden appeared to him once again. 'I am deeply grieved to see you in such distress,' she said, 'but I am not permitted to come to the lower world to meet you. But go to the Og Yŏn Dong, the Lotus Garden, and I will come and see you there.'

Sŏn-Gŏn was overjoyed at her words, and immediately regained his health. He told his parents that he must go away on some pretext or other, and made preparations for the journey. Then he set out accompanied by one servant. He had no idea where the Og Yŏn Dong was to be found, so he wandered here and there, visiting many places of historical interest, and renowned beauty spots.

One day he travelled far up a mountain valley, and came upon a lovely palace set among the trees. Inscribed over the gate he saw the words 'Og Yŏn Dong'. He could hear the sweet strains of the harp from within, and he made haste to enter. There he found the Heavenly Maiden for whom he had languished so long. She paused in her playing and welcomed him most profusely, and took him into her room. They talked most happily together, and time sped by as in the sweetest dream. There they became as man and wife, and so the Heavenly Maiden could not return to Heaven. So Sŏn-Gŏn took her home to his parents' house, and told them his secret. They readily pardoned him, and welcomed the Maiden with open arms. They held a formal marriage ceremony, and adopted her as their daughter-in-law.

For a few years they lived happily together, and a son and a daughter were born to them. Now the time came for Sŏn-Gŏn to go to Seoul to take the High Civil Examination, and he set out for the Capital. That night however a man's voice was heard whispering in the Heavenly Maiden's room. It was Sŏn-Gŏn himself, who had slipped back unnoticed, because he could not bear to be parted from his wife. Next morning he set out again, but once more even a few hours parting was more than he could bear, and in the evening he returned again. Several days passed in this fashion.

The maid-servant Mĕwŏl knew what was going on and was

consumed with jealousy. She had been intimate with Sŏn-Gŏn before the Heavenly bride had been brought to the house, but thereafter she had been cast aside, and utterly neglected. As she listened to these nocturnal whisperings a base and deceitful idea came to her. One night she introduced a young man into the house, and went and told Sŏn-Gŏn's father that his daughter-in-law was being unfaithful to his son. So he came to investigate, and sure enough he heard a man whispering in the room, and afterwards he saw a man running away. He was furious and next morning he summoned the Heavenly Maiden to him and upbraided her severely. She knew nothing about Měwŏl's plot, and strongly denied the accusation, but her father-in-law would not listen to her. He had her beaten and locked up. In her agony she cried, 'Father, I am innocent. This bodkin will prove the truth. Throw it in the air, and if I am guilty it will fall on me and plunge deep into my bosom. But if I am innocent it will fall on the stone doorstep, and penetrate it. Please make this test, Father.'

Her father-in-law took the bodkin and threw it in the air. To the astonishment of all it fell on the door-step and penetrated deeply into it. His wife believed in the truth of this miracle, and begged her husband, 'Do wait till Sŏn-Gŏn comes back. Surely her innocence is proved.' But, convinced by what he had seen with his own eyes, he obstinately refused to change his mind.

Next morning the Heavenly Maiden was found dead. She had taken her own life, and left her two children motherless. Her countenance was calm in death, and from her body came a sweet and lasting fragrance. Her mother-in-law repented of the harsh treatment meted out to her, but it was too late. The servants came to put her in a coffin, but the body would not release the dagger from its hand, and adhered so tightly to the floor that it could not be moved. So there was nothing they could do but await the return of Sŏn-Gŏn.

Sŏn-Gŏn passed the examination, and came home full of pride at his success. He was overwhelmed with grief when he heard of the tragedy which had occurred. There was nothing he could do but try and arrange a proper funeral for her. The very night of his return he sat in vigil in the room where his wife was lying.

He fell asleep and dreamed. His Heavenly wife appeared to him and told him everything. 'While you were away,' she said, 'I was forced to take my own life. On the death of my mortal body I came up to Heaven and was taken before the Heavenly King. He spoke to me sternly but not unkindly. "I did not intend that you should fall in love with that young man," he said, "for the time had not yet come for you to be married to a mortal. In my opinion you fully deserve all that has befallen you. Since, however, your love for your husband is so sincere I am going to allow you to go back and live with him." So I will most gladly return to you and be your wife. If you can induce the maid-servant Měwŏl to repent of her misdeeds, so that she is forgiven by Heaven, then I shall be restored to life.' And then she disappeared once more.

Sŏn-Gŏn was deeply affected by his dead wife's words in his dream. He secretly summoned Měwŏl to him, and earnestly appealed to her to repent of her malice towards his wife. So strongly did he implore her that she was moved by his sincerity, and felt her jealousy slip away. Thereupon she repented of her wickedness and humbly apologized, kneeling beside the corpse of the Heavenly Maiden, and weeping bitter tears of remorse. Immediately the body, which lay cold and stiff like a great white candle, was suffused with blood, and a blush appeared on her cheeks. Her eyes opened, and the wound in her throat was healed. She sat up and the dagger she had grasped so long in her hand fell to the floor.

So she was restored to life, and Sŏn-Gŏn was beside himself with joy. The tragic cloud passed away, and the family were reunited in happiness.

Told by Gim Gi-Hwan; Tong-yŏng (1940).

PART THREE
FAIRY TALES

64

The Mallet of Wealth

LONG, long ago there lived a very poor boy. He used to go out into the mountains every day to cut firewood. His parents used to sell the wood he gathered to buy food.

One day he went out to the mountain to cut wood as usual. As the afternoon wore on he began to feel very hungry, and so he looked around for something to eat. By good fortune he soon found a walnut tree growing in the forest, and climbing it he began to pick the nuts.

He picked one and put it in his pocket. 'This is for Father,' he said. He picked another. 'This is for Mother,' he said.

Then he picked a third. 'This is for my brother,' he said.

Picking a fourth he said, 'This is for my sister.'

'And now, one for me,' he said, and picking the fifth nut he put it in his mouth and ate it. Then he picked more, until his hunger was satisfied.

When he set out for home the sun had set and it was already growing dark. So he stopped to pass the night in a wayside shrine. He sat on the floor quite alone. It was eerie sitting there on the floor, and he felt quite frightened. So he climbed up into the rafters to await the dawn.

In the middle of the night he was surprised to hear the clamour of voices outside, and then a crowd of goblins rushed into the hall talking animatedly to one another.

'Where have you been to-day?'

'I hung on the tail of an ox.'

'I have been looking for a filial son. But it's very hard to find one these days, isn't it?'

'I have spent the whole day teasing a bad boy.'

'I have been jumping in a ditch and blowing bubbles in the mud.'

'I have been sleeping in the crevices of a stone wall.'

'I have been dancing under a floor.'

Every goblin recounted his doings of the day. Then one of them who seemed to be the leader cried, 'Enough! Let us have a drink. I suppose you are all very hungry, aren't you?'

One goblin took a mallet from his belt, and striking the floor with it chanted, 'Tudurag-tag-tag, come out, cooked rice.'

Immediately a great dish of cooked rice appeared from nowhere. 'Tudurag-tag-tag, come out, wine.'

At once a cask of wine appeared in the middle of the hall. In the same way they got fish, meat, eggs, cake, fruit, and as many other delicacies as they wished. So they feasted on all the good things.

The boy hiding in the rafters looked down on the scene of revelry by the dim light that penetrated the paper windows, and he too began to feel hungry. So he took a walnut from his pocket and cracked it in his mouth. Startled by the noise he made all the goblins shouted, 'Help! Help! The roof is falling. We must get out at once.' They all rushed in a panic from the hall, abandoning all the food and their mallet.

The boy came down from the rafters and ate his fill. Then he picked up the magic mallet and tried it out. He struck the floor with it and said, 'Tudurag-tag-tag, come out, clothes.' Immediately there appeared a full suit of clothes. Then he struck with the mallet again and wished for a pair of shoes. These too appeared. The boy was thrilled by his unexpected find, for he guessed that this was the celebrated 'Mallet of Wealth', of which he had often heard, though no man had ever seen it before.

At day-break next day he hastened home with the mallet. His parents and the neighbours had worried greatly over his failure to return home the previous night, and now with great relief they listened to his story, walnuts, shrine, goblins, mallet, and all. His parents were delighted to get the mallet, for now they could live at their ease, and in the end they became quite rich.

Now there was in the same village a greedy and selfish boy. When he heard that his friend had suddenly become rich he came to him and asked him the secret of his good fortune. The honest filial boy told him all about his experiences.

So the selfish boy, who was really quite well-off, and who had never in his life gone out into the mountains to cut wood, went out to look for the walnut tree. At last, after a long weary search, he found it, and, being by now very hungry, he picked a nut and ate it. Afterwards he picked some nuts for his father and mother, and then rushed off to the wayside shrine while it was still light, so impatient was he. He waited in the hall until it got dark, and then he climbed up and hid among the rafters.

In the middle of the night the goblins came in and, striking the floor with a mallet, began their feast. The selfish boy was too impatient to wait until the wine had befuddled their wits, and, taking out a walnut, cracked it in his mouth. This time the goblins were not at all alarmed by the sound, but merely looked up and said, 'There he is up there. We are not going to be tricked a second time. Pull him down before he spoils our entertainment.'

So the selfish boy was dragged down from the rafters. The goblins sat round him on the floor and put him on trial.

'What shall we do with this idle greedy fellow?' asked the leader of the goblins.

'Hang him! Hang him!' shouted the others.

'That would be too severe. After all he is only a boy. I suggest that we stretch his tongue.'

The assembly agreed with this suggestion, and so one of the goblins tapped his tongue with a mallet and intoned, 'Tudurag-tag-tag, come out this tongue, one hundred feet long.' Immediately his tongue began to grow, until it was one hundred feet long. Then the goblins kicked him out of the hall.

In his pain and weariness he could hardly stagger along carrying his tongue on his back. He came to a river, and saw that there was no bridge. So he stretched out his tongue across the river, so that it formed a bridge that people could walk on. He had repented of his selfishness, and had made up his mind to serve others. Travellers walked gratefully across the bridge he had formed, but one man let some burning tobacco fall on his tongue. He jumped with the pain and fell into the river.

The filial boy heard the news and came to his rescue. With great difficulty he managed to save him, and then he took his mallet and tapped the enormous tongue. 'Tudurag-tag-tag, draw in, tongue,' he said, and at once the tongue returned to its proper size. Thus he was cured, and never again did he do anything selfish as long as he lived.

Ondoru Yawa, told by Zŏng Bog-Sul; Ŏnyang (1913).

65

The Three Sons

LONG, long ago three sons lived with their sick father in a house at the top of a mountain. Though the family had once been comfortably off they had fallen on evil days and in the end the sons were so poor that they could hardly even buy medicines for their father.

At last the old man lay dying. He called his sons to his bedside, and bade them farewell with tears in his eyes. 'You have toiled hard for me these many years,' he said. 'While your mother was alive I was rich and had much property. But now I have nothing left but the few things that I will give you as tokens to remember me by. To my eldest son I leave my hand-mill with its grinding stones. To the second I leave my bamboo stick and a bowl made of half a gourd. And to the third I leave my long drum with the narrow waist. I shall not last much longer, and when I am gone you need live in this lonely mountain retreat no longer. May Heaven's blessing light upon you all!' With these words he breathed his last.

After the funeral the three brothers agreed to leave the house. They set out carrying the gifts their father had left them, and before long they came to a crossroad in the mountains where three ways met. They agreed to meet again after ten years at that spot, and then they parted, one going down one of the three roads. The eldest son took the right hand road, the second son the middle road, and the youngest the road to the left.

Carrying the heavy millstones on his back the eldest son walked on until night fell. He was still in the mountains, very tired and very hungry. At last he felt that he could walk no further and lay down under a big tree by the roadside to pass the night. It was a pitch black night, and he began to feel afraid. He feared that some wild animal or a robber might come and attack him if he stayed there, so he climbed up into the tree still carrying the millstones.

In the middle of the night, as he sat drowsily in the tree he heard two men quarrelling on the ground beneath him. He listened and soon realized that they were two robbers arguing over the division of their loot. He heard the clink of coins being counted. Then he began to make water on them out of the tree, and at the same time he rubbed his two millstones together so that they made a noise like thunder. Frightened by the thunder and rain the robbers ran away, still shouting abuse at one another. 'The punishment of Heaven has fallen upon you, you scoundrel,' said one. 'It has fallen fair and square on your head.'

The eldest son climbed down out of the tree and found a big wooden chest full of money and jewels. Next morning he set out again with the box. Before long he came to a village, and he decided to settle there. He built a big new house and married one of the girls of the village, so that he lived happily there.

The second son walked straight ahead along the middle road, thinking sorrowfully of his father and mother. As night fell he came to an old graveyard and decided to stay the night there. In the middle of the night he heard someone walking toward him, but in the darkness he could not see who it was. He was frightened and shrank back behind a burial mound. Then the unseen walker suddenly said, quite near him, 'Come on, skeleton. Let's take a walk before dawn. Wake up there, I say, sleepyhead.' It was evidently a goblin.

So the second son replied, 'Where are you going to-night? I'll be glad to come with you.'

Hearing a human voice the goblin was displeased and cried, 'You are not dead, are you? Your voice sounds wrong. What has happened? Let me touch your skull.'

So the second son held out into the darkness the gourd that he had received from his father. In a cracked voice he said, 'Here it is. Feel it. You will see that I am a skeleton.'

The goblin ran his hand over the gourd and said, 'That's all right. No hair at all. Must have been dead a long time. Let's see your arm.'

So the second son held out the bamboo stick and said, 'Here it is. You are hard to please, aren't you?'

The goblin felt the stick and said, 'Ah, very thin indeed. You must have starved to death. Very well, let us go. To-night we are going to steal the soul of a rich man's only daughter. Aha!'

They hurried to a village and stopped outside the gate of a large house. Then the goblin said, 'You wait outside here, skeleton. I'll go and get the daughter's soul while she's asleep.' Then he went into the house.

So the second son waited outside the house and in a few minutes the goblin came back, apparently holding something in its hand. 'This is her soul,' it said. 'It is a very nice one indeed, you know. By the way, have you a purse or something?'

'Oh yes, I have,' answered the second son. 'I'll put the soul in it so that it can't escape.'

He took the daughter's soul very carefully and put it in his purse. Then he drew the strings tight and went back towards the graveyard with the goblin. Before long they heard a cock crow, and the goblin said, 'It is time for me to leave you. I'll meet you again soon. You had better keep the soul for the time being.'

The goblin vanished and the second son waited for dawn. When it grew light he saw that his purse was swollen as if there was some living thing inside it. Then at sunrise he went back to the village, and heard that the only daughter of a rich man had died suddenly in the night, leaving her parents overcome with grief. They called in all the doctors, but to no avail, for they could not even establish the cause of death. So the second son hid the purse at his breast and went to the dead girl's father. He kept his secret to himself and said, 'I think I may be able to bring your daughter back to life. Will you let me try?'

'You may if you like, stranger,' replied the bereaved father. 'If you can restore her to me you will earn my undying gratitude.'

'Let me see her then, and let no one else as much as peep into the room while I am at work. If you will accept these conditions I will start at once.'

The father accepted his offer and took him to the room where his daughter lay. The second son locked the door securely on the inside and pasted paper over the tears in the windows. He put a screen around the bed, and going behind it he held his purse right under the dead girl's nose. Then he loosened the strings and her soul flew out of the purse and into her nostrils with a whistling sound. She opened her eyes at once, and was completely restored. He unlocked the door and the girl's parents came in. They embraced her and wept in their joy. In his gratitude her father offered the second son her hand in marriage, and he accepted. So they were married, and he lived happily as the son-in-law of a wealthy house.

The youngest son set out along the road to the left. As he walked along through the mountains he amused himself by beating with his hand on the long drum which he' carried slung from his neck. The mountains rang with the rhythm of the drum and the melody of his voice raised in song. Before long he saw a big yellow tiger come out of the forest and dance to his music. He was terrified at its appearance, and realized that he could not stop playing, for if he did the tiger would assuredly fall upon him and eat him up. So he went on playing to keep it in good humour, and walked backwards so that he could face it and watch what it might do.

Before long he came to a village. All the villagers were very amused to see him, with the tiger dancing before him. It seemed to be quite tame, for it attacked no one, and people began to throw money to the youngest son. He was surprised and pleased to find what a success he was, and so he led the tiger up to the capital, beating his drum and making the tiger dance.

The King was greatly interested by what he heard of this unusual happening and summoned the youngest son to come and perform at the palace. One of the King's daughters fell in love with him, and the King consented to their marriage. And so the youngest son became the husband of a Royal Princess, and the tiger was made a Royal pet.

When ten years had gone by the three brothers, to whom their father's tokens had brought such good fortune, went back to the place where they had parted. There they told one another of the adventures which had befallen them and went together to visit the graves of their parents.

Ondoru Yawa, told by Zŏng In-Mog; Ŏnyang (1915).

66

How Foolish Men Are!

LONG, long ago there was a poor boy who had been left an orphan. He was employed as a servant in a house, and worked very diligently and honestly.

One day he went out into the mountains to cut firewood. He worked steadily until sunset and then set out for home. On the way back he lost his way in the forest, and so had to spend the night in a hollow in the ground. In the middle of the night he heard strange voices talking. 'What is your news to-day?' said the first.

'How foolish men are!' replied the other. 'You know the village down there, don't you? They go to all the trouble of fetching water from a long way off, when all the time they could have a nice well right by the willow tree.'

'Indeed you are right. Men appear to be clever, but often they are very foolish indeed. You know the poor starving old widower? He doesn't know that there is an earthen pot full of money buried in his kitchen right by the kettle.'

'Yes, indeed. That is quite true. By the way, I came past the rich man's house just now. His daughter is lying seriously ill. He is spending vast sums of money on medicine, but I am convinced that it is quite useless. I suspect that there is a great centipede lurking under the pile of firewood in the yard, and that she has been overcome by the noxious vapours it emits. But no one has thought of that possibility. How foolish men are!'

The boy guessed that what he had overheard was a conversation between two goblins. In the morning he returned home, and saw the women of the village with water jars on their heads going off as usual to the distant well. He asked his master's permission and began to dig beside the willow tree in the centre of the village. Before long he struck water. Then all the villagers came and helped him in his digging, and before long there was a fine well right in the middle of the village. All the people were very grateful to him.

Next he went and knocked on the door of the poor old widower, who was so poor that he could only earn a mere pittance by making straw sandals. The boy told him that he knew of a way to help him, and started to dig up the kitchen floor. Before long he found the pot, and it was indeed full of money. The old man was overjoyed and offered to share it with the boy, but he refused.

Then he went to the rich man's house, where the daughter was lying sick in bed. He offered to do his best to cure her, and her father accepted his offer. So he asked for a big pot to be filled with oil and boiled, and got a big pair of iron tongs. Then he had the firewood moved aside and there he found a big black centipede. He picked it up with the tongs and dropped it in the boiling oil. While the centipede was dying the sick girl groaned with pain, but no sooner was it dead than she recovered completely. As a reward her father offered the boy her hand in marriage, and he accepted. So they were married, and the boy became the rich man's son-in-law.

Now the boy had a friend who was of a most deceitful nature. He heard of the boy's good fortune and came to ask him about it. 'How did you find out all these things?' he asked. 'Won't you tell me?'

So the boy told him how he had stayed all night in the mountains and had overheard the goblins' conversation. So the second boy went off into the mountains so that he too might have the good fortune to hear the goblins too. He hid behind a rock, and in the middle of the night he did indeed hear the goblins talking.

'You know that poor boy has made his fortune? He must have heard us the other night. But he is a nice boy, isn't he?'

'Oh yes, honest and hard-working. But do you know that greedy ill-natured friend of his? He is consumed with jealousy now. He doesn't even know his own good fortune. How foolish he is!'

'You mean the jewels under the paving stone by the south-east pillar of his house?'

'That's right. He *is* a fool!'

Thereupon they burst out laughing. The boy was very excited to hear the goblins, and carefully remembered every word they said. When they had disappeared he hastened home and began to dig under the paving stone as they had said. He made so much noise that he woke his parents. They were most alarmed to hear the sound of digging in the middle of the night. So his father got up to catch the thief, as he imagined it must be, but to his great surprise he found it was his son. The boy was beside himself in his eagerness to get on with his digging, and would not listen to his father's advice to give up the idea. 'Father, you don't understand,' he said. 'I am going to find a great fortune. Let me do as I wish.'

So his father gave up and the boy went on with his digging. For the first time in his life he was dripping with sweat. At last his spade struck something hard. He thought that it must be what the goblins had meant, and he tugged at it with all his might. At last it came away, the pillar collapsed, and the whole house came crashing down in ruins. The bricks all fell on the boy and crushed him to death.

The thing he had found was merely one of the stones of the foundations of the house.

Ondoru Yawa, told by O Sŏg-Gŏn; Ŏnyang (1915).

67

The Magic Cap

THE goblins of Korea used to wear magic caps, called Horang Gamtĕ, which had the power of rendering them invisible.

Now there once lived a man who was most diligent in his worship of his ancestors. He was always holding services to their memory, with lavish offerings of delicious food and drink. One day, when he had held such a service, a group of goblins came to his house, and ate up all the good things set out on the altars. And on every following occasion they did the same. Of course they were invisible, for they wore their magic caps, and so the offerings just disappeared. The man was very gratified at first to see his offerings eaten, for it seemed to prove that his ancestors relished them. So he spent more and more money to provide even more lavish feasts until he was almost ruined.

At last his wife complained of his extravagance. 'There must be something wrong,' she said. 'The spirits of our ancestors would never eat so much as to leave us almost ruined. There must be thieves coming in and stealing them while we are occupied with the ceremonial and bowing before the altar. In future I think we ought to keep a careful watch.'

So one night the husband hid behind a screen by the altar. He held a stout cudgel in his hand. In the middle of the night he heard the sound of whispering and of food being eaten. He peeped over the screen and saw the food steadily disappearing from the dishes. Yet he could see no one by the table. So all of a sudden he rushed out brandishing his cudgel and rushed round the altar and into all the corners of the room. Alarmed by his violent onslaught the goblins ran away, but the man touched óne of them with his cudgel and knocked his cap off. When the goblins had gone the man saw a red cap lying on the floor, the like of which he had never seen before. He picked it up curiously and put it on, and then began to shout 'Thief! Thief!'

His wife heard his shouts and came into the hall. But she could not see her husband, though she could hear him beside her gasping breathlessly, 'The thief got away, but he left a very strange cap behind. See?' His wife just stood there bewildered and said, 'But where are you, my dear? I can't see you.' Her husband took her by the hand and said, 'I'm here. What's the matter?' She felt him take hold of her, and tried to grasp him. She chanced to knock off the cap which he had put on his head. No sooner had it fallen to the floor than she saw him standing beside her.

She picked up the cap and said, 'Is this the cap you mean?' It must have made you invisible. So that's how the thief got in unnoticed. Let me try it.' She put it on her head and immediately vanished. 'This must be Horang Gamtĕ, the magic cap. I'm sure of it!' she exclaimed. 'The thief was no man, but a goblin.'

Having made this remarkable find they determined that they would turn it to their profit. From that day on they went from house to house in the village, stealing all that they could lay their hands on. Many complaints were made to the authorities, but though a strict watch was kept not a single clue could be found, so stealthily were the thefts committed.

They continued their activities for more than a year, and became very rich. But one day the husband went to a jeweller's shop. It was not open yet, so he waited by the door. In a little while the jeweller came along and opened the door and the thief slipped in behind him. The jeweller took his money from the safe and began to count it. While he was counting it he was amazed to see the coins disappearing one by one. He searched the whole shop, on the floor, and in every corner, but could find no trace of them. Then he looked up, and saw a piece of thread moving slowly in the air. He grabbed it with his fingers, something dropped on the floor, and there beside him he saw a man. The magic cap was beginning to wear out, and a thread had come loose from one of the seams.

The jeweller seized him with both hands, but when he returned all the money he had stolen and offered him the magic cap he let him go. Then the jeweller neglected his business and began himself‾ to use the magic cap as the other had done. One day in the harvest time he went to a rich farmer's house, wearing the magic cap on his head. The yard was full of labourers threshing rice with flails. As he passed through the yard to the house one of the flails knocked the cap off his head, and it fell in tatters to the ground. So he was discovered, and immediately arrested.

He was brought to trial, and the husband and wife as well. They were all condemned to imprisonment, and shortly afterwards died in prison.

Ondoru Yawa, told by Zo Sŏng-Gab; Ŏnyang (1913).

68

The Story-Spirits

LONG, long ago there lived a boy who very much liked to be told stories, much more even than eating rice. But although he enjoyed hearing stories so much he would never tell stories to others. He stored each story jealously in his memory, and would never utter so much as a word of it to anyone. He was the only child of wealthy parents, and to make him happy they saw to it that there was always someone to tell him a new story. After his parents died the faithful servant who took care of him continued to tell him a story every night.

In a corner of his room there hung an old purse, its mouth tightly fastened with string. It had hung there on a nail for years, completely forgotten. But every time a new story was told its spirit went into the bag and stayed there. It could not escape from confinement because the boy refused to tell stories to others. Every day one more spirit went into the purse, for every day he heard a new story. At last the bag was filled to suffocation, so that the story-spirits could hardly move.

When the boy was fifteen years old his uncle arranged for him to marry the daughter of another rich family. On the eve of the ceremony he was out with his friends and his faithful servant was stoking the fire beneath his room to make it warm for him. Suddenly he was astonished to hear whisperings inside the room. In great curiosity he listened carefully to what they were saying.

'He's getting married to-morrow, isn't he?' said one.

'That's right,' replied another. 'And we are almost suffocating to death in here.'

'Quite so. Isn't it time we got our own back on him?'

'Certainly. Indeed we should.'

The servant peeped into the room through a small hole in the paper window. There was no one in the room, but the voices were coming from the old purse on the wall. It was swelling and heaving as if there was some living thing moving inside it. The conversation continued—

'He will ride on horseback to the bride's house. It is quite a long way, isn't it? It will be a thirsty ride. I will be a well by the roadside, full of clear water with a gourd-cup floating on it. If he drinks he will die.'

'That's a good plan,' said another. 'Just in case he does not drink, I will be a field of delicious strawberries a little further on. If he eats them, he will die.'

Then a third said, 'If you two should fail, I will be a red-hot poker in the sack of rice husks on to which he will get down from his horse at the bride's house.'

'In case you should all fail,' said a fourth, 'I will be a little poisonous snake under the mat in the bridal chamber. I will bite him while he is asleep.'

Then once more silence reigned. The old servant was horrified, but he realized that it was quite to be expected that after such long confinement the story-spirits would try to harm his master. He was afraid to touch the purse before the ceremony was over, nor did he dare to tell his master when he returned what he had overheard.

Next morning everything was ready for the procession to the bride's home for the ceremony. Two horses had been prepared, one for the bridegroom and one for his uncle, who was acting as his guardian. There was a groom to lead each horse. Then the faithful servant came forward and earnestly begged that he be allowed to lead the bridegroom's horse. He was determined that in one way or another he would protect his master from the dangers that beset him. At first the uncle would not agree, and ordered him to stay behind and

mind the house, but he insisted so vehemently that in the end he
was allowed to come.

They set out with the bridegroom riding at the head of the procession and his uncle in the rear, according to the custom of those times.
The faithful servant led his master's horse so fast that his uncle protested at the unseemly haste, but the servant refused to slow down.

When they had gone about half a mile the bridegroom complained of feeling thirsty, and asked his servant to stop for a few
minutes at a well by the roadside. 'The water is very clear,' he said.
And there is a gourd floating on it. Please go and bring me some.'

But his servant merely urged on the horse and said, 'No, sir.
We will be late if we stop.' Thus he got his master safely past the
first danger. Before long they came to a field where the bridegroom
saw some ripe strawberries. 'I see some strawberries over there,' he
cried. 'They look delicious. Go and get me some to ease my thirst.'

Again his servant refused. 'No sir,' he said. 'They would be bad
for you. You will get better ones at the bride's house. After all you
are only a child. It is better not to eat anything on the way.'

By now the bridegroom's uncle was getting rather angry. He
upbraided the servant for his insolent behaviour to his master. 'You
would not bring him water, and now you refuse to fetch strawberries for him. I will see that you are soundly punished for this
after the ceremony.' But none the less he refused to stop, and so
safely negotiated the second peril.

About noon they arrived at the bride's home. The whole garden
was covered with an enormous tent so that if any bird of ill-omen
should fly over its shadow would not fall on the ceremony and bring
bad luck to the wedded pair. Before the door there was a sack filled
with rice husks to make it easier for the bridegroom to dismount.
But no sooner had he stepped on to the sack that his servant kicked his
feet away and he fell heavily on the ground. The bridegroom's uncle
was furious at this final act of insolence, on top of his earlier refusals
to obey orders, but he could not take any action just at that moment.

So they all went into the tent. In the centre was a table, and on
the table were a cock and a hen, half enveloped in embroidered
cloth, and each tied to a wine cup, one by a green thread attached
to its leg, and the other by a crimson thread. The bridegroom stood
on the Eastern side in front of a decorated screen. On a table beside
it was a wooden duck, the symbol of the go-between. There he

waited till the bride came in on the Western side, with two girls as her attendants. Then they bowed to each other and exchanged wine-cups, and the ceremony was complete.

Afterwards the bridegroom was led away to the main room of the house and the bride to her own room. All their relations came to visit them in each room. And in each room there was a big table laden with rich food and wine. So they feasted to celebrate the wedding. Everyone was happy, except the bridegroom's faithful servant, full of anxiety for his master's safety, and resolved to watch over him the whole night long.

No sooner had the newly-married couple retired for the night than his servant came and knocked at the door. To the astonishment of bride and bridegroom he came in armed with a sword, and tearing up the carpet he uncovered a snake and killed it with one blow. Then he threw the body out into the garden.

This commotion woke everyone in the house and they came to see what was the matter. They went and fetched the bridegroom's uncle from the house where he was sleeping. Then the old servant explained his strange behaviour. He told him about the old purse hanging on the wall, the story-spirits and their malevolent whisperings, of the poisoned well and strawberries. And he went and fetched the sack of rice husks and tore it open. Inside he found a red-hot poker which had already burnt up most of the husks. The bridegroom's uncle understood everything, and instead of punishing the old servant he warmly commended him for his fidelity.

The young man learnt his lesson and from that day on was always willing to tell stories to others. And he went and untied the purse and then burnt it.

Ondoru Yawa, told by Mun Czang-Zun; Ŏnyang (1920).

69

The Old Tiger and the Hare

THERE was once an old tiger in the hills in Gangwŏn province. One day he chanced to meet a hare and said, 'I am hungry, I am going to eat you up.'

The cunning hare answered, 'My dear Uncle! Where are you going? I have some delicious food for you. Won't you come with me?'

So the tiger followed the hare into a valley. Then the hare picked up eleven round pebbles and said with a smile, 'You have never tasted anything so delicious as this before in all your life.'

'How do you eat them?' the tiger asked with great interest.

'Oh, it's quite simple,' answered the hare. 'You just bake them in a fire until they turn red, and then they are most delicious.' He lit a fire, and put the pebbles in it. After a while he said to the tiger, who was gazing hungrily at the fire, 'Dear Uncle, I will go and get you some bean sauce. It will make them ever so much better. I'll only be a few minutes. Don't eat them till I get back. There are just ten altogether, for us both, you know.'

So the hare ran off and left the tiger alone. While he was waiting the tiger counted the pebbles, which had already turned deep red. He found that there were eleven, not ten, as the hare had said. So he greedily gobbled one of them up, so as to get more than his share. It was so hot that it scorched his tongue, his throat, and his stomach. The pain was unbearable and he rushed madly through the hills in his agony. He had to spend a whole month without eating before he recovered.

One day the tiger met the hare standing by a bush in the middle of a field. He roared at him angrily, 'You tricked me last time. You made me suffer terribly and I have starved for weeks. This time I will certainly eat you up.'

The hare trembled with fear but managed to say calmly, 'Look here, Uncle. I'm chasing these sparrows now. Don't you see? If you look up at the sky and open your mouth I will drive them into it. You will get thousands of them. Wouldn't that be a much better meal for you than I would make?

The tiger looked and saw many sparrows fluttering about the bush. He relented somewhat. 'You are not trying to trick me again, are you?' he said. 'If you mean what you say, I will do as you suggest.'

'Oh yes, I mean it all right,' replied the hare. 'Just stand in the middle of the bush and open your mouth, Uncle.'

So the tiger went into the middle of the bush and looking up at the sky opened his mouth. Then the hare set fire to the bush. The crackling of the flames sounded like the twittering of a thousand sparrows. The hare shouted, 'There's hundreds coming, Uncle. Can't you hear them?' Then he ran away and left the tiger alone in the burning bush. He began to notice that he was getting hot, and then suddenly realized that he was surrounded by fire. It was only with great difficulty that he escaped. All his fur was burnt off, and he could not go out in the cold. He had to stay in his cave for weeks, furious that the hare should have tricked him a second time.

One winter day, when at last his fur had grown again, he went down to a village to look for cattle. He came to a river and there on the bank he met the hare once again. He was furiously angry and roared, 'You insignificant wretch! That's twice you have tricked me, and yet you are still alive. What have you got to say for yourself?'

The hare answered most humbly, 'Uncle, you don't understand. I've only been trying to help you, but you would not follow my advice. Yet I have come here to get you some fish. The river is full of them, and in winter I live on them. Uncle, have you ever tasted fish? It's the most wonderful thing you ever tasted.'

The tiger was curious about fishing, and asked, 'How do you catch them? You are not trying to trick me again, are you? This is the last chance I'll give you.'

'Do trust me, Uncle,' said the hare. 'You know the proverb which says, "Try three times, and you will be successful." You see those fish down there? Just dip your tail in the water and close your eyes. If you open your eyes, you will scare the fish away. Just keep still, and don't move your tail until I tell you. It makes a fine fishing rod!'

The tiger saw the fish in the river, and so he dipped his tail in the cold water. He stood there patiently with his eyes closed. The hare waded up and down in the river and shouted to the tiger, 'I'm chasing the fish over to your tail. The water is very cold, but keep still just the same. Your tail will soon feel very heavy.'

It was now evening. It was very cold indeed and the water in the river began to freeze. Soon the tiger's tail was frozen fast. The hare shouted, 'Uncle! I think you should have caught quite a lot by now. Just lift your tail, and you will see.' The tiger tried and found that his tail was very heavy indeed. With a happy smile he said, 'I must have caught a lot. It's so heavy I can't move it.'

Then the hare shouted as he ran off, 'Uncle Tiger! You have tried to kill me, but you are caught now, and you will never get away.'

Then the tiger realized that his tail was frozen firmly in the ice, and so he could not go back to the mountains. In the morning the villagers found the tiger still squatting on the ice and a hunter caught it without the slightest difficulty.

Ondoru Yawa, told by Bag Mal-Bong; Ŏnyang (1925).

70

The Young Gentleman and the Tiger

LONG, long ago a young gentleman went on a journey riding on a horse. Before he had gone very far a May-beetle came flying towards him. 'Hullo, young gentleman!' it said when it reached him. 'May I come with you?'

'Certainly,' answered the young man. 'Do come with me.'

So the May-beetle alighted on the horse and they both rode on together. Then an egg came rolling along the road towards them, and it too said, 'Hullo, young gentleman! May I come with you?' And the young gentleman answered, 'Certainly. Do come with me.' So the egg got on the horse too.

The young gentleman, the May-beetle and the egg went on their journey on the horse. Then a crab came sidling along and asked, 'Hullo, young gentleman! May I come with you?' And once more the young gentleman answered, 'Certainly. Do come with me.' So the crab got on to the horse.

The young gentleman, the May-beetle, the egg, and the crab went on their journey on the horse. Then a rice-ladle came hopping along the road. 'Hullo, young gentleman!' it cried. 'May I come with you?' And the young gentleman answered, 'Certainly. Do come with me.' So the rice-ladle got on the horse.

The young gentleman, the May-beetle, the egg, the crab, and the rice-ladle went on their journey on the horse. Then an awl came hopping along the road, and said, 'Hullo, young gentleman! May I come with you?' And the young gentleman answered, 'Certainly. Do come with me.' So the awl got on to the horse.

160

The young gentleman, the May-beetle, the egg, the crab, the rice-ladle, and the awl went on their journey on the horse. Then a mortar came tumbling along the road. 'Hullo, young gentleman!' it said. 'May I come with you?' And the young gentleman answered, 'Certainly. Do come with me.' So the mortar got on the horse.

The young gentleman, the May-beetle, the egg, the crab, the rice-ladle, the awl, and the mortar went on their journey on the horse. Then a rolled-up straw-mat came rolling along the road. 'Hullo, young gentleman!' it said. 'May I come with you?' And the young gentleman answered, 'Certainly. Do come with me.' So the straw-mat got on the horse.

The young gentleman, the May-beetle, the egg, the crab, the rice-ladle, the awl, the mortar, and the straw-mat went on their journey on the horse. Then a wooden pack-carrier came stalking along the road. 'Hullo, young gentleman!' it cried. 'May I come with you?' And the young gentleman answered, 'Certainly. Do come with me.' So the pack-carrier got on the horse.

So the young gentleman, the May-beetle, the egg, the crab, the rice-ladle, the awl, the mortar, the straw-mat, and the pack-carrier went on their journey together, all riding on the horse. In the evening they came to a house in the mountains and knocked at the gate. No answer came from the house. So the young gentleman opened the gate himself and went in. In a room he found a young girl sobbing bitterly.

'What is the matter?' he asked. 'Why are you sobbing?'

'There is a tiger in the mountain behind the house,' she answered. 'It has come down every night, and already it has eaten my father, my mother, my brother, and my sister. It will be my turn to-night. That is why I am crying.'

So he said to soothe her, 'Poor girl! Do not be alarmed. My friends and I can help you.'

He called the May-beetle and told it to wait in the corner of the room and to blow out the candle when the tiger rushed in. He told the egg to go and bury itself in the ashes of the kitchen fire and burst out in the tiger's eyes when it came near. Then he posted the crab by the kitchen sink and told it to scratch out the tiger's eyes. He hid the rice-ladle behind the kettle, and told it to beat the tiger in the face. Then he put the awl under the floorboards by the door of the girl's room and told it to pierce the tiger's feet. He told the mortar to climb up on to the roof, and to throw itself down on the tiger to crush it. He sent the straw-mat and the pack-carrier to hide in the store-room, and told them to come out afterwards and carry the tiger away.

When he had sent them all to their posts the girl went to her room and lit a candle, while the young gentleman went and waited in the stable in the dark with his horse. Before long the tiger came down from the mountain and went into the house. It sprang into the girl's room and tried to seize her. At that moment the May-beetle blew out the candle with its wings. So the tiger said, 'My dear girl, the light has gone out. I can't see where you are.'

The girl answered, 'You can't eat me in the dark. You had better go into the kitchen and blow the fire to get some light.' So the tiger went to the kitchen and bent down to blow at the embers of the charcoal fire. Then the egg burst out and blew ashes in the tiger's eyes. 'Oh, my eyes!' the tiger screeched in its pain, and rushed over to the sink to bathe them in the water. Then the crab jumped out and gouged out the tiger's eyes with its claws. Blinded, the tiger rushed from the kitchen in a frenzy, and as it passed the kettle the rice-ladle jumped out and hit it violently in the face. Then it tried to get back to the girl's room, but when it stepped on the floor the awl pierced its foot. So it leapt out of the house on to the ground, and the heavy mortar jumped on to it from the roof, and crushed it to death. The straw-mat came and wrapped up the body, and the pack-carrier came and carried it off to the river and threw it into the water.

So the tiger was killed and the girl's life was saved. The young gentleman married her, and all his friends lived with them in the house.

Told by Gim Du-Ri; Tong-Yŏng (1949).

71

Four Sworn Brothers

LONG, long ago there lived a man who had the misfortune to have no son. One day, however, he found a baby boy lying abandoned outside his house. He took it in and cared for it. It was a most unusual baby, for instead of milk it could eat cooked rice, and it grew up at a phenomenal speed. When he was but a month old the boy asked his foster-father to make him a pack-carrier, for he wanted to set to work cutting firewood in the mountains. So his father made him one of corn-stalks, but he said scornfully, 'This is no use.' So his father made him one of wood, but again he was not satisfied, and said, 'This is not strong enough.' So his father went and got a smith to make him one of iron. This time he was satisfied and went off to the mountain with it on his back. A little later his father was astonished to see a mountain of wood moving towards him. Then he saw his son underneath it, and realised that it was no mountain but a load of wood that his son was carrying on his back.

After this the son used to go often to the mountains and brought back many great logs, and built a large house with them. Then he went and quarried stone to build gate-posts for it. He was by now so strong that he wore iron shoes, and so earned the nickname of 'Iron-shoes'.

One day he left home to set out on a journey. He sat on a hill to rest, and suddenly noticed that a tall tree in a neighbouring field was behaving in a most peculiar manner. It kept on falling down and rising up again immediately afterwards. So he went over to investigate. When he came near the tree he saw a boy sleeping under it. He was snoring loudly, and when he breathed out his breath was so strong that it blew the tree over, and when he breathed in the tree stood up again. Iron-shoes shouted at the boy to wake him up, but without success. So he kicked him on the nose, and he woke up. He sat up yawning and scratching his head. Then Iron-shoes suggested to 'Nose-wind' that they should swear to be as brothers thenceforth. He agreed, and they wrestled together. Nose-wind was victorious, and so became the elder brother.

Then they went on their way together. One day they saw a great mountain suddenly crumble, and in its place a level field. So they went nearer, and saw a boy with a long iron rake raking over the soil. So they invited him to be their brother, and he agreed. Then each of them in turn sat on his rake. When they sat on it he could not move it at all, and so 'Long-rake' became the youngest brother.

So now the three sworn brothers went on their way to seek adventures. They came to a river and found it swollen with brown water, which struck them as odd, since there had been no rain lately. So they followed the bank upstream until they found a boy making water in a valley. He it was that was responsible for the rushing torrent. To test him one of the three took him by the neck and shook him. At once a great waterfall almost drowned them. So they begged 'Waterfall' to be their eldest brother, and he readily agreed.

Now the four sworn brothers set out on their travels together. They wandered all day in the mountains and at nightfall they saw a big house with a tile roof. They went up to it and knocked at the door and asked for something to eat. An old woman came and welcomed them, and invited them to come inside. She led them to a room with stone walls, and brought them supper. They were astonished to see the food, for it was human flesh. They did not eat any of it, and were alarmed at what might happen to them. Then they heard the door being locked on the outside.

They pretended to go to sleep, and then in the middle of the night they overheard a noisy conversation.

'Mother, I can smell them,' said a voice. 'How many have you got?'

'Four. They look delicious,' was the reply. 'What have you got?'

'I only got two deer, Mother,' said the first voice. 'My three brothers got nothing at all. So will we cook them, or yours, Mother? We are all very hungry.'

'They should be asleep by now. We will have them if you like.'

When they heard this conversation the four brothers realized that the old woman and her four sons were not human but tigers in disguise. They kept silent, lest they should do themselves some harm by precipitate action. Soon they felt the stone floor of the room getting hot. The tiger-brothers had lit a great fire underneath to roast the four sworn brothers. Nose-wind calmed his brothers' fears and blew with might and main to keep the room cool. After a while the tigers opened the door of the room and were amazed to find the four brothers still alive and unharmed. So they had to eat the two deer instead, puzzled as they were by the mysterious survival of the brothers.

Next morning the old woman came and suggested that the four brothers have a wood-cutting contest with her four sons. She told the four sworn brothers to go and cut pine trees in the mountains, while her sons would pile them by the house. The losers in the competition would be put to death.

So the four sworn brothers went out and tore pine trees up by the roots. They hurled them down beside the house, where the four tiger-brothers started piling them up. In no time at all the tigers seemed to be in danger of defeat, for the four sworn brothers were sending logs down far faster than they could pile them up. So the old woman shouted to them to change over. The tigers went up into the mountain to chop trees down and the sworn brothers began piling up the logs. But they piled them so fast that they were forced to stop and wait for more to come down from the mountain. The old woman feared that her sons would lose the contest and set fire to the pile of logs to burn the four sworn brothers who were standing on top of it. Her four wicked sons were delighted to see the flames and came down from the mountain to enjoy their rivals' discomfiture. They stood round the pile of wood with their mother, clapping their hands with fiendish glee.

The four sworn brothers were greatly taken aback by the old woman's unexpected treachery. But they soon pulled themselves together and worked out a plan to save themselves and at the same time punish these wicked creatures. Waterfall made water and soon put out the fire. More than that he made a great flood that submerged the others up to their necks, though the four sworn brothers were safe up on top of the pile of logs. The old woman and her four sons suddenly changed into their proper tiger shape. They were almost drowning, with only their heads and fore-paws showing above the flood. They cried out piteously, 'Have mercy on us. We are very sorry that we tried to harm you. Spare our lives, we beseech you.'

But the brothers took no notice of their entreaties. The second brother, Nose-wind, blew on the water with his cold breath, and the flood suddenly turned to ice. So the tigers were frozen to death. Their heads and forepaws still showed above the surface of the ice.

The third brother, Iron-shoes, was most amused by the unusual sight. He got down on to the ice, and began to skate on the vast expanse. The heads and forepaws of the wicked tigers had frozen quite stiff, and snapped off when the iron shoes touched them. They went rolling hither and thither over the ice.

At last the youngest brother, Long-rake, took his steel rake and broke the thick ice into little pieces and threw them far and wide. Thus he restored the ground to its former condition and no trace remained of the great flood. And then the four sworn brothers returned home safely.

Ondoru Yawa, told by Zo Zĕ-Ho; Saczŏn (1925).

72
The Nine-Headed Giant

ONCE upon a time a giant with nine heads lived in a retreat far away in the mountains. From time to time he used to go down to the nearest village and carry off one of the inhabitants. All the villagers were in a state of great alarm, and were constantly trying to devise some scheme to overcome him.

One day a beautiful woman and her maid-servant went to the well to draw water and were carried off by the giant. When the news was brought to her husband he immediately went off into the mountains to find his wife and rescue her. He came to a thatched cottage in the woods, and asked the old woman who lived there where the nine-headed giant was. She told him to go on over the hill until he came to a woman who would be washing radishes in the valley. So he crossed the hill and in the next valley he found an old woman washing radishes. He went up to her and asked her where he could find the nine-headed giant. Thereupon the old woman gave him a radish and said, 'That giant is exceedingly strong. So eat this radish and go and lift that heavy stone over there.'

It was not a radish but a magic ginsen. The man ate it and tried to lift the stone. But it was very heavy and he could move it only with great difficulty. So the old woman gave him another radish which was really a ginsen, and he found he could lift it to his knees. He ate one more, and then he could lift the stone without the slightest difficulty. Then the old woman gave him a big sword and said, 'Go over the next hill until you find a big flat stone. Lift up that stone and you will find the entrance of a big cave. Inside the cave you will find a road which will lead you to the giant's home. With the strength you have now acquired I am sure you will kill him.'

So the man crossed over the hill and found a big flat stone just as the old woman had said. He lifted it up and went into the cave. It was an underground world. At first the road was very narrow, but before long it widened and at last he came out into the open in front of a big tiled house surrounded by a wall with nine gates. He went in through one of the gates and climbed a willow tree which stood beside a well. He stayed hidden in the branches to see what would happen.

In a short time a girl came out to draw water with a water jar on her head. She drew a gourd full of water from the well and sighed, 'Oh, when shall we be able to go back home?' The man saw from his hiding place that she was the maid-servant who had been carried off with his wife. When she had filled her jar he dropped a few leaves in the water she had drawn. 'It seems very windy to-day,' the girl grumbled, and tipping out the water drew more water and filled the jar again. When it was full the man again dropped leaves in it. Once more she complained and filled the jar again. The third time she looked up in the tree and saw her master hidden in the branches. She was overjoyed to see him, and called to him to come down. Then she led him into the house, and hid him in a secret room. 'The giant is away just now,' she said, 'but you had better wait here while I go and tell the mistress.' So she went and told his wife, who came running to see him. She told him all about the horrible giant. 'His habits are peculiar,' she said. 'He goes away for three months and ten days, and then comes back and sleeps for three months and three days. He is due to return in just three months from now. Until then you had better drink *zanggun-su*, the 'general's draught', so that you will gain enough strength to overcome him.' Then she led him to a cave outside the house closed with a stone door. Inside the cave was a spring whence flowed crystal clear water. He drank this water everyday for a week. Then his wife brought him a big sword and said, 'This is the giant's sword. Are you strong enough to use it?'

The man tried, but the sword was too heavy. So he went and drank more of the water from the spring. After a few weeks he became so strong that he could flourish the heavy sword without the slightest difficulty. When he had been there only a month he could wear the giant's wooden shoes and leap in the air in them. When he had been there two months he could toss the giant's iron balls in the air, and at the end of three months he was so strong that he could don the heavy helmet and armour of the giant, carrying two swords. In the end he could even hold the giant's long pipe between his teeth, without supporting it with his hand.

Now the time drew near when the giant was due to reappear. One day the air was filled with a sound like thunder and the maid came and told her master that the giant was half a mile away. Almost immediately there was a second report and the giant was a quarter of a mile away. Then in a few moments there was a deafening thunderclap and the nine-headed giant strode into the house through the main gate. He scowled and roared, 'I smell a man.'

The woman answered, 'Nonsense! You are mistaken. You must be very thirsty after your journey. I have some excellent wine here. Do drink some, and relax.' She had prepared specially strong wine for this very purpose, and the giant drank nine barrels of it, one barrel with each head. When he had finished he lay down and immediately fell into a drunken sleep.

The man came into the room and dressed in armour and carrying the two swords. The giant's body was covered with scales as hard as iron, and so seemed to be invulnerable to any sword-thrust. So the man kicked him hard on the shin and all the scales stood up on end, so that he was able to thrust his swords into one of the necks. The giant started up with a groan and lashed out furiously. He leapt high in the air and the man followed him. High in the clouds they joined in mortal combat. The two women on the ground could not see them, but the clash of steel rang in their ears. They trembled in fear, and prayed that the giant might be overcome.

Before long two or three of the heads fell crashing to the ground. Rolling their eyes in fury they sprang back into the air to join their body, and as they went they cursed, 'You hateful women, to deceive me thus!' And so the desperate struggle continued high in the air. Then the women went and fetched ashes in their skirts and when next a head fell to the ground they smothered the severed neck with ashes, so that it closed its eyes and died. And when the other eight heads fell down they smothered the severed necks with ashes. At last the giant's body crashed to the ground with a heavy thud, and lay lifeless before them. After it the man came down, his face dripping with sweat. He thanked his wife and her maid most profusely for the valuable help they had given him.

Next morning they went and looked in the dead giant's store-houses. One they found full of gold and silver, another full of rice, and a third full of silk. They also found human bones hanging from the rafters, and one or two of the giant's victims on the point of death. They tended those who were still alive, and offered them all the treasure they wanted.

Happy once more now that they had escaped from the clutches of the giant they set out for home. Before they left they set fire to the house. On the way back the man tried to call on the two old women who had helped him on the way out, but he could find no trace of either of them.

Ondoru Yawa, told by Zŏng Sŏg-Gwŏn; Yangsan (1925).

73
The Mountain Witch and the Dragon-King

LONG ago there lived a warrior. One day as he was walking on the seashore he saw seven boys standing round a big three-tailed turtle and arguing violently with one another. They were going to cut the turtle up with a big knife, saying, 'We seven caught it, so we should cut it into seven pieces.' The poor turtle looked very sad, so the warrior asked the boys to sell it to him. They agreed and he paid one *yang* to each of the boys. Then he took the turtle and released it in the sea. Before it dived under the waves it turned and said, 'I am deeply grateful to you. I am the Dragon-King from under the sea. I came up to-day to take a look at the world of men, and those hateful boys caught me. If you are ever in danger, come to this shore here and call me. I will do anything I can to help you.'

Some time afterwards the warrior set out on a journey. One evening, when he was deep in the mountains, he lost his way. He came upon a solitary cottage, and knocked on the door. An old woman answered his knock and he asked her whether he might pass the night there. She agreed to let him stay, and served him supper. He asked her the way across the mountain, and she replied vehemently, 'Do not cross this mountain. There is an evil witch who lives on the summit, and she is a fox one thousand years old.

I used to be the goddess of this mountain, until she came with her magic and usurped my position. She will surely do you harm if you go near her.' But the warrior waved aside her protestations and replied, 'No warrior would fear a creature like that.'

Next morning he set out again and went on up the mountain. When he came near the top a beautiful woman came towards him clad in a gorgeous robe. She seemed to glide swiftly over the ground, and when she came near him she said with a winning smile, 'I am the goddess of this mountain. My house is quite near at hand; come with me and rest a while.'

The warrior went with her, wondering who she could be, and rather suspecting that she might be the witch that the old woman had warned him of. She served him rich food and wine, and then tried to embrace him. 'I am very lonely living here on my own,' she said. 'Stay here and let us live together.' The warrior repulsed her and replied firmly, 'It is not right that a woman should make advances to a man. Your behaviour is most discourteous and unbecoming.'

The woman was furious at this unexpected answer. 'I see you do not like me,' she snapped. 'You will repent of your unfriendly attitude, for I shall kill you, and you will not escape. I will demonstrate my magic, and then you will consider again.' She wrote some signs on a piece of paper and threw it in the air. The sky suddenly darkened and countless swords of flame came out of the air and threatened the warrior. He begged her to give him a week to consider, and she granted his request.

He hastened forthwith to the seashore where he had set the turtle free. He stood at the water's edge and called on the Dragon-King in a loud voice. Immediately a mysterious boy came up out of the sea and welcomed him. He turned and recited a magic formula and the waters parted and a wide road appeared between them. The boy led the warrior to the Dragon Kingdom and into the presence of the Dragon-King. The warrior told the King of the peril which beset him and the King agreed to help him. He immediately dispatched his three brothers to kill the mountain witch. The warrior took hold of the tails of the three dragon brothers and was whisked back to the mountain in an instant. They seemed to glide over the ground without touching it with their feet.

The three dragon brothers raised a terrible black storm to destroy the witch's house. But the witch came out and laughed aloud. 'You went to the Dragon-King for help,' she chortled. 'His magic is nothing to me. Just you watch.' She threw a piece of paper inscribed with magic signs into the air, and immediately three pillars of flame flashed through the air and felled the three dragon brothers to the ground each severed in two parts. Then the sky lightened and the wind dropped.

The witch took the warrior by the hand and said, 'Now you must do as I wish. Come and stay with me and keep me company.' But the warrior wrenched his hand away and asked her to allow him a month to make up his mind. She agreed reluctantly and said, 'If you try to overcome me again, and are defeated, I will not give you a third chance. Do you understand?'

So the warrior returned once more to the palace of the Dragon-King and told him what had happened. The King sighed sadly and replied. 'The witch is too strong for me to overcome. The only thing we can do is to go and ask the Heavenly King to punish her.' So the Dragon-King went to the Heavenly Kingdom attended by his warriors and humbly begged the King to punish the witch. The King granted his request and immediately dispatched three warriors from Heaven.

When they reached the mountain the Heavenly warriors filled the air with raging gales and pelting rain. The witch came out and threw her magic paper into the air, but to no avail. A thunderbolt fell on the house with a deafening crash and immediately a dead fox appeared where the witch had been.

The warrior thanked the Heavenly warriors profusely, and the kind old woman whom he had met in the first place reigned once more as the goddess of the mountain.

Told by Gim Han-Yong; Gimhě (1919).

74

The Fox-Girl and Her Brother

LONG ago there lived a rich man who had a son but no daughter. He longed to have a daughter, and so he spent much money consulting fortune tellers and visiting temples to pray. After a few years his prayers were rewarded, and a girl was born. Her parents treasured her like a precious jewel. She grew up a healthy child and never suffered a day's illness.

When she was about five years old a strange affliction fell upon the household. They possessed many hundred head of cattle, but now one cow died every night. The bodies showed no sign of disease nor any trace of wounds. So the herdsmen reported these mysterious deaths to their master, who ordered that a strict watch be kept at night.

So a herdsman hid in a dark corner of the cow-shed and waited. In the middle of the night his master's daughter came stealthily into the shed and went up to a cow. She greased her hand with sesame oil and slipped it into the belly of the cow. Then she withdrew her hand and the watching herdsman saw that she was holding the cow's liver. She ate it with great relish, while the cow fell down dead on the spot.

The herdsman was horrified to see this incredible sight. In the morning he went to his master and told him what he had seen. But his master refused to believe it. 'Nonsense! What a disgraceful suggestion!' he cried. 'My daughter would never dream of doing such a thing. You shall pay dearly for this falsehood.' So he had the herdsman put to death. Then he ordered another herdsman to keep watch and find the true cause of the mysterious death of the cattle. This servant too saw the girl take the liver from a cow and eat it. But when he reported it to his master he too was disbelieved and put to death. Then a third herdsman brought exactly the same report, and yet his master would not believe. So every night one of the cattle died, and not only cattle but horses and pigs, while the herdsmen who reported what they had seen were put to death. In the end there were no more herdsmen, for no one in the village would accept employment on the rich man's farm.

So the rich man sent his only son to keep watch. He hid one night in the shed, and saw his sister come in and take the liver from a cow and eat it. He went and told his father, but his mother who was sitting nearby scolded him and said, 'Why must you speak so ill of your sister? Everyone is jealous of her. I can't stand it any longer.' And the father drove his son from the house, though he still lavished all his affection on his daughter.

When all the cattle were dead the evil girl began to kill men in the same way. So the villagers were terrified and in the end they all fled from their homes. In the end her father and mother too were found dead, so that the village was completely deserted and haunted by the spirits of the dead.

When his father drove him from the house he wandered off into the mountains. He met an old Buddhist priest and with him studied the laws of magic that governed the world of spirits. A few years went by and one day he began to feel homesick, and longed to see his parents once more. So he took his leave of his master and set out for home. Before he left the old priest gave him three bottles, one red, one white, and one blue. 'These are for you to use if you encounter danger,' he said. So the boy hid the three bottles at his breast and rode on horseback to his native village. He found the village deserted and his own home desolate. He went into his old home and found it overgrown with dense grass and covered with moss. His sister was sitting in the sun catching lice and eating them. She welcomed her brother with a happy smile. She seemed to be very hungry and was apparently waiting for some new victim to fall into her clutches. She looked at her brother with a queer expression and asked, 'Where have you been all these years, Brother? I have missed you so much.'

Her brother asked her, 'Where are father and mother?'

'They are in their graves,' she replied. Her brother began to suspect that she might have been in some way responsible for their deaths, and so he made up his mind to run away before she could kill him too. So he said, 'Sister. I am very hungry. Won't you cook something for me, say the leeks in the front garden? They would suit me very well.'

His sister took a reel of thread from her pocket and said, 'You must not run away again, Brother. Tie this thread round your waist and I will hold the other end while I go and get them. So that she might not suspect him he did as she asked. But as soon as she was out of sight he tied the thread to a post and crept away. He got on to his horse and galloped off.

When his sister found he had gone she rushed after him with all speed. 'Brother!' she shouted, 'Stop! Stop!' She almost caught up with the horse and reached out her hand to seize its tail. So her brother took the red bottle from his breast and hurled it straight at her. It burst into a mass of flame, and she was severely scorched. But she managed to pass through, and nearly caught up again. This time he threw the white bottle, which barred the way with a mass of needles. This obstacle too she managed to pass, and so her brother threw the blue bottle at her. It formed a mighty sea, and she was drowned. When her body floated to the surface he saw that it was a fox, which had taken the form of his sister.

Ondoru Yawa, told by Zo Gyŏng-Gu; Ŏnyang (1925).

75

The Traveller, the Fox, and the Tiger

ONCE upon a time a traveller went on a journey and lost his way in the mountains. While he was still wandering about he was overtaken by night, and at last made his way to a cottage at the foot of a hill. A pretty woman invited him in and kindly brought him food. She was living alone in the house, and there was no sign of anyone else.

In the middle of the night the traveller awoke to hear the woman grinding a sword in the kitchen. The eerie darkness alone was enough to make his hair stand on end, and this evil sound struck terror into his heart. So he crept noiselessly from the room and out the back door. But the woman heard him go and, half transformed into a fox, pursued him with the sword in her hand. He saw a tall tower in front of him, from which came the strains of music. So he rushed into the tower and shouted for help. But the master of the tower said sternly, 'Why should I help you when you have vexed my mother so?' and ordered his servant to seize him. Then the servant pushed him roughly into a small room and locked the door. The traveller was sure that he must have fallen into the clutches of the son of the fox.

A little later the fox's son came in to kill him with a sword. As his last request the traveller begged him to bring him some water. 'I am terribly thirsty,' he pleaded. 'Won't you bring me a big jar of water?' So the fox's son brought him the water he had asked for, and complained, 'You are a glutton to want to drink such a big jar of water.' Then the fox's son went and waited outside the room while he drank the water. As soon as he was alone the traveller poured the water on the earthen wall of the room to soften it, and then kicked a hole in it

174

and escaped. But unfortunately the tower stood on the very edge of a steep cliff, and the traveller fell over the edge. As it happened a tiger was passing beneath the cliff at that moment, and he fell fair and square on its back. The tiger was alarmed by this unusul occurrence and ran off to its den with him on its back. There the tiger saw the man and seized him with its claws. The tiger was accustomed to bring its prey back to its den for its cub, and so it scratched the traveller's face that its cub might drink his blood. Then he fell half dead on the floor of the cave, until the tiger went out hunting once more. Then he came to his senses, stood up, and killed the tiger cub. He made his way out of the cave and climbed up a tall tree nearby.

The foxes thought that the tiger must have seized the traveller and carried him off and went into the tiger's den to look for him. At that very moment the mother-tiger came back and found her cub lying dead. She thought at once that the foxes must have killed it, and so she attacked them fiercely. A desperate struggle followed in which the tiger tore the foxes to pieces. But in the fight the tiger too was mortally wounded, and before long it too lay down and died. The traveller climbed down from the tree, and went and explored the foxes' house and tower. There he found much treasure, gold and silver and precious things, so that he became rich and lived in comfort ever after.

Told by Mo Yun-Sŭg; Hamhŭng (1933).

76

The Toad-Bridegroom

LONG ago there lived a poor fisherman in a certain village. One day he went fishing in the lake as usual, but found he could not catch as many fish as he was accustomed to. And on each of the following days he found his catch growing smaller and smaller. He tried new baits, and bought new hooks, but all to no avail. At last even the water of the lake began to disappear, until in the end it became too shallow for fishing. One afternoon in the late summer the bottom

The Toad-Bridegroom

of the lake was exposed to view, and a big toad came out from it. The fisherman immediately thought that it must have eaten up all the fish and angrily cursed the *samʒog* or three families of the frog, its parents, brothers, wife and children, for it is popularly believed that the toad is a relative of the frog. Then the toad spoke to him gently, rolling its eyes, 'Do not be angry, for one day I shall bring you good fortune. I wish to live in your house, so please let me go with you.' But the fisherman was annoyed that a toad should make such a request and hastened home without it.

That evening the toad came to his house. His wife, who had already heard about it from her husband, received it kindly, and made a bed for it in a corner of the kitchen. Then she brought it worms and scraps to eat. The couple had no children of their own, and decided to keep the toad as a pet. It grew to be as big as a boy, and they came to love it as if it were their son.

Nearby there lived a rich man who had three daughters. One day the toad told the fisherman and his wife that it would like to marry one of the three daughters. They were most alarmed at this most unreasonable request and earnestly advised it to forget such an impossible ambition. 'It is utterly absurd,' they said. 'How can poor people like us propose marriage to such a great family? And you are not even a human being.'

So the toad replied, 'I don't care what the rank of the family is. The parents may object, but yet one of the daughters may be willing to accept me. Who knows? Please go and ask, and let me know what answer you receive.'

So the fisherman's wife went and called on the mistress of the rich man's house and told her what her toad-son had asked. The lady was greatly displeased and went and told her husband. He was furiously angry at such a preposterous suggestion and ordered his servant to beat the toad's foster-mother. So the poor woman returned home and told the toad of her painful experience.

'I'm very sorry that you have been treated like that, Mother,' the toad said to her, 'but don't let it worry you too much. Just wait and see what will happen.' Then he went out and caught a hawk and brought it home. Late that night he tied a lighted lantern to its foot, and crept stealthily to the rich man's house. He tied a long string to the hawk's foot and then climbed a tall persimmon tree which stood by the house. Then he held the end of the string in his hand and released the hawk to fly over the house. As it flew into the air he solemnly declared in a loud voice, 'The master of this house shall listen to my words, for I have been dispatched by the Heavenly King. To-day you rejected a proposal of marriage, and now you shall be punished for your arrogance. I shall give you one day to reconsider your decision. I advise you to accept the toad's proposal, for if you do not, you, your brothers, and your children shall be utterly destroyed.'

The people in the house were startled by this nocturnal proclamation from the sky, and they opened the windows to see what was going on. When they looked up into the sky they saw a dim light hovering overhead. The master of the house went out into the garden and kneeled humbly on the ground looking up into the sky. Then the toad let go of the string he held in his hand, and the hawk soared skywards with the lantern still tied to its foot. The rich man was now convinced that what he had heard was spoken by a messenger from Heaven, and at once resolved to consent to the toad's marriage to one of his daughters.

Next morning the rich man went and called on the toad's foster-parents, and apologized humbly for his discourteous refusal on the previous day. He said now that he would gladly accept the toad as his son-in-law. Then he returned home and asked his eldest daughter to marry the toad, but she rushed from the room in fury and humiliation. Then he called his second daughter, and suggested that she be the toad's wife, but she too rushed from the room without a word. So he called his youngest daughter and explained to her that if she refused she would place the whole family in a most difficult position indeed, so stern had been the warning from Heaven. But the youngest daughter agreed to marry the toad without the slightest hesitation.

The wedding took place on the following day, and a great crowd of guests attended consumed by curiosity at such an unusual happening. That night, when they retired, the toad asked his bride to bring him a pair of scissors. She went and got a pair, and then he asked her to cut the skin off his back. This strange request startled her greatly, but he insisted that she do so without delay, and so she made a long cut in his back. Then, lo and behold, there stepped forth from the skin a handsome young man.

In the morning the bridegroom put on his toad skin again, so that nobody noticed any difference. Her two sisters sneered contemptuously at the bride with her repulsive husband, but she took no notice of them. At noon all the men of the household went out on horseback with bows and arrows to hunt. The toad accompanied them on foot and unarmed. But the party had no success in the hunt and had to return empty-handed. The bridegroom stripped off his toad skin and became a man when they had gone, and waved his hand in the air. Then a white haired old man appeared and he bade him bring one hundred deer. When the deer came he drove them homeward, once more wearing his toad skin. Everyone was most surprised to see all the deer, and then he suddenly stripped off the toad skin and revealed himself as a handsome young man, at which their astonishment knew no bounds. Then he released all the deer and rose up to Heaven, carrying his bride on his back and his parents on his arms.

Ondoru Yawa, told by Zŏng Bog-Sun; Ŏnyang (1925).

77

Sweet Dung, the Cake-Tree, and the Bugle of Life

ONCE upon a time there lived a poor man who had a little dog, a persimmon tree, and a bugle.

One day he went out into the mountains to cut wood, and chanced to find a bees' nest full of honey. He took the honey home and put it in a closet. Then in the night, while he was asleep, his little dog found it and lapped it all up. When he found what had happened the man was furiously angry and kicked the little dog with great violence. It was terrified and excreted a small amount of dung. The dung smelt remarkably sweet, so the man dipped his finger in it and tasted it. He found to his surprise that it was very sweet indeed. So he took the little dog out into the street, and shouted, 'Sweet dung! Won't you buy some sweet dung? This little dog makes sweet dung. Come along and buy some! Very cheap!' People came and tasted it and then they bought some. Then a gentleman came by and offered to buy the little dog. So its owner sold it for one thousand *yang*.

178

Next day the gentleman invited a crowd of guests to a special feast of sweet dung. When they were all seated he drew the little dog from his sleeve, and served them all himself. He squeezed its belly with his fingers, so that it excreted dung into each dish. But when his guests started to eat it they all pulled wry faces and cried out angrily. The little dog had been fed on cooked rice and its dung smelt as unpleasant as usual. The gentleman realized that he had been swindled, and rushed off to find the man who had sold it to him.

The original owner had guessed that the gentleman would sooner or later come to complain, and so he told his wife to cook a lot of rice cakes and hang them high in the bare branches of the persimmon tree. Before long the gentleman came rushing into the house with the dog, intending to demand the return of his money. The husband received him affably and said to his wife, 'The gentleman has come. We have nothing much to offer him, but you may as well go and pick some cakes from the cake tree. We haven't had a very good crop this year, but you may find some on the lower branches.'

The gentleman was very intrigued to hear of the cake tree, and forgot his anger. Overcome with curiosity he went out and looked at the tree in the garden. It was quite laden with cakes, and the woman climbed up and picked them. He had never seen anything so wonderful in his life. So he said nothing of the little matter of the dog, and when he had tasted the delicious cakes he proposed that he should buy the cake tree. The husband agreed at once, and sold it to him for one thousand *yang*, and the house with it. The gentleman went back home very pleased with himself, and proud of the remarkable tree he had bought. And the very same day the husband and wife moved to another village.

The gentleman told his wife of the cake tree, and the wonderful bargain he had got, but she was most sceptical and would not believe that any such tree existed. So the next day he took her to see it, and then they found that it was just an ordinary tree with cakes hung on it. The gentleman was furious at being swindled a second time, and hastened to the village where the couple had gone.

They had however already planned another trick to play on him. The husband had killed a dog, and his wife hid its entrails at her breast. Then when the gentleman came and called to the husband from the gate, the wife pretended to be angry and complained

Sweet Dung, the Cake-Tree, and the Bugle of Life

loudly that his visit was most inconvenient. So her husband abused her roundly, and shouted, 'This is my affair and nothing to do with you. I will not have you being rude to my guests.' Then he picked up a mallet and pretended to beat her most cruelly. In a minute or two she threw out the dog's entrails on to the ground and fell down apparently dead. The gentleman was most alarmed by this violent onslaught, and the woman's death, but her husband merely went and got his old bugle. He applied it to his wife's anus and blew. At once she appeared to revive and in a few moments sat up quite unharmed.

The gentleman was very relieved to see this awkward situation resolved so easily. The bugle seemed to him to be something infinitely precious. So he offered to buy the bugle and the husband readily sold it to him for another thousand *yang*, so that he had made three thousand *yang* in all by these transactions. He also extracted a pledge from the gentleman that he would not come and complain about his purchases any more.

The gentleman was very proud indeed of the bugle. But when he took it home his wife was more displeased than ever by yet another foolish bargain and told him off in no uncertain terms. So the gentleman got very angry and beat her to death. All the family were terrified by his sudden madness, but he merely smiled and poked the bugle under her skirt. Then he blew and confidently expected that she would be restored to life. But however hard he blew she would not revive, and in the end he too fell down in a faint and died.

Ondǫru Yawa, told by Czoe Sǒ-Bang; Ǒnyang (1914).

180

PART FOUR
FABLES

78

The Ungrateful Tiger

ONE day a tiger was trapped in a pit, and asked a passing traveller to rescue it, promising to reward him. So the traveller poked a long branch down into the pit, and the tiger crawled out. But when it was safe again it turned on the traveller and roared with its mouth wide open, 'I am very hungry and I am going to eat you up.' The traveller protested and chided the tiger. 'You are most ungrateful,' he said, 'you must not do that.' But the tiger ignored his protests and so the traveller appealed to a toad which lived under a nearby rock.

The traveller told the toad of the tiger's ingratitude, but the tiger insisted that it was hungry and meant to eat the traveller. 'I must look into this more closely,' said the toad. 'Will you show me the place where it happened?' So they took it along to the pit. Then the toad asked the tiger, 'How did it happen? Let me see just where you were.' So the tiger jumped down into the pit and said, 'I was down here at the bottom, see.' But the traveller took the branch out of the pit and said, 'Of course, this wasn't there then.'

The toad turned to the traveller and said with a smile. 'You had better go now, and in future don't help such ungrateful creatures.' And looking down at the tiger in the pit it said, 'You ungrateful wretch! You can stay down there now.'

The traveller thanked the toad and went on his way. The tiger trapped in the pit roared in fury, but the toad went back to its home under the rock and refused to help it.

Ondoru Yawa, told by Gim Gwang-Sŏb; Ŏdĕzin (1925).

183

79
The Tiger and the Persimmon

ONE night a tiger came down to a village. It crept stealthily into the garden of a house and listened at the window. It heard a child crying. Then came the voice of its mother scolding it. 'Stop crying this very minute! The tiger is here!' But the child took no notice and went on crying. So the tiger said to himself, 'The child is not the least bit afraid of me. He must be a real hero.' Then the mother said, 'Here is a dried persimmon.' And the child stopped crying immediately. Now the tiger was really frightened and said to himself, 'This persimmon must be a terrible creature.' And he gave up its plan of carrying off the child.

So it went to the outhouse to get an ox instead. There was a thief in there, and he mistook it for an ox and got on its back. The tiger was terrified, and ran off as fast as it could go. 'This must be the terrible persimmon attacking me!' it thought. The thief still rode on its back and whipped it up so that he might get away before the villagers saw him stealing an ox.

When it grew light the thief saw he was riding on a tiger and leapt off. But the tiger just raced on to the mountains without looking back.

Told by Ma Hĕ-Song; Gĕsŏng (1925).

80
The Rat's Bridegroom

ONCE upon a time there lived a family of rats. When the eldest daughter grew up her parents decided that they must find the most powerful bridegroom in the world for her.

So one day they went and called on the Sun. 'Good day, Mr. Sun,' they said. 'Our daughter has grown up and it is time she was married. So we are looking for the most powerful person in the world to ask him to be her husband. By your high position and great power you

The Rat's Bridegroom

seem to be the most powerful of all, and so we have come to invite you to be her bridegroom.'

But the Sun shook his head and said with a smile, 'It may seem to you that I am the most powerful, but it is not so. Mr. Cloud is more powerful than I am, for he can cover my face and keep me from shining. So I recommend Mr. Cloud to you.'

Mr. and Mrs. Rat thought over what the Sun had told them, and decided that Mr. Cloud must indeed be the most powerful of all. So they called on him and said, 'Good day, Mr. Cloud. Our daughter has grown up, and it is time she was married. We wish to invite the most powerful person in the world to be her husband, and so we have come to welcome you as her bridegroom, for you can cover the face of the Sun and keep him from shining.'

Mr. Cloud smiled and shook his head. 'Yes, I can cover the face of the Sun and keep him from shining,' he said. 'Yet I am not the most powerful, for Mr. Wind blows me away, whether I wish to go or not. He is far more powerful than I, and so I recommend him to you.'

Mr. and Mrs. Rat thought it over, and decided that Mr. Wind must indeed be more powerful than Mr. Cloud. So they went to him and said, 'Good day, Mr. Wind. Our daughter has grown up and it is time she was married. We wish to invite the most powerful person in the world to be her husband, and so we have come to welcome you as her bridegroom, for you can blow Mr. Cloud away, whether he wishes to go or not.'

But Mr. Wind shook his head and laughed. 'I appreciate your kind offer,' he said. 'I am indeed very powerful, but there is one more powerful than I. It is the Stone Buddha, in Ŭnzin, in the Province of Zŏlla. His feet are planted so firmly on the ground that, blow how I will, I cannot budge him in the slightest. He has a hat on his head, but I cannot even blow that off. He is surely the most powerful of all, so I recommend him to you.'

So Mr. and Mrs. Rat went off and called on the Stone Buddha of Ŭnzin. Mrs. Rat said to him, 'My daughter is old enough to marry now, and we invite you to be her bridegroom, as you are the most powerful of all.'

The Stone Buddha smiled and answered in a gentle voice, 'Thank you for your kind offer. But there is one yet more powerful than I. He is the young rat who lives beneath my feet. One day he will undermine me completely and I will fall. Mrs. Rat, I am at the mercy of the rats.'

Mr. and Mrs. Rat were happy and realized at last that the only fitting bridegroom for their daughter was a young rat. So they returned home and married their daughter to a young rat.

Told by Zŏng Mi-Og; Seoul (1945).

81
Three Corpses, Money, and a Wine-Bottle

ONE day an old man said to his grandson, 'Once upon a time three corpses lay on a mountain-side, and beside them were a large sum of money and a wine-bottle. Can you tell me why?'

'No, I don't know,' replied the boy.

Then the old man explained. 'The three corpses were three thieves,' he said. 'They had stolen the money and came to the mountain to share it out. Before they did so they sent one of their number to a village to buy wine, so that they might drink to celebrate their success. But while he was away the other two thieves decided to kill him when he returned, so that the money might be divided among two instead of three. So when their companion came back with the wine they fell upon him and killed him. Then they drank the wine their companion had brought, and immediately they too died. The thief who had been sent to the wine-shop had also decided to kill his companions so that he might take the whole of the spoils, and so had put poison in the wine. Thus three corpses, money, and a wine bottle were left lying on the mountainside. You understand now?'

The old man's grandson thought it was a good story and smiled.

Told by Sa Gong-Hwan; Gunwi (1920).

82
The Aged Father

LONG, long ago, when a man passed the age of seventy it was the custom to take him out to the mountains and leave him there to die.

One day a man carried his father, who had passed seventy, out into the mountains on a pack carrier. When he thought he had gone far enough away he put the old man down and abandoned him there with a certain amount of food and the pack carrier. But when he turned to return home, his son, who had gone with him, picked up the pack-carrier to take it back home. His father scolded him and said, 'You mustn't take that home. It must be thrown away too.'

But his son answered, 'When you are old I will use this pack carrier to carry you away too. So I think it would be silly to throw it away now.'

Then his father, deeply moved by his son's words, lifted his aged father on to his back and carried him back home. And from that day the evil custom itself was abandoned.

Told by Sŏ Zu-Sig; Ŏnyang (1916).

83

The Judgements of a Magistrate

ONE day an old man was walking along a road. A young man came up and asked him to lend him his pipe. The old man agreed, but when the young man had finished smoking he refused to return it. The old man was greatly displeased and said, 'Give it back. It's mine, isn't it?'

The young man then retorted angrily, 'Certainly not! It's my pipe.'

So they wrangled bitterly over the pipe, and in the end the case came before the local magistrate.

'This is a most ridiculous quarrel,' said the magistrate. 'It is utterly absurd to bring such a case before me.' Then he handed the old man a pipe. 'You can have this pipe,' he said. 'Now let us settle this amicably. What about a friendly smoke?'

So the three of them, the magistrate, the old man, and the young man, sat down together for a smoke and a chat. There was an ashtray where they could knock out their pipes when they went out. When the young man stretched out his hand to press down the tobacco in his pipe he did not reach out far enough. The magistrate noticed this and reasoned that he was accustomed to smoke a shorter pipe. So he immediately ordered that young man to be put in prison, and returned the pipe to its rightful owner.

One day two merchants came to the magistrate with a roll of cloth. Each of them claimed that it belonged to him. The magistrate said to them, 'This is a very difficult case to decide. Unroll the cloth and each of you take one end. Then pull as hard as you can and the winner can take the cloth.'

So they did as he told them. One of them tugged with might and main, but the other pulled only with great reluctance lest the cloth be damaged. The magistrate immediately deduced that the one who pulled harder had stolen the cloth and was trying to make sure of his ill-gotten gains, so he had him put in jail and returned the roll of cloth to its rightful owner.

So the magistrate acquired a great reputation for wisdom and was highly respected by the people.

Told by Gim Tĕ-O; Seoul (1947).

84

Poisonous Persimmons

A BUDDHIST priest once kept a big store of dried persimmons in a cupboard in his room. He planned to eat them all himself, and so he told his young disciple, 'These are deadly poison. If you eat even the smallest part of one you will die within the hour. See that you leave them well alone.'

But one day the young disciple went and ate all the persimmons in the cupboard. Then he broke the holder of his master's inkstone, which was his most highly prized possession. Then he went and lay on his bed and covered himself with blankets.

A little later the priest returned. When he saw his disciple he cried, 'Whatever is the matter with you?' His disciple answered, 'Through my miserable clumsiness I dropped the holder of your inkstone and broke it. I realize that that was an unpardonable

188

crime. The only thing left for me to do was to put an end to my life, and so I went to your cupboard and ate all the poison you keep there. Now I lie here waiting to breathe my last.'

The priest was so tickled by his disciple's ingenuity that he could not help laughing and said no more about the matter.

Told by O Wi-Yŏng; Ŏnyang (1917).

85

Lazybones

THERE was once a terribly lazy man. He was too lazy even to feed himself, and so his wife had to put the food into his mouth with spoon and chopsticks. One day she had to go away for a few days and so she cooked some rice cakes and hung them round his neck on a string. 'Those are for you to eat when you are hungry,' she said.

Then she went off and came back a few days later. She found her husband lying starved to death, with the cakes still hanging round his neck. He had been too lazy to lift his hand and put them in his mouth.

Told by Gim Gi-Tĕg; Tong-yŏng (1930).

86

The Bride Who Would Not Speak

ONCE upon a time a man said to his daughter when she was setting out to go to her wedding, 'A daughter-in-law's life is very hard. She must pretend that she does not see the things that are to be seen, that she does not hear the words spoken around her, and she must speak as little as possible.

So for three years after her marriage the girl spoke never a word. Her husband's family thought she was deaf and dumb, and so they decided to send her back to her father's house.

As she went back riding in a palanquin she chanced to hear a mountain pheasant call, and she said, 'Dear pheasant! I have missed your voice these long years.' Her father-in-law, who was walking beside the palanquin, was overjoyed to hear her speak and took her back to her husband at once. Then he sent his servants to catch the pheasant.

As she cooked the pheasant the daughter-in-law sang, 'The wings that protected me I will serve to my father-in-law. The nagging beak I will serve to my mother-in-law. And the rolling eyes will do for my husband's sister.

Told by O Hwa-Su; Ŏnyang (1920).

87

A Clever Old Bride

IN olden times early marriage was the rule, and very often the bride was considerably older than the bridegroom.

Once a rather elderly bride was married to a child-bridegroom. She tried to treat him as her husband, but he gave her no end of trouble by his childishness. She was ladling rice out of the pot one day when her husband came and asked her to give him the burnt rice at the bottom. She felt ashamed that her husband should be so childish, and so she snapped at him, 'A gentleman mustn't ask for such things in the kitchen.' Thereupon the boy burst into tears. She was greatly embarrassed by this, so she picked him up and put him on her back and started to soothe him like a baby. Before long he stopped crying.

Just then her husband's father came along. So she went to the door and told the boy to climb up the thatched roof where the gourds were growing. Then she said loudly, 'Pick me a good ripe one please.' She did this to show her father-in-law that she had not been carrying her husband like a baby, for if it had been known she would never have been able to hold up her head again.

Told by Zŏng Dŏg-Zo; Ŏnyang (1913).

88

The Bald Old Man

LONG, long ago an old man had a young mistress, though he kept the affair secret. He let her pull out all his white hair, so that he might not look so old. His wife noticed that he had less white hair, and guessed that he must be keeping a mistress. So she abused him roundly for deceiving her.

Her husband feigned ignorance and protested, 'Certainly not! I would never do a thing like that.' Then to prove his innocence he let his wife pull out his black hair. In her jealousy she pulled it all out, so that he might no longer be attractive to his mistress. And so the old man became completely bald.

Told by Gim Du-Ri; Tong-yŏng (1950).

89

A Selfish Husband

ONCE upon a time an old man lived with his wife. One day, after he had held a service in memory of his ancestors, one of their neighbours sent them a present of some food. He sent them cooked rice and vegetables, but only one cake. They were unwilling to divide it, and so they agreed that the first to speak should forfeit the cake. So they left it on the table, and sat gazing at it in silence.

Just then a thief broke into the house, and when he saw the old man and his wife sitting there in silence he concluded that they must be blind and deaf. So he calmly helped himself to everything he could find, and then began a violent assault on the old woman. But her husband just sat and watched in silence. At last his wife could stand it no longer. She shouted at him, 'You heartless old man! You sit there quietly while this fellow beats me!'

Then the old man said, 'The cake is mine.' and coolly popped it into his mouth.

Told by Son Zin-Tĕ; Gupo (1925).

191

90
A Talkative Old Woman

LONG ago there was a stupid widow. One day she heard that her daughter's father-in-law had died, and so she went to his house to join in the mourning. As she bewailed, 'Aigo! Aigo!' she imagined she was mourning for her own departed husband, and cried loudly, 'Take me with you, my dear. I wish to be with you.' All the other mourners burst out laughing. But she took no notice and went on crying out in the same way.

At last her daughter, who was standing beside her, prodded her gently with her forefinger. Then the silly woman noticed that she was in her daughter's home and not her own, and that the dead man was not her husband but her daughter's father-in-law. So in an attempt to divert attention from her mistake she said brightly to her daughter's relations, 'How are you all? Is everybody well?' They looked at her rather strangely and replied, 'We are all very sad. Father died suddenly, you know.'

The silly old woman found herself in an even more awkward situation. So she said, 'Did he die of illness?' 'No,' she was told. 'An awl fell on to him from the shelf.' 'Fancy that!' she said. 'Very dangerous indeed. I hope his eyes didn't get hurt.' Then the lady of the house said severely, 'Nothing could be worse than death.' Then the old widow began to blush for her stupidity.

She was still looking for a chance to cover up her shame. All the other ladies went out into the garden. So she went after them, and when she came to the door she found no shoes but her own. (In Korea it is customary to take off one's shoes on going indoors and to put them on again on going out.) 'What has happened to everybody else's shoes?' she cried. 'I'm glad mine are still here anyway.' All the ladies out in the garden burst out laughing at her words.

So now she decided that she must be very careful in what she said, and not to speak without due consideration. Then she saw a magpie perching on a tree and turned to her daughter's mother-in-law. 'Tell me,' she said, 'Is that magpie one of your fowls?'

So in spite of all her efforts the others still roared with laughter at her.

Told by Yŏm U-Gyŏng; Gŭmhwa (1938).

91
A Foolish Mourner

THERE was once a very stupid man, who was called one day to visit Mr. Gong, one of his neighbours, and join him in mourning for one of his relations who had just died. His wife was afraid that he would make a fool of himself, and so she gave him detailed instructions on how to behave. 'When you get there,' she said, 'You must first make sure you have come to the right place. You will hear the dog barking, "gong, gong," which will remind you to ask, when they open the door, "Is Mr. Gong at home?" When you go inside and come to the room where the mourners are congregated you must look out of the window at the mountains. They will appear to recede, saying "I go, I go." This will remind you how to lament. Just pretend to weep, and cry "Aigo, Aigo." When the lamentation is at an end, they will bring in tables laden with salt fish. Then you should have no difficulty in remembering to say, "I am so *sorry* you have suffered this grievous loss." Do you think you can remember all that?'

Her foolish husband answered readily, 'Oh yes, of course!' and left the house. As he walked along he turned the three phrases over in his mind to impress them on his memory. Unfortunately he had to cross a river, and in the fuss of taking off his shoes and socks, rolling up his trousers, and wading across, he managed to forget them completely. To make matters worse he absent-mindedly left his shoes and socks behind on the bank before he crossed, and then walked barefoot to Gong's house.

When he reached the gate he heard a dog bark. It happened to be an old dog that barked 'mŏng, mŏng.' So the silly man called out, 'Is Mr. Mŏng at home?' Gong was most embarrassed, but nevertheless came out himself to welcome him wearing his mourning clothes. Then he led his guest to join the other mourners. The stupid fellow looked out of the window at the mountains and thought they looked rather *rug*ged. He was all at sea by now, and in his confusion he started crying out 'Lucky, lucky.' Gong and the others were very puzzled when they heard him.

Then the tables were brought in with the salt fish. He remembered that the fish was to remind him of something, but he could not for the life of him remember what. He felt sure that it must be to thank his host, so he said, 'Thank you for the fish.'

The three *faux pas* were too much for Gong, and he burst out laughing in spite of himself. Then the silly guest suddenly noticed that he was barefooted. He shouted angrily at his host, 'You villain! You have stolen my shoes and socks, and you think it funny, eh? Give them back to me at once.'

The host was so overcome with laughter that he just got a new pair of socks and handed them to him on the spot.

Told by Gim Bong-Zib; Pyŏng-yang (1935).

92
Three Foolish Brides

THERE were once three sisters. The eldest sister refused to undress on her wedding night, because she felt too bashful. The bridegroom thought she must dislike him and got up and left the house, never to return.

When the second sister married she remembered her sister's failure. So on her wedding night she went in to her husband naked, carrying her clothes over her arm. He was astounded that she should behave in such an outlandish fashion, and he too left the house at once, never to return.

The third sister was very worried after her sisters' two failures, and so on her wedding night she stood at the door of the room and asked her husband, 'Shall I come in dressed as I am, or must I undress first and come in naked?' Her husband was so embarrassed by her strange question that like the others he too got up and left the house for ever.   Told by Gim Yun-Gi; Gŭmze (1924).

93
Three Foolish Wives

ONE day three women who had been driven out by their mothers-in-law met in a certain place. They started to chat together and then asked each other why they had been cast out.

194

The first woman said, 'It was a trifling matter really. One night my mother-in-law asked me to knock the ashes out of her pipe. So I took it out into the garden and tapped it hard on a round stone. Unfortunately it wasn't a stone, but my father-in-law's bald head shining in the moonlight. She sent me away for that.'

The second woman said, 'It was nothing really. One day my mother-in-law asked me to bring her a light for her pipe. So I brought her hot ashes in a sieve, and she sent me away at once.'

The third woman said. 'I didn't do anything either. There were a lot of lice in my clothes, so I boiled them in the rice pot. And then she sent me away!'

Told by Gim Bog-Hi; Tong-yŏng (1933).

94

Two Lies

ONCE there was a Minister who was so fond of being told lies that he announced, 'Any man who can tell me two lies that I find interesting shall marry my only daughter.' So all the leading liars in the Eight Provinces came to his house. But with all the stories they told he was never satisfied, and refused to give his daughter to any of them.

One day, however, a young man came and said, 'It will be very hot in summer, you know. So you should go out now and dig a great pit under the main street of Seoul. Then when the hot weather comes you can sell it and make your fortune.'

'That's a wonderful lie,' answered the Minister as usual. 'And the next?'

The young man took an old document from his pocket. 'This is a bond of debt amounting to one hundred thousand *yang* which your late father borrowed from me before he died. I have come to demand payment.'

Now the Minister was in a quandary. 'If I say its a lie,' he said to himself, 'I must give him my daughter. But if I say it is not a lie, I must pay all that money.' In the end he had to say, 'It's a lie,' and the young man married his daughter.

Told by An Zŏng-Og; Seoul (1940).

195

95

A Grain of Millet

ONE evening a young man on his way to Seoul to take the civil examination went to an inn-keeper and gave him a grain of millet. 'This is a most valuable thing,' he said. 'Guard it carefully till I ask for it back.'

In the morning he asked the inn-keeper to give him his grain of millet. 'But a rat ate it up in the night,' replied the inn-keeper. 'Then bring me the rat!' said the young man. So the inn-keeper went and caught a rat and brought it to him. Then the young man went on his way with the rat.

The next evening he stayed at another inn and handed the rat to the inn-keeper. 'This rat is most important,' he said. 'Please look after it for me till I need it again.'

In the morning he asked the inn-keeper to give him back his rat. 'A cat ate it in the night,' replied the inn-keeper. So the young man said, 'Bring me the cat,' and the inn-keeper gave it to him. Then he went on his way with the cat.

When he reached the next inn he left the cat with the inn-keeper. But in the morning the inn-keeper told him that it had been kicked to death by a horse. So the young man demanded the horse, and the inn-keeper gave it to him. Then he set out again with the horse.

At the next inn he asked the inn-keeper to look after his horse. But in the morning he was told that an ox had gored it to death. So he took the ox instead and drove it off to Seoul. Again he stayed at an inn, and left the ox in the care of the inn-keeper. But in the morning the inn-keeper came to him and apologized profusely. His son had sold the ox to a Minister by mistake. So the young man demanded that the inn-keeper bring the Minister to him.

So the inn-keeper was obliged to go to the Minister and explain humbly what had happened. The Minister said, 'If he has the nerve to summon me he must be an interesting fellow. Bring him to me.' So the young man was taken to the Minister. 'Give me back my ox,' he demanded at once. 'I'm afraid it's already been killed and eaten,' replied the Minister. 'Then bring me whoever ate it,' the young man persisted stubbornly.

The Minister was most impressed by the young man's fearless and persistent character, and welcomed him cordially and offered h'm his daughter in marriage.

Told by Gim Yang-Ha; Zŏng-pyŏng (1928).

96
Two Unfaithful Husbands

ONCE there was a profligate husband who used to· leave his wife alone every night. So naturally enough she too found a lover.

One night her husband came back stealthily and found his wife's lover lying in a drunken sleep. So he made his wife bring boiling oil and pour it in her lover's ear. In fear and trembling she obeyed and so killed him. Then her husband told her to take the body secretly to the mountains and bury it there. Then he ran on ahead by another path and waited for his wife to come past. When she appeared he jumped out at her and shouted, 'Who is this?' so that she was terrified by the unexpected voice.

Then he said sternly to his wife, 'You have killed this man, and so you must take the body to the magistrate and confess your crime.' The miserable woman grovelled on the ground and begged him to spare her. So he took her, still with the body on her back, to the dead man's house. When they arrived before the gate he disguised his voice and shouted, 'Open the door.' But the woman would not open the door, and said in a voice full of jealousy, 'Certainly not! You can go and stay the night with your beloved.' So he repeated his request two or three times, but the woman still refused to open the door. Then he said, 'I will hang myself from the gate-post.' The woman inside answered, 'Do as you please. I don't care.' So he put a rope round the corpse's neck and hung it from the gate-post. Then he went home with his wife.

After waiting a few minutes in silence the dead man's wife opened the door and looked out. To her astonishment she saw her husband hanging dead. She wept bitterly, for though he too was unfaithful she loved him as a wife should.

Told by Son Zin-Tĕ; Gupo (1930).

PART FIVE
OLD NOVELS

97

The Two Sisters, Rose and Lotus

I N Czŏlsan, in the province of Pyŏng-An, there lived long ago a certain Bĕ Mu-Yong. He was quite a rich man, and held in high esteem by his neighbours, for he was the headman of the village. He was childless, which caused him and his wife much unhappiness.

One day his wife fell asleep, and dreamed that a divine being descended from Heaven and offered her a branch of beautiful flowers. She held out her hand to take it, but it changed into a fairy, and then entered her body, while a mysterious wind sprang up. Before long she became pregnant, and in due course gave birth to a beautiful girl. Though they would have preferred a son the parents were delighted with their daughter, and named her Rose. Three years later a second daughter was born to them. She too was very pretty, and they gave her the name of Lotus.

Some years later a grievous misfortune befell the family. The mother was taken ill, and no treatment was of any avail to cure her. At last, as she lay on her death-bed, she said to her husband, 'I shall be leaving you soon, and I go with no regret for the past. But I am worried for my daughters, though you will marry another good wife.' With these words she died, leaving her husband and her two daughters stricken with grief at their loss.

Not long after her death Bĕ married again. His second wife was young, but by no means beautiful. Her face was pock-marked and ugly, she was bad-tempered and quarrelsome, and very conceited because she had three sons of her own. And so, as time went on, Bĕ thought more and more of the gentle and loving wife he had lost, and was drawn by bonds of sympathy ever closer to his daughters. When she noticed this, the stepmother became madly jealous of the two girls, and all the loving care their father lavished upon them.

They were cleverer than her sons, too, and so she determined to kill them. She began to treat them very harshly. Her good-natured husband remonstrated with her, and asked her to treat his daughters more kindly, but she took no notice of his entreaties, and treated them as roughly as she could, especially when their father was away. Rose and Lotus became very unhappy, and often wept in each other's arms, so that their father was forced to speak sternly to their stepmother for her hard-heartedness.

At last the stepmother could bear the girls' presence no longer, and so she resolved to bring a false charge against Rose. She planned to make it appear that she had disgraced her family, and contrived a faked abortion. She caught a big rat and skinned it. Then she took the gory mass of flesh and hid it in Rose's bed. That night she went to her husband, and told him that his elder daughter had disgraced him. 'For weeks I have been watching her,' she said, 'for I suspected she was up to no good. But so far I have said nothing because I was afraid you would not believe me. Now, however, I have proof, and a leading family will be utterly dishonoured if people come to hear of it.'

She took her husband to see what was in Rose's bed. He was astounded, and much against his will had to agree that his wife's charges were true. Of course Rose denied strongly that she had done any such thing, but with the evidence of his eyes before him, he ignored her protests. That day the two sisters wept in their room the whole day long, remembering their dear departed mother in the grave.

The wicked stepmother gave her husband no peace, and demanded that he take some positive action to settle the matter. She suggested that he send Rose to stay with her maternal grandmother. At last he agreed, and late that night called Rose to him. 'I can understand your feelings since your mother died,' he said. 'It must all have been very painful to you. I am sending you to your grandmother for the present, and you can stay with her till you have recovered from your unhappiness. She will be very glad to see you. In fact she has been wanting you to go for some time past. You will leave at once, to-night.'

Rose was appalled by her father's words, and begged him not to send her away. 'Father, I have never been there before,' she said. 'And besides it is very late. If you send me away, my sister Lotus will be very lonely without me.'

Ignoring her plea her father told her to leave at once. 'My mind is made up,' he said. 'You must obey your father's orders. Your brother Zang-Sŏn will take you there now.'

The wicked stepmother had, unknown to her husband, hatched an evil plot with her eldest son. He was waiting outside with a horse, and his mother urged Rose not to delay. Before she went, however, she entered her sister's room, and told her what her father had ordered. 'Dear Lotus,' she said, 'I will be back in a few days. Look after yourself well while I am away. Good night, and farewell, dear sister.' Lotus sobbed, 'Where are you going, and how shall I endure alone? Come back soon, I shall be waiting for you.' Then her stepbrother seized her, and put her on the horse, and rode off with her. They vanished into the darkness, unseen by anybody in the village.

They rode far into the mountains, and deep into the dense forest. While it was yet dark they came to a lake, where her stepbrother told Rose to get down from the horse. She was alarmed, and said, 'Why do you want me to get down? This cannot be our destination, and it is still very dark.' Zang-Sŏn said roughly to her, 'This lake is your future home. Have you forgotten you have sinned and brought disgrace upon your family? I don't want to kill you, but that is what Father and Mother have told me to do.'

Rose was completely taken aback, and cried, 'Woe is me! I can remember no such order. This is indeed a plot to bring dishonour upon me. May Heaven some day absolve me of this disgrace! I am doomed to sink below the waters of this lake. My dear lost Mother, now I come to join you. But oh, my poor Lotus, how lonely and forlorn you will be without me! Now I shall become a spirit of the waters. . . .'

Her heartless brother Zang-Sŏn seized her roughly and tried to thrust her in the lake, but she tore herself free and plunged herself into the deep blue waters of the lake. At that very moment a strange chill wind arose, and a great tiger sprang out of the undergrowth. Zang-Sŏn turned in alarm and tried to escape, but it tore him from his horse, and ripped off his ear, arm, and leg, so that he fell off and rolled down into a valley.

At home his mother waited for him to return, and to her great alarm his horse came back riderless. So she called the servants and went with them to look for him with lanterns. At last they found him lying crippled and unconscious in the valley where he had fallen, and carried him home. When he came to his senses in the morning he told his parents secretly the night's happenings by the lake. The father repented of his cruel and heartless act, and his affection for his younger daughter Lotus increased greatly. But his wife only treated her more and more harshly, and even began to consider how she might murder her too.

For a few days Lotus waited in vain for her sister to return, and then asked her stepmother what had happened to her. Her stepmother answered with a sneer, 'Your precious sister was eaten by a tiger. Can't you see what happened to your brother Zang-Sŏn? He is crippled for life.'

Lotus retired to her room in the utmost distress. Weeping bitterly, so that she was drenched with tears, she called her sister repeatedly by name. After a while she fell asleep, and in a dream she saw Rose rise up from beneath the waters of the lake in the form of a great yellow dragon and set out towards the Northern Sea. So she cried out to her, 'Dearest sister, Rose, where are you going, leaving me alone with my cruel stepmother?'

Her sister answered, 'My dearest Lotus, I am now in the world of the dead. On the orders of the Heavenly King I am on my way to the Mountain of the Three Genii to fetch a magic potion. I can stay with you no longer now, for I must make haste, but we will be reunited before long.'

The loud cry of the yellow dragon awoke Lotus from her dream. She told her father what she had seen, and he wept bitterly. She thought that the circumstances of her sister's death were highly suspicious, so she questioned Zang-Sŏn cautiously about it, and learned that Rose had killed herself by throwing herself into the waters of the lake. She resolved thereupon to go to her sister by throwing herself likewise into the lake. She went to her room, and prayed alone. 'Dearest Rose!' she cried. 'Now I see that you are the spirit of the waters while I am left alone in this miserable world. They say that death brings regrets even to those who have lived their full span of seventy years and more, but you were plucked off in the flower of youth when you were seventeen. And moreover you were dishonoured by the deceitful plots of a scheming woman. . . . Dearest Rose, I shall join you there!'

She did not know where the lake was, nor could she have found the way even if she had known. One day, as she was pondering on this problem, a blue bird came fluttering and twittering before her eyes. She guessed that it might have been sent to show her the way, and so that night she wrote a note for her father, and stealthily left the house, and followed the blue bird.

When she reached the lake she heard a sad voice rising from the water, 'Dearest Lotus! Please do not end your life. Once you have died, you can never return to the world of men.' It was the voice of her dead sister. She replied that she preferred to sacrifice herself, and boldly plunged into the deep waters of the lake. And people who passed by the lake afterwards said that they could hear the two sisters crying reproaches on their cruel fate.

Now the magistrate of Czŏlsan died suddenly one night. It was rumoured that the ghosts of the two sisters had appeared and caused his death. His successor died in the same way, and likewise the next two who were appointed. The sisters appeared to them not to cause their deaths, but to draw attention to their own unhappy fate. But being of weak constitution and horror struck by the pitiable apparitions, they died of the shock they caused. The Governor of Pyŏng-An Province reported the repeated tragedies to the King, and he sent a high official named Zŏng Dong-Ho to investigate.

Zŏng went to Czŏlsan, and alone in the brightly lit hall of the official residence read aloud the Book of Changes. At the dread hour of midnight the air in the hall gradually became colder, and there appeared a girl in a green jacket and crimson skirt. The magistrate asked what he could do for her. 'I am the daughter of Bĕ Mu-Yong, who lives in this district,' replied the apparition. 'My name is Lotus, and my elder sister is Rose. We were shamefully treated by our step mother Hŏ, after our own dear mother had died. One day our step mother plotted to disgrace my sister, and contrived a faked abortion with a skinned rat. So my sister was compelled to commit suicide by throwing herself in the lake.' With these words the girl disappeared.

The next morning Zŏng began his investigation. He learned all about the family of Bĕ in detail, and of the mysterious murmurings from the lake. He had Bĕ and his wife arrested and immediately brought to trial.

'How many children have you?' he asked Bĕ.

'Two daughters and three sons,' was the reply. 'But my daughters died long ago.'

'How did they die?'

'Of sickness, Sir.'

'Tell me the truth,' said the magistrate. 'Do not try to deceive me.'

Then the step-mother Hŏ interrupted, 'The elder daughter Rose brought disgrace upon herself and dishonour on the family. She had a miscarriage, and committed suicide. Then the younger, Lotus, ran away from home, and we have heard nothing of her, Sir.'

'Have you proof of this miscarriage?' asked the magistrate.

'Yes Sir, I have it here,' answered the stepmother at once, taking a dried up piece of flesh from her breast. In shape it looked as if it might be human. So Zŏng adjourned the trial that the matter might be investigated further, and the couple were allowed to return home.

That night the two sisters appeared to Zŏng, and told him how he might expose their step-mother's duplicity. They assured him that their father was innocent, and disappeared riding on the back of a blue crane.

Next morning Zŏng re-opened the trial, and summoned the couple before him. He ordered that the lump of flesh be cut open, and in it they found rat-dung. Thereupon Bĕ confessed his stupidity and errors, but his wife refused to admit the truth.

The magistrate Zŏng sent his report to the Governor in Pyŏng-Yang, and he made the final decision. The step-mother was sentenced to be decapitated and dismembered, and her eldest son to be strangled, but Bĕ was acquitted and released.

Bĕ went and searched for his daughters' bodies in the lake. He found them still intact, with their faces serene as in life. He selected a suitable spot on the mountain for a grave and buried them there. Close by he built a monument of stone.

The magistrate Zŏng won great renown for his successful handling of the case. The spirits of Rose and Lotus appeared to him again and thanked him for his wise judgement. Moreover he was promoted to the rank of Field Commander.

A few years later Bĕ took another wife. She was the daughter of a leading man in the neighbourhood, by name Yim Gwang-Ho. She was of a sweet and gentle disposition, and seventeen years of age. One night Bĕ's two daughters appeared to him in a dream and

said, 'Father, we were spirits of the water for some time, and then
we were taken up to the Heavenly Kingdom. To-day, however,
the Heavenly King has ordered us to be born again as your
daughters. How happy we shall be to be with you again?'

He tried to take his daughters by the hand, but just then a cock
crowed and he awoke from his dream. So he went into his new wife's
room, and found her holding a rose and a lotus. He asked her what
had happened, and she answered, 'A Fairy Queen came and gave
me these two flowers, saying, "These are a gift from the Heavenly
King. Tend them with the greatest care. May happiness be yours."
And I awoke, and found these in my hands.'

They put the flowers in a vase. Bě's wife became pregnant, and
when twin girls were born the flowers disappeared. They called
their daughters Rose and Lotus. When they reached the age of
fifteen years they looked exactly like the other Rose and Lotus.
They married the twin sons of a powerful man of the neighbourhood, Yi Yŏn-Ho. Their husbands both passed the High Civil
Examination, and attained high rank as scholars.

From *Gaⱬe Zib*, by Gim Dong-Hŭl.

98

The Story of Hong Gil-Dong

IN the days of King Se-Zong there lived a minister named Hong,
who was of noble descent. In his youth he had passed the Civil
Examination, and had by successive stages been promoted to the
highest and most honourable rank.

One night he dreamed that a blue dragon surrounded with
thunder and lightning came out and challenged him. When he
awoke he went to his wife Yu and told her of his dream. 'Surely
Heaven will grant me a noble son,' he said, 'for it was a dragon that
I saw in my dream.' His wife, however, was already with child, and
would not accept his advances.

Filled with regret at her display of ignorance he left her room.
As he was coming out he chanced to see one of his maid-servants,
Czun-Sŏn, a girl of seventeen who served tea to his guests. So he

called her to him, and she could in no wise refuse his request, for he was her master. Thus she became the concubine of the Minister Hong, and conceived, and in due course gave birth to a son. Now Hong had two sons, the elder, born to Yu his wife, he called In-Hyŏng, and the second, born to Czun-Sŏn, he called Gil-Dong.

The younger son Gil-Dong was a lad of heroic mien, and of a strong and upright character. By the time he was eight years old he had displayed a most unusual degree of wisdom, and his insight was remarkable. Hong was very proud indeed of his outstanding son, though he always regretted that he was born of such a humble mother. Yet he never allowed his son to call him father, or to call In-Hyŏng his brother, because of his illegitimate birth. The servants often jeered at him because of this, and in the course of time he became very unhappy.

One autumn evening, in the middle of September, when he was ten years old, Gil-Dong sat reading in his room. The moon was shining brightly in the sky, and so he closed his book, and went for a stroll in the garden. He began to think of his future, and said to himself, 'I was born a man, and yet I am not allowed to address my father and brother as such. If I may not study the doctrines of Confucius and Mencius then it were better that I should study strategy. Thus I might gird on the sword of a General, and win renown in battle for my country. Is not this a noble aspiration for a man?' And immediately he began to make flourishes as if he were brandishing a sword there in the garden.

It happened that Hong too was in the garden enjoying the moonlight, and he saw his son. He realized that Gil-Dong was dissatisfied with his lot, and asked him the reason. 'I was born as a man, but I am not yet accepted as a man,' replied his son. 'You are not the only one who has been born of a humble mother in the family of a Minister,' replied his father in a tone of reproof. 'Beware lest you show too much conceit, or I shall be forced to punish you.'

That night Gil-Dong tossed sleeplessly, and in the morning went to Czun-Sŏn, his mother, and told her of his unhappiness. She too said to him, 'You are not the only one of humble birth. This stubbornness of yours is a great grief to me, and only makes both of us unhappy.'

Gil-Dong then spoke to her of his ambition, and of the difficult situation they were both in. 'Mother,' he said, 'I have heard that in the days of old there was a certain Zang who was of humble birth. He went to Mount Unbong and there devoted himself to study, so that in the end he attained great renown, and his fame has endured even to this day. I intend to follow his example. We are both in danger here. For there is Gogsan, who is jealous of the Minister's affection for you. I am afraid that she is planning some mischief for us. So Mother, do be careful.'

This Gogsan was a former dancing girl, who had been known as Czoran in those days. She had become the concubine of Minister Hong but, being childless, had fallen from favour. She was jealous because of the birth of Gil-Dong, and now determined to have him done away with. In order to see how this could be brought about she consulted with a woman who was one of the most famous physiognomists in the land and who lived outside the Hŭng-In Gate. She bribed her with silver to the sum of fifty *yang*.

The very next day this physiognomist knocked at the gate of the Minister's residence, and offered to read Gil-Dong's face. Permission was readily granted, and she set to work. When she finished she gave a cry of alarm, and, going into the next room, told the Minister in strict confidence, 'He is a very rare type, the type of a hero or a great man, for he shows great energy between his eyes. But he is lacking in wisdom, and so may meet with some disaster, which will bring ruin to the honour of this house. I advise you to watch him with the greatest care.'

So Hong had Gil-Dong taken to a mountain retreat where he was kept under strict guard. There he devoted himself to reading works on magical strategy, astronomy, and geography. When this was reported to Hong his anxiety became even greater, and in the end he fell seriously ill.

Gogsan then went to a necromancer and intrigued with him to bring about the death of Gil-Dong. Then she went to Hong's sick-bed, and earnestly advised him to take some positive action to settle the question of Gil-Dong. 'It was anxiety over Gil-Dong that made you ill,' she said. 'Any fool can see that. I have consulted a famous necromancer and his advice is that Gil-Dong should cease to be. If you do not take stern measures immediately the result will be dire misfortune for you and your house.'

Hong was barely conscious in his pain, and did not understand what she said, but his wife Yu and his eldest son In-Hyŏng, who were weeping at his bedside in their distress, were persuaded by her words and authorized her to take any steps which could cure his illness. So Gogsan hastened to the necromancer, who had already got in touch with a famous assassin named Tŭg-Zĕ, and paid him the sum of one thousand *yang*.

Far away in his mountain retreat Gil-Dong spent many sleepless nights. Many times he thought of escaping, but he was unwilling to disobey his father's orders, and so he spent many a weary night reading. One night he sat up reading the Book of Changes by the light of a candle when he heard a magpie call three times. He said to himself, 'This is a bird that shuns the night, and yet it cries out at this hour. Surely this is an omen that presages some dire misfortune.' So he turned to divination, and at once there appeared the shadow of an assassin.

At midnight the assassin Tŭg-Zĕ came into the room with a big sword. At once Gil-Dong recited a passage of scripture and immediately a dismal wind sprang up. It whisked the house away, and there all around stood the high and craggy mountains. Tŭg-Zĕ was terrified by Gil-Dong's magic, and tried to sheath his sword and run away. But whichever way he turned the path vanished and a steep cliff rose up, or a deep valley appeared that blocked his way. Suddenly he met a boy riding on a donkey and playing a flute of crystal. 'Why are you trying to kill me?' asked the boy, 'the judgement of Heaven will surely fall upon you.' Then dark clouds appeared and covered the sky, and rain came pelting down mixed with sand and gravel. Now Gil-Dong stood in front of Tŭg-Zĕ, who recalled his evil intention and made a sudden attack upon him. 'Make no mistake,' he cried, 'You are doomed. Gogsan sent me to kill you, and the Minister gave his approval.'

Then with his magic Gil-Dong snatched Tŭg-Zĕ's sword away and said, 'You devil! You would murder an innocent person for money. You heartless unfeeling devil!' And with one blow of the sword Tŭg-Zĕ's head fell to the ground.

Gil-Dong took the sword and hastened home. He ran to Gogsan's room, but she was not there. So he went to his father's bedside, who was now a little better, to bid him farewell. 'I stayed in the house in the mountains as you ordered Sir,' he said. 'But a treacherous fellow came to murder me, and so I must go away.'

His words made the Minister very sad and he said, 'I quite

understand how you feel, but you are too young to go out into the world just yet. Stay here with me a while. From now on you may call me "Father" and In-Hyŏng "Brother".'

At this Gil-Dong began to weep. 'Oh, Father!' he cried. 'My dear father. For the first time you allow me to call you father. How happy you have made me! But I have made up my mind to go out into the world and seek my fortune. Please take care of yourself and of my mother until we meet again, Father.'

Then Gil-Dong went to meet his mother, who tried at first to dissuade him from his intention. He refused to yield to her entreatie and left the house.

Now Gogsan, who had been waiting in a remote house for news of the assassin Tŭg-Zĕ, heard that he had been found dead, and that Gil-Dong had escaped. This news she reported to Yu, the Minister's wife, and her son In-Hyŏng told his father what had happened. He told him the whole plot that Gogsan had devised. Now Hong understood everything, and cast Gogsan from his house. Overcome with shame at this discreditable episode, he even resigned his post as Minister.

When he left his home Gil-Dong wandered far and wide. One day he came to a deep valley in the mountains where he found a great stone gate. He opened the gate and went inside. There he saw hundreds of houses standing in a broad field, and in an open space a great crowd of men were holding a banquet. They were startled to see this unexpected intruder, and looked at him suspiciously. Then one of them asked him who he was. He had guessed that Gil-Dong must be a boy of unusual character. 'How did you get here, my boy?' he said. 'We appreciate adventurous lads. I will test you. Can you carry that heavy rock there?'

'I am the son of the concubine of Hong the Minister in Seoul,' replied Gil-Dong. 'My name is Hong Gil-Dong. I was ill-treated by my family, and so I left home to seek my fortune in the world. Born a man as I am, how can I refuse your request?' With these words he picked up the heavy rock, which must have weighed a thousand *gŭn*, carried it about twenty paces and threw it on the ground. The others were amazed, and one of them said, 'In truth, none of us could carry it. We have been looking for a leader, but so far we have not found one. To-day Heaven has sent us our General.'

They were a group of bandits. Young as he was, Gil-Dong

accepted their offer of leadership, and remained with them. For a few months he trained them in military tactics.

One day a member of the band came to him and told him that they had once planned to seize the Hĕ-In Temple in Hyŏb-Czŏn but the attack had been unsuccessful. They now asked his advice on a second attempt. So he decided to go to the temple to spy out the land. Wearing a blue robe tied with a black belt he went to the temple riding on a donkey, accompanied by a few attendants. He met the chief priest and said to him, 'I am the son of the Minister Hong in Seoul. I have come here to study. In return I will send you a gift of unhulled rice, and one day I will come and dine with all the members of the temple.'

When he left the temple and returned to his band he sent the rice as he had promised, and fixed a day for the feast. On that day he went back to the temple. A lavish spread of food and drink had been prepared. All the priests assembled in the great hall of the temple, and Gil-Dong ate and drank with them. As he was eating his rice he suddenly bit on a few grains of sand. He had mixed them in the rice for just this purpose. Trembling with rage he shouted, 'You scoundrels! Who cooked this rice? You have put gravel in my food to insult me!' And he immediately ordered his attendants to arrest all the priests there. They were full of apologies for their careless-ness, but the sand was plain to see, and they could not refute the charge. While they were thus held, the bandits broke into the temple and carried off all the treasures stored there.

One priest escaped to the village and reported the robbery to the authorities. A detachment of soldiers was dispatched at once to catch the bandits. As they came near the temple they saw a priest standing on a grave who shouted to them, 'The bandits have just got away. They ran off up that path there to the north.' The priest was really Gil-Dong in disguise, and so the soldiers ran off on a false trail, while the bandits, following Gil-Dong's instructions, came safely back to their cave in the south.

After this exploit Gil-Dong called his band 'Hwal Bin Dang' or 'Band of Helpers of the Poor'. They went about seizing the ill-gotten gains of corrupt officials throughout all the eight provinces of Korea and used the vast sums they gained in this way to alleviate the sufferings of the common people.

The Governor of the Province of Ham-Gyŏng was a most

corrupt official. So Gil-Dong went to his castle and set fire to some houses outside the South Gate. While the governor and his officials and all the people were fighting the flames hundreds of Gil-Dong's men burst into the castle and plundered the storerooms. They seized money, grain, and weapons and withdrew through the north gate. On the gate they pasted a paper on which was written, 'Hong Gil-Dong, Leader of the Band of Helpers of the Poor.' When he returned and saw this the Governor sent his troops to capture the bandits.

Using the Hiding Armour Magic Gil-Dong and his men returned safely to their cave. Then, summoning the whole band he addressed them as follows. 'Men, we robbed the Temple of Hě-In of its treasure and plundered the stores of the Governor of Hamgyŏng. Sooner or later I will be captured, for the authorities know that I was responsible for both. But now I will demonstrate to you my tactical superiority.' So saying he made seven dolls of straw and on each of them he pasted a soul-label. Then he recited a passage of scripture relating to strategy, and the seven dolls changed into seven living Gil-Dongs. They stretched out their arms, and shouted together. Now there were eight Gil-Dongs, for the real one was among them, and no man could distinguish which was real and which was false. Then the whole band divided into eight groups, identical in number and appearance, each under the leadership of one of the 'Gil-Dongs'. The groups parted and went one to each of the eight provinces of the whole country. And the same night they attacked many towns and villages simultaneously, using the same magical tactics and attended by violent winds and rain.

So to Seoul there came reports from the governor of every province, each describing an identical attack at the same hour on the same day. Each attack was carried out in the same manner, and in each case the plunder was the same. A most serious state of affairs was apparent, which might well lead to the total destruction of the country. So the King consulted with his two Marshals, the Marshal of the Right and the Marshal of the Left. 'It is most uncanny,' he said. 'Every case is identical and carried out in exactly the same way. I cannot understand how one man could be responsible for them all. He must be possessed of most unusual magical powers, the like of which has never been heard of before. Difficult though it is, however, we must do something about it. This state of affairs cannot be allowed to continue.'

The Marshal of the Right, Yi-Hyŏb, then spoke up. 'Your Majesty,' he said, 'I will devote all my efforts to settling this affair. I do not think that all your forces will be needed. I will use the troops under my command, if Your Majesty so wishes.'

The King gave him his assent, and the Marshal of the Right ordered his troops to assemble on the lofty hill of Mun-Gyŏng on a certain day, and went in disguise to a wine shop in a country village, accompanied by several officers of his staff. As he was sitting in the shop a young boy rode up on a donkey and greeted him politely. With a deep sigh he said, 'There is not a piece of land, however small, that does not belong to His Majesty, and not a single man who does not owe him allegiance. But now a robber called Hong Gil-Dong is wreaking havoc throughout the eight provinces. The people are suffering terribly from his depredations, and yet he is not caught. It is indeed a most regrettable state of affairs.'

His words pleased the Marshal greatly. He seemed to be a strong and capable lad and so the Marshal said to him, 'You look a very fine young fellow. Won't you join us and help us bring our enemy to justice? But first I would like to test your strength.'

So they went up a hill until they came to a big rock. The boy sat on it and challenged the Marshal to kick him off. So he tried his hardest, with both his feet, but he could not make the boy budge even an inch. So the Marshal was satisfied with the boy's unconquerable spirit, and took him with him when he went on his way. The boy led him up a deep valley in the mountains, until they came to the entrance of a cave.

Then the boy said, 'I think this must be a bandit's lair. You wait here while I go in alone and investigate.' He went in alone and the Marshal waited outside. Suddenly thousands of bandits appeared and thronged the valley. They surrounded the Marshal and took him prisoner. He was completely taken by surprise and hardly realized what was happening. When he collected his scattered wits he found he was in a vast hall and surrounded by warriors wearing yellow caps. A stern-faced King sat on a lofty throne, and roared at him, 'You are indeed a stupid soldier! What hope have you of catching General Hong? You shall be imprisoned in Pung-Do.'

Then the Marshal bowed down humbly and begged for mercy. 'I am but a poor feeble-minded man, Your Majesty,' he said. 'Have pity on me, I beg of you.'

Thereupon the King laughed long and loud, so that the hall rang with his mirth. 'You poor fool!' he cried, 'Look at me. I am Hong Gil-Dong, the Leader of the Band of Helpers of the Poor. To test your courage to-day I disguised myself as the young boy in the blue robe. You may go home now, but remember that you say not a word of this meeting to anyone, or it will go ill with you.'

He then entertained the Marshal with wine, and gave orders that he be released. When he tried to stand up, however, he found he could move neither his arms nor his legs. He was tightly bound in a small leather bag. At last he managed to free himself, and then he found he was on Mount Bug-Ag, the rocky mountain behind the capital. There on the ground beside him he saw three more leather bags. He untied them and out stepped his three officers. He asked them what they were doing there, for his orders had been to assemble on the hill of Mun-Gyŏng in the province of Gyŏngsang.

'We waited some time for you to return to the wine shop in the village, Sir,' one of them said. 'We must have fallen asleep. All of a sudden a great wind swept us up, as in a dream, enveloped in rain. And then the next thing I knew was when I saw you here. I cannot understand it at all. Hong Gil-Dong must be endowed with limitless supernatural speed. We'll never catch him, sir, I'm afraid. But if we go back now empty-handed the King will punish us for our failure. So we had better go and lie low somewhere for a few months.' So the four of them went away from Seoul and wandered about the country.

Reports were constantly being brought to the King of further ravages by Gil-Dong and his men, but as yet no strong counter-measures had been taken. So the King summoned his ministers for consultation. 'Hong Gil-Dong must be in league with some demon,' he said. 'He has so far gone completely unpunished. Is there anyone among you who knows the secret of this remarkable person?'

One of the Ministers replied, 'This Gil-Dong is the illegitimate son of a former minister, Hong. His brother, Hong In-Hyŏng, holds an important position in the Ministry of the Army. So I suggest that the best policy will be to arrest both these men.'

So Hong the former minister and his elder son were thrown into prison. Then the King ordered In-Hyŏng to be brought before him. In stern tones he said to him, 'It has come to my notice that this bandit Gil-Dong, who is causing so much trouble everywhere, is your illegitimate brother. How do you account for it? It is my command that you go out and bring him to justice. If you fail in this, I shall sentence both you and your father to execution.'

Humbly In-Hyŏng answered, 'I had indeed a brother born of a mother of low degree. One day, however, he murdered a man and ran away. It has caused great grief and anxiety to my father who has been lying sick in bed as a result of his worries. Yet Gil-Dong persists in his evil ways. If Your Majesty would be so kind as to release my sick father from prison I will undertake to do the best I can to bring Gil-Dong to justice, so that Your Majesty's mind may be set at rest.'

So the King released his father and appointed In-Hyŏng governor of the province of Gyŏngsang, with orders to arrest Gil-Dong. As soon as he arrived at his post he issued a proclamation to be read in every part of all the provinces in the land. This proclamation was as follows: 'The Virtues of Morality are the basis of the life of men, and disloyalty and disobedience to one's father are not to be tolerated for one moment. My brother Gil-Dong knows this as well as any man. So to him I say that his father is seriously ill as a result of his misdeeds, and the King greatly troubled. Therefore I advise him, Gil-Dong, to surrender to me, In-Hyŏng, whom His Majesty has been pleased to appoint Governor of the province of Gyŏngsang with orders to arrest him. I ask him to surrender to me at once, and repent of his past misdeeds, so that his punishment may be less, the honour of his family saved, and His Majesty's mind set at rest.'

A few days went by and then there came to call on the Governor a boy riding on a donkey and accompanied by many attendants. It was none other than his brother Gil-Dong. The Governor met him alone in a room, and in tears appealed to him to drop his evil ways at once. Gil-Dong agreed at once, saying, 'It was for the sake of my father and brother that I came here to-day, so how can I refuse your request? If Father had let me call him "Father" and you "Brother" in the first place all this would never have happened. The past is all over now, and so I ask you to arrest me and send me to Seoul, my dear brother.'

So Hong Gil-Dong was arrested and led away to the Capital, under a strong guard of officers. Thousands of spectators lined the way to watch the procession pass. But, strange to relate, eight Gil-Dongs were brought in from the eight provinces and the King and his Ministers could not tell which was the real one, for the eight were constantly quarrelling among themselves, each claiming to be real and accusing the others of being nothing but straw dummies. So once more the King summoned Hong, the father of Gil-Dong, from his sickbed. When he came to the court the King asked him which was his real son. So Hong turned and looked at the eight figures and said, 'My son has a red spot on his left leg, and so I can easily identify him among the eight. You must not try to deceive me in the presence of His Majesty.' But at that very moment blood gushed forth from his mouth and he fell dead on the floor.

The King was greatly taken aback, and sent for the Royal Physician, but in vain. He was quite unable to revive Hong. Then the eight Gil-Dongs each took a pill from his pocket and put it in the dead man's mouth. After about three hours had elapsed he recovered. Then the eight Gil-Dongs appealed to the King. 'We were born of a humble mother,' they said, 'and were not properly accepted into the family. So in the end we went and joined a group of bandits. But we have never troubled ordinary law-abiding people. Many of Your Majesty's officials are corrupt, and those we have punished for the common good.' No sooner had they finished speaking than the eight fell on the floor, and it was seen that they were nothing but dolls made of straw. So once more the King dispatched officials with strict orders to take immediate steps to capture Hong Gil-Dong.

Now Hong Gil-Dong gave up the use of straw dolls, and went himself and pasted on four castle gates a notice which read: 'Hong Gil-Dong will be glad to be arrested, or if so desired, undertake to leave Korea, if the King will but appoint him Minister responsible for the defence of the Realm.'

When this offer came to the ears of the King he summoned his ministers and consulted them as to what he ought to do. After some discussion they recommended that he should not agree to the proposal, for to confer so high a dignity on a mere rebel would undoubtedly bring discredit to the Government. So the King summoned once more In-Hyŏng, Governor of the Province of Gyŏngsang, who had been appointed for the sole purpose of arresting his brother, Gil-Dong.

So one day Gil-Dong descended out of the sky in his brother's presence and said, 'Dear Brother, I am the real Gil-Dong. It is due to me that you are in a most difficult position, so now arrest me and send me to Seoul, if you please.'

His brother the Governor examined his left leg, and found a red spot on it. So without more ado he arrested him, and had him bound hand and foot, and imprisoned him in a strong iron drum. Then he was carried up to Seoul, under a strong military guard, in a cart fitted with a cage of heavy iron bars. But no sooner had they arrived before the Royal Palace than Gil-Dong burst out of the drum and the cage, and ascended to the cloudy sky, as easily as a snake sheds its skin.

This was reported to the King, and once more he consulted with his ministers. One of them suggested now that the best course would be to offer him the title he had requested, for he had undertaken to leave the country if this were done. The King assented to this proposal, and notices were posted up everywhere conferring the title of Minister responsible for the Defence of the Realm upon Hong Gil-Dong.

No sooner had this been done than Gil-Dong appeared in the main street of Seoul, wearing the uniform of his post, and the cap and belt of a gentleman. The high officials of his department went out into the street to welcome him, and attended him on his way to the Palace to pay his respects to the King. But other officials planned secretly to kill him with an axe outside the Palace gate as he came away from the audience.

When he was admitted into the Royal presence Gil-Dong apologized humbly to the King and repented of his past misdeeds. 'Your Majesty has been kind enough to pardon my crimes,' he said, 'and has been pleased to confer on me a title of great honour. I am fully satisfied, and true to my word will now leave Korea. May the blessings of Heaven rain upon Your Majesty!' With these words he rose into the sky, and disappeared, wrapped in clouds. The King was delighted, and trusting in the sincerity of Gil-Dong's words, gave orders that the special measures ordered for his arrest should now be cancelled.

Hong Gil-Dong returned to his cave, and told his men that he was going to leave the country. He ordered them to desist from further raids, and to wait there till he returned, and to have no communication whatsoever with other people. Then he rose up into the air, and proceeded southwards until he reached a kingdom called Yug-Do. It was a fairly thickly populated country, set among beautiful mountains and rivers. It seemed to him to be a delightful land to live in. And there he saw the island of Ze-Do, with the mountain of O-Bong, most beautiful to behold, surrounded with fertile farm-lands, seven hundred *i*, or thirty-five miles, in circumference.

So he returned to his cave where his men were waiting, and bade them assemble on a certain day by the Han River, near Seoul, with many boats. He promised that he would get them one thousand *sŏg* of unhulled rice from the King.

Peace now reigned throughout the land of Korea, and the King was very pleased. One moonlight September night he was strolling in the Palace garden, when a breeze suddenly sprang up and he heard a sweet melody played on a flute of crystal. Then all of a sudden there appeared before him a young boy. The King was startled by this unexpected apparition, and asked, 'Who is this fairy child who has come down to the world of men at this hour of the night? Tell me what you desire, and I will do all in my power to help you.'

The boy answered humbly, 'I am he whom you appointed to be Minister for the defence of the Realm. Hong Gil-Dong is my name, Your Majesty. I have lately travelled southwards from Korea, and I have found a suitable place to make my home. I intend to take my thousands of followers there to live in peace. We should all be deeply grateful to Your Majesty if you would send one thousand *sŏg* of unhulled rice to Sŏ-Gang on the Han River.' The King granted his request and at once the boy vanished.

The following day about three thousand of Gil-Dong's followers embarked on many boats in the Han River and set sail. As they went they shouted, 'Hong Gil-Dong appointed by His Majesty to be Minister responsible for the defence of the Realm, is now leaving Korea. He bears as a gift from His Majesty one thousand *sŏg* of unhulled rice. Farewell, land of our fathers!'

So Hong Gil-Dong sailed across the sea to the island of Ze-Do, and established there a new country of his own. He built houses and developed agriculture, taught his men to read and write, and had them manufacture weapons.

One day he set out to go to the mountain of Mang-Dang, to get a special herb which should be applied to arrow-heads. On the way he came to Nag-Czŏn, where there lived a rich man named Bĕg Yong. He had one daughter, who was most beautiful and clever. She was also trained in the art of swordsmanship. She was unmarried, for her parents could not find any man sufficiently qualified to be a suitable match for her.

While Gil-Dong was in the village a strange storm sprang up and attacked Bĕg Yong's house. His daughter was carried off, and all agreed that some baleful magic influence was at work. Bĕg Yong and his wife were overcome with grief, and to any man who could find their daughter they offered her hand in marriage, and a lavish reward as well.

Hong Gil-Dong set out once more on his journey and soon came to the mountain where the magic herb grew. He found it growing in clumps here and there, and wandered about picking it until it grew dark. Then he saw a brightly lit house, whence came the sound of voices. He went up to the house and peeped into the room. Inside he saw many of the monsters that are called Uldon. He shot an arrow into the room and wounded one of them, whereupon they all ran away. He followed the wounded monster for some distance but soon lost track of him in the darkness. As he was retracing his steps he met three more monsters who said to him, 'Who are you? No man has ever come here before.'

Without the slightest hesitation Gil-Dong replied, 'I came here from Korea to seek the magic herb that grows here, for I wish to use it as a drug to cure illness.' At his words the monsters seemed to be very pleased and one of them said, 'Our King was holding a banquet to celebrate his wedding, but suddenly he was wounded, as if by the punishment of some god of Heaven. If you can cure his pain, we will be most grateful indeed.'

Gil-Dong guessed that they might be referring to the monster whom he had shot with his arrow and readily agreed to go with them. He was taken to a great tower, and there led to the King's bedside. He examined the wound and found it was less serious than he had expected. So he took some tablets of poison from his pocket and dissolved them in a cup of water, which he gave to the monster to drink. In a few moments the monster was stricken with paralysis, and with a scream of agony he died.

The other monsters realized that they had been deceived and made a rush at Gil-Dong, but, calling upon the Spirit of the Winds to help him, he soared up into the air. Hovering over them he shot many arrows at the monsters and slew them all. Then he came down and thoroughly searched the tower. In a stone cell he found two girls who were on the point of death. At first he took them too for monsters, and raised his hand to kill them, but they cried out to him that they were girls whom the monsters had carried off. One of them was the daughter of the wealthy Běg Yong of Nag-Czŏn, and the other was the daughter of one more rich man, Zo-Czŏl, of the same place.

Gil-Dong restored both girls safe and sound to their parents. In their gratitude both families entertained him lavishly and offered the two girls to him to be his wives. And so he married them, taking Běg's daughter as his first wife, and Zo's as his second

After a few days he returned to the island of Ze-Do, and his people welcomed him and his wives from their hearts. One summer day, however, Gil-Dong began to think longingly of the parents he had left so long before. He grew very sad as he thought of them, so that his wife asked him what made him so unhappy. He told her of everything that had caused him grief in the past, of his mother's humble station, and how he had not been fully accepted into his family, of his sick father, of his career as a bandit, and finally his exile to the island.

The next morning he climbed up the mountain of Wŏl-Bong, and after searching for a while he found a suitable spot for a graveyard where his father might lie. He sent men to build a mausoleum, using only the finest stones. When the work got under way he cut off his hair and disguised himself as a Buddhist priest. Then he set sail for Korea, where he feared that his father might be dangerously ill, and on the point of death.

His father, the former Minister Hong, was over eighty years of age, and summoning his wife and eldest son to his bedside he said to them, 'I am about to die, and I know not whether my son Gil-Dong is alive or dead. If he is living, it may be that one day he will come and visit you. If he does, let there be no distinction between my sons, the legitimate and the illegitimate. Let Gil-Dong receive the same treatment as In-Hyŏng, and let his mother be well cared for too.' With these words he breathed his last.

Not long afterwards a priest knocked at the gate and began to cry lamentations for the dead minister in a loud voice. In-Hyŏng received him as a guest in the room where his father lay in state, and asked him who he was. 'Don't you recognize your own brother?' the priest exclaimed, and indeed it was Gil-Dong. So In-Hýŏng took him to meet his mother Yu, and his own mother Czun-Sŏn too. They told him of his father's last words, and he was well content. Then he told them of his own experiences since his departure from Korea, and insisted that his father should be buried in the graveyard that he had established on the island. His request was granted, and moreover it was agreed that his mother Czun-Sŏn should go with him.

Next day Gil-Dong set out to return to his island. He took his mother with him, and his brother In-Hyŏng came too, to look after his father's coffin, which they loaded on to the ship. Many boats came out from Ze-Do to meet them, and when at last they arrived his mother and brother were delighted with the scenery of the island. Moreover they were well pleased with the modesty of Gil-Dong's two beautiful wives.

Gil-Dong held a most magnificent funeral for his father. His mother and brother were most impressed by the mausoleum he had prepared, and his brother In-Hyŏng returned to Seoul well satisfied. He told his mother all that Gil-Dong had done for his father, and she was well content.

For three years Gil-Dong mourned twice every day for his father, morning and evening as custom demanded. When this period of mourning was over he turned his attention to the problem presented by the neighbouring kingdom of Yug-Do. It was a wealthy and powerful country, and presented a serious threat to the people of his island. So Gil-Dong set about raising a great and well-armed army, and when his preparations were complete he launched an attack on his menacing neighbour. His army reached the slopes of Mount Czŏl-Bong without being detected, and took the governor Gim Hyŏn-Czung completely by surprise. After a brief show of resistance he retreated and took refuge within his castle. Then Gil-Dong ordered his Chief of Staff Ma-Sug, and the four generals, East Blue, South Red, West White, and North Black, to seize the castle with fifty thousand of his magic soldiers, and this they did without difficulty. Then Gil-Dong sent an envoy to the King of Yug-Do calling on him to surrender, since his most powerful fortress of Czŏl-Bong had fallen.

The Story of Hong Gil-Dong

On hearing this dread news the King of Yug-Do took his own life, and his Queen and his son did likewise. So Gil-Dong entered the capital at the head of his army, and ascended the throne of Yug-Do on the ninth day of the First Month. He appointed new ministers and promoted those officials who pledged him their loyalty. Then he reformed the administration completely and before long had established an ideal kingdom. After three years the new kingdom of Yug-Do was firmly established, and one day Gil-Dong whispered to his mother, 'If the assassin had succeeded in killing me that day long ago, this happy day could never have come to pass.'

Now that he was firmly established Gil-Dong sent his father-in-law Běg Yong to the King of Korea with a letter thanking him for his generosity and goodwill, and recalling the days gone by. He also sent one thousand *sŏg* of unhulled rice, in repayment of those the King had given him. The King was delighted to have this unexpected news of Gil-Dong after all these years, and showed the letter to his elder brother In-Hyŏng, who was now a deputy Minister. He dispatched In-Hyŏng to Yug-Do with his letter in reply, and granted him one year's leave of absence. So In-Hyŏng set out with his mother and came to the court of his brother Gil-Dong. In-Hyŏng and his mother, accompanied by the leading families of the Kingdom of Yug-Do, went out to his father's grave and paid their respects there.

When they had been in Yug-Do for a few months the mother of In-Hyŏng was taken ill and died and was buried beside her husband. Six months later In-Hyŏng returned to Seoul and after the prescribed three years of mourning had elapsed was appointed Minister.

Soon afterwards Gil-Dong's mother died, and he mourned her for three years. Then when he had reigned for thirty years and had reached the age of seventy a spirit came from Heaven and appeared to Gil-Dong. It told him that the time had come for him to depart from this world, and so he rose up into Heaven, followed by his two Queens. His three sons and two daughters mourned his departure, and his eldest son ascended the throne and reigned in his stead.

By Hŏ Gyun.

223

99

The Legend of Zŏn U-Czi

LONG ago there lived beside the Sung-In Gate in Song-Gyŏng a scholar named Zŏn U-Czi. By assiduous study he had acquired supernatural powers and had attained a remarkable proficiency in magic. He was careless of worldly fame, however, and never made any public display of his powers, so that no one knew of his capabilities.

Now for some years the harvests had been bad in the lands along the south coast, and moreover a plague of vipers assailed the land, so that the people were in dire distress. But the officials and leading citizens took no measures to relieve the suffering of the people, for they were more interested in amassing wealth for themselves by intrigue and quarrelling among themselves.

Zŏn U-Czi, on the other hand, was grieved to see the wretched conditions in which the people were living, and so at his own expense he undertook measures for their relief. Before long his own resources were exhausted, and so he turned his attention to magic. One day he transformed himself into a superhuman being wearing a golden crown, and, accompanied by two small boys dressed in blue, he mounted upon a cloud and rode through the air towards the Royal Palace. It was the second day of the First Month, and all the courtiers had come before the King to offer him New Year greetings. Zŏn U-Czi descended at their head, before the King, and solemnly proclaimed, 'I, Emperor of the Heavenly Kingdom, declare to you, King of this land, that it is my intention to build in Heaven a "Palace of Peace" dedicated to the memory of all those men and women who had the misfortune to die in poverty. I call upon every country to prepare one beam of gold. I shall return to receive it on the last day of the third month.'

So the King consulted with his advisers and sent orders to the eight provinces of the land that they should collect gold and send it to the capital. Then the beam was cast at the Royal Foundry. Then on the appointed day the King mounted a high platform and waited. The two Heavenly boys came riding on a cloud and pulled the beam up on to it. Then they rode away, and gradually disappeared into a rainbow.

Zŏn U-Czi took the beam and sold one half of it in a foreign country in the west. With the proceeds he bought a hundred thousand *sŏg* of rice. He carried it back on the spring wind, and distributed it to a hundred thousand starving families. And the following year he distributed provisions and seed to the farmers.

One day he took the remainder of the beam to sell it in the open market in Seoul. An army official came up to him and asked him how much he wanted for it.

'Five hundred *yang*,' replied Zŏn U-Czi.

'I havn't that much with me now,' said the official, 'but I will bring it to you to-morrow. Where do you live?'

'My home is in Bu-Zu, in South Korea,' said Zŏn, 'and my name is Zŏn U-Czi.'

The official reported his conversation to the commander of the garrison. The matter seemed to be very mysterious, and the commander decided to buy the gold at the price asked, so that he could investigate its origin. He strongly suspected that it was part of the beam of gold, and his investigations seemed to confirm his suspicions. So he sent soldiers to arrest Zŏn U-Czi and bring him before him, but he refused to submit, saying, 'I have done no wrong, and I refuse to go with you. Tell the commander that he has no authority to arrest me, except on the express orders of the King.'

So the commander of the garrison stationed five hundred soldiers to guard Zŏn's house, and sent a report to the King. Thereupon a detachment of police was sent from Seoul to arrest Zŏn to bring him before the King. They seized him and bound him with iron ropes and set out for the capital. But before they had gone very far Zŏn U-Czi cried out, 'Who is that you have arrested instead of me?' So they looked and saw that they had a pine tree bound with iron ropes, and that Zŏn was standing free beside it. They were utterly perplexed, and at a loss what to do. Then Zŏn said, 'If you want to arrest me, let me get into this bottle,' and he placed a bottle in the road. So they seized him once more, and he got into the bottle. It was so heavy that they could hardly move it. At last with much effort they managed to take it into the King's presence, and the King was very pleased to see it. 'I have heard that Zŏn U-Czi was a practitioner of magic,' he said, 'but now I see that he is well and truly trapped in a bottle.' And he gave orders that the bottle should be put in a cauldron of boiling oil. Then Zŏn U-Czi spoke from inside the bottle, 'Thank you, Your Majesty. I have been shivering from the cold, and now you are so kind as to give me warmth.'

The King was angry at his words, and ordered the bottle to be broken in pieces. But from every piece there came the voice of Zŏn U-Czi exhorting the King to take a more active interest in the welfare of his people. The King was more angry than ever, and ordered that the bottle be ground to powder.

One day Zŏn U-Czi met a white haired old man in the street. The old man said to him in a voice broken by sobs, 'One of my neighbours called Wang accused another, Zo by name, of intrigue with his wife, and attacked him violently. My son was passing at the time and tried to stop their quarrel, but to no avail. Zo felled Wang with a mighty blow and left him lying dead on the road. Then the dead man's cousin went to the magistrates and accused my son as the murderer. The Minister of Justice, Yang Mun-Dŏg, sentenced my son unjustly for the crime, and let the actual murderer go free, for it happens that he is an intimate friend of the Minister.'

So Zŏn U-Czi assumed the likeness of the murdered Wang and went to the Minister's residence. He appeared in a mirror in the Minister's presence, and said, 'I am the ghost of Wang, who was most shamefully murdered. You have thrown an innocent man into prison, and have let the guilty man go free. You have erred most grievously in your judgment.'

The Minister was terrified at the apparition and instantly released the innocent man from prison and arrested Zo instead.

One day Zŏn U-Czi heard the sound of music as he passed by a luxurious restaurant. He went in and found several gentlemen dining on rich food and being entertained by pretty dancing girls. He asked that he might be allowed to join the party. 'I am a traveller, and my way happened to take me past this house. Will you permit me to sit a while and listen to your music?' he asked.

There were two among them who seemed to be most over-bearing, Un and Sŏl by name. 'You may if you like, rustic,' they sneered. 'Have you ever seen such a party, such varieties of food, such beautiful girls as we have here?'

'No Sir, never,' replied Zŏn, 'It is indeed amazing. But I think that there is something missing. You have no water-melons, no sweet grapes, no peaches even.'

Then all the guests burst out laughing. 'Ridiculous!' they exclaimed. 'It is early spring now, and those fruits are nowhere to be found. Do you mean to tell us that you can get them?'

'Yes indeed, gentlemen,' replied Zŏn. 'I have just seen a tree that bore all kinds of ripe fruits. If I bring them to you now, what will you give me?'

'If you bring them to us we will bow to you, and if you do not we will have you stripped naked and soundly beaten,' the haughty ones replied.

So Zŏn U-Czi went out and climbed a near-by hill. There he plucked a branch of peach blossom and recited over it a magical text. Immediately the flowers were transformed into peaches, grapes, and water-melons. He took them back to the house.

The guests were most amazed, but Un and Sŏl refused to bow to him as they had promised, and merely offered him wine. So Zŏn said in a solemn voice, 'You two have failed to keep your word. May the wrath of the gods fall upon you!'

After a few minutes Un went outside to relieve himself, but found to his consternation that he could not pass water. He cried out in alarm, and Sŏl went after him to find out what was the matter, and then found that he was himself in a like predicament. And the same thing happened to the prettiest of the dancing girls.

So terrified were they by their misfortune that they came to Zŏn and humbly begged him to pardon them for having behaved so discourteously to him, and bowed so low before him that their noses touched the ground. Zŏn was mollified and accepted their apologies as sincere. So he summoned his two Heavenly boys and bade them climb up to Heaven by a thread that was hanging down there and to send down three Heavenly peaches. The boys went off into the sky, and soon peach leaves came fluttering down. Then three peaches, each as big as a man's head, fell unharmed on the ground. Then Zŏn handed one to each of the three and said with a smile, 'You had better eat these. They will cure you at once.'

So they were cured, and never again did they despise others without reason or fail in their word.

One day Zŏn U-Czi met a filial young man named Han Za-Gyŏng who was so poor that he could neither hold a proper funeral for his father nor feed his aged mother. Zŏn took from his sleeve a small gourd such as was used for fetching water and gave it to him. Then he said, 'If you call to this gourd, "Ho, servant" it will answer "Yes sir." Then you may ask it to bring you one hundred *yang* and it will bring you that sum. That will suffice for the funeral expenses. Thereafter you must not ask it to bring more than one *yang* each day, which will be enough to keep your aged mother.'

The young man Han thanked him for his kindness and asked his name. Zŏn replied, 'I am Zŏn U-Czi, from the city of Nam Czam.'

Han hurried home and looked inside the gourd. There he saw the picture of a big storehouse and a boy holding a key. He shouted, 'Ho, servant!' and the boy answered 'Yes sir'. So Han commanded, 'Bring me one hundred *yang*.' And in an instant the money appeared. So he was enabled to hold a funeral for his father, and thereafter he asked for one *yang* a day for the support of his aged mother.

This went on for some time, but one day he asked for one hundred *yang*, which he wanted for some purpose or other. The boy took no notice. So Han repeated his request two or three times, and then the boy unlocked the door and let him enter the storehouse. He took one hundred *yang* and tried to come out, but he could not, because the door was locked. He shouted for the boy to open it, but there was no reply, so he began to kick the door.

Now one of the servants of the Minister of Finance went and reported to his master that he could hear someone shouting in the storehouse where the money was kept. So the Minister gave orders that someone should go and arrest the man. When the door was opened they found a man there holding money in his hands.

'Who are you, stealing money here?' demanded the Minister.

'Who are you to come and arrest me in my own house?' demanded Han in reply, and then the truth began to dawn on him. He realized that it was indeed the Minister and that he was himself in a most difficult position. So he explained about Zŏn U-Czi and the gourd.

So the Minister went and looked in the safes in the storehouse and found them full of green frogs and yellow snakes instead of gold and silver. This was immediately reported to the King. Then more dread portents were seen. The rice in the Royal storeroom was found to have been transformed into worms, and the dwellings of the ladies in waiting were invaded by tigers.

So Han was brought to trial as the accomplice of Zŏn U-Czi.

'You say you got the gourd from this Zŏn U-Czi,' said the King. 'When was it, and where?'

'Five months ago, Your Majesty, in the street,' replied Han.

At that moment a violent wind sprang up, and Han vanished in the twinkling of an eye. The King turned to his ministers and asked them what course they thought he ought to take. One of them spoke up and suggested that Zŏn might modify his attitude if he were granted some official rank. The King accepted this suggestion and ordered that notices to this effect be posted on the four gates of the castle.

Zŏn U-Czi saw the notice and went to the Palace. The King was very pleased to have found him so easily, and appealed to him to co-operate with the government. Zŏn was moved by the King's appeal, and determined that thenceforth he assist him, and from that time he served the Court faithfully.

Now there was a bandit who lurked on the slopes of Mount Ga-Dal and terrorized the neighbourhood, plundering and murdering. The local authorities repeatedly sent soldiers to capture him, but without success. At last the King came to hear of it, and Zŏn U-Czi at once offered to go out and bring the bandit to justice. With a few officers he rode out on horseback, and came to the mountain. The first thing to do was to spy on the enemy to see how the land lay. So Zŏn transformed himself into a kite and flew up the mountainside to the bandit's lair. There he saw Ŏm Zuni, the leader of the band, out hunting with about a hundred of his followers. He was a tall man, with a red face and rolling eyes.

Zŏn flew back, and assuming once more his proper shape donned a suit of yellow armour and a double helmet. Then he took leaves from the trees, and transformed them into soldiers armed with spears and swords. Then mounting his swift black horse he led them against the enemy's camp. He recited a magic formula, the castle gate flew open, and he rushed inside, followed by his troops.

The bandits were at that moment feasting in the grounds. So Zŏn transformed his men and himself into kites and swooped down. They snatched up all the rich food, and a violent wind sprang up and swept aside their embroidered screens. Then Zŏn and his men assumed their human form, and the bandits rushed fiercely at them. Zŏn made one of his men take his own form and impersonate him at the head of his troops, while he himself soared into the air. While the false Zŏn was engaging the enemy in mortal combat the real Zŏn swooped through the air, brandishing his sword that flashed like lightning. The bandits were terror stricken and tried to run away, but Zŏn stood before them and blocked their path. They turned, and there found another Zŏn pursuing them behind. So they were trapped, and surrendered abjectly. The King was delighted at Zŏn's success, and he was held in high respect at Court for his exploit.

Among the courtiers, however, there was a most jealous man, Wang Yŏn-Hi by name. Envious of Zŏn's reputation he falsely accused him to the King, so that he might be put to death. So Zŏn transformed himself into the likeness of Wang Yŏn-Hi and went to Wang's house while the real one was away. In the evening the real Wang came home, and his family were greatly perplexed, for now there were two Wangs, exactly alike. Then Zŏn poured abuse on the newcomer, and said, 'This must be a fox a thousand years old, transformed into human shape. Be off at once, you scoundrel!'

'Who is this impudent fellow, who has intruded into my house?' demanded the real Wang. 'You be off, and never come here again!'

Then Zŏn recited a magic formula and ordered the servants to grind laurel bark to powder and blow it on Wang. This they did, and Wang changed instantly into a nine-tailed fox. They rushed upon it and tried to beat it with sticks, but Zŏn bade them desist. Then he ordered them to bind it tightly and put it in prison. Wang tried to protest, but he could only bark like a fox, and so they shut him up. He was almost frantic with despair, and in a few days it seemed that he would die. So Zŏn went to him and advised him not to be so jealous in future. Then he released him, and spoke some magic words. At once Wang assumed his proper form and apologized most humbly for his infamous conduct.

Zŏn U-Czi was anxious to serve the King to the best of his ability, but among the courtiers there were many who were jealous of him, and turned the King against him. He was very disturbed that he did not enjoy the full confidence of the King, and so often wandered unhappily about the country. One day he came across a group of boys playing in a village. He found their games most amusing, and decided to do something to entertain them in return for the pleasure they had given him. So he drew out from his sleeve a cup in which was carved the image of a girl holding a bottle.

230

Holding it in front of him he said, 'Come out Miss Zu Sŏn-Dang, and give these boys some of your sweet wine.'

At his words a beautiful fairy girl stepped out of the cup and poured out wine for each of the boys, to their very great pleasure. Just at that moment it happened that a rich traveller, by name O Sĕng, passed that way, and the girl served him too with a cup of wine, and then went back into the cup. O was deeply impressed, and offered to buy the cup, and Zŏn accepted his offer. It was arranged that he should call at O's house on the following day to receive payment. .

O took the cup home and hung it on the wall of his study. Next morning he said, 'Miss Zu, how about getting me a cup of wine?' Then the fairy girl appeared before him and served him as he expected. He drank several cups and the wine began to go to his head. He was captivated by the girl's beauty and taking her by the hand set her on his knee. Just at that very moment his wife Min came into the room. She was furiously angry to see her husband's infidelity and made as if to strike the girl, who at once squeezed herself back into the cup. In her fury Min seized the cup and dashed it in pieces on the floor, to the great disappointment of her husband.

Just at that moment Zŏn arrived to receive payment for the cup. O came out and told him what had happened, and begged to be excused from paying the full price they had agreed upon. Zŏn left an image of himself to bargain with O and went himself to rebuke his wife for her wanton behaviour in breaking so priceless a cup. When he mentioned the question of payment she protested vigorously that she would never agree to it, and so Zŏn resolved to make use of his magic powers to teach her a lesson and cure her of her arrogant bad manners. He transformed her into a great monster that completely filled the room. O came in and was terrified by what he saw. He apologized most profusely for having shown such meanness in spite of his wealth, and announced his readiness to pay the full sum he had promised. Perceiving that he did indeed repent sincerely Zŏn relented and refused to accept any money from him, and released his wife from the spell.

One day Zŏn U-Czi went to call on a scholar named Yang Bong-Hwan, who had been one of his own schoolmates. He found him lying sick in bed. Yang told him that he was unhappy because he loved a beautiful young widow about twenty-two years of age, living near the south gate in Hyŏng-Dong, who was of an obstinate character and seemed little disposed to accept him.

Zŏn sympathized deeply with his old friend in his misfortune and said, 'I am now thirty years old, but have as yet had no experience of love. But I have noticed that when once a man is affected by it he finds it exceedingly difficult to recover from it. I will, however, see what I can do to help you. Just relax and worry no more, and I will go and bring her to you.' With these words he left his friend's bedside.

The widow lived with her aged mother, in poverty and extremely unhappy. She was so miserable that she often wished that she might die. One day she heard a voice speaking solemly out of the sky. 'The young mistress of this house must heed the Star of Fate,' it said. 'You are cordially invited to a feast in Heaven. You are to come at once.'

The widow bowed her head humbly and said, 'It is not right that I should attend, now that I have lost my husband. I am no longer pure, but sullied by earthly desire. How can I accept your invitation?'

The voice answered from the air, 'Do not drink the water of the earth in defiance of the Heavenly wish.' At once a Heavenly boy came down and offered her a cup containing a mystic liquid. It gave off a sweet perfume and she drank it. Then she rose up into the air wrapped in clouds of many colours, while her mother looked on helplessly.

Now a noble spirit called Gang Im Doryŏng disguised himself as a beggar and mingled with the other beggars in the market-place to beg alms. He looked up at the cloud as it floated overhead and pointed at it with his forefinger. Immediately a beautiful woman fell from it to the ground unharmed. Zŏn happened to be passing through the market place and was astounded by this unexpected accident. He was even more surprised when one of the beggars standing by rebuked him saying, 'Ah, poor Zŏn! I see your magic is still mischievous, though sometimes you use it to do good. You must not carry out your plan with this woman. It is fated that she is to remain chaste for the rest of her life.'

Zŏn drew his sword to challenge the beggar, but it suddenly changed into a big tiger and leapt on him. So he tried to run away, but he could not, for his feet were rooted to the ground, and his magic was of no avail. Thus he was worsted by the strange beggar,

232

and kneeling down before him begged for mercy. And so he failed in his attempt to help his friend in his ill-starred love.

After this defeat Zŏn U-Czi went to visit Sŏ Hwa-Dam, a scholar renowned in Taoism, who lived in a simple thatched cottage in a small patch of land on Mount Ya-Ge. He was known as the Earthly Genie. Zŏn went to him and asked him to instruct him in magic. So Hwa-Dam welcomed him warmly, and introduced him to his younger brother, Sŏ Yong-Dam, who was also his pupil.

Sŏ Yong-Dam challenged Zŏn U-Czi to a contest of magic. Zŏn immediately turned Yong-Dam's hat into iron threads, and Yong-Dam turned Zŏn's hat into tiger hairs. Then the iron threads turned into a white dragon, and the tiger hairs turned into a blue dragon. The two dragons rose up into the air breathing clouds and fogs and fought furiously together. At last the blue dragon was defeated and fled towards the south-east.

Seeing this Sŏ Hwa-Dam burst out laughing and threw up into the air the water container of his inkstone which was lying on his desk. Then the two dragons came down and changed into their proper shape. Hwa-Dam apologized to Zŏn for his brother's lack of courtesy. He turned to his brother and said, 'You must not challenge my guest without my permission. And you might well have been defeated, for you gave him a blue dragon and he gave you a white dragon. Blue is the colour of Wood, and white is the colour of Metal. In the Five Elements Metal always prevails over Wood. How then can wood defeat metal? You were at fault there!'

One day Sŏ Hwa-Dam said to Zŏn, 'By the Southern Sea there stands a mountain called Hwa-San. On that mountain there lives a famous Taoist called Un Su Sŏnsĕng. He was my teacher when I was young. I would like you to take him this letter for me. It may take you some time, for the mountain is very high, and stands in a remote land. On the way you will encounter great obstacles.'

Zŏn agreed to do as he was asked, but he felt a little displeased that Sŏ Hwa-Dam still did not believe in his ability. He took the letter and set out, but when he came to the sea a huge net blocked his way. He tried to leap over it, but the higher he jumped the higher the net stretched, until it spread from the surface of the sea right up to the sky. He struggled for ten days, but in the end had to admit defeat and returned without accomplishing his mission.

Zŏn was greatly ashamed at failing so abjectly, and tried to run away. He turned himself into a sea-bird and flew off, but Sŏ Hwa-Dam turned himself into a kite and pursued him. So Zŏn turned himself into a leopard, but his pursuer then turned into a lion. The lion fell upon the leopard and began to maul it, so that before long it fell down defeated. Then the lion roared, 'I can see by your running away that you are still too conceited. You must come back and study with me. Magic must only be used for the good of mankind. I intend to go and live on Mount Tĕ-Bĕg and study harder than ever. You must come with me too.'

So Zŏn was forgiven, and went with his master Sŏ Hwa-Dam. They built a simple cottage on Mount Tĕ-Bĕg and devoted themselves to study, writing books and storing them in a cave.

Nothing was heard of them for years until a certain Yang Bong-Nĕ, from the Province of Gang-Wŏn, came across them when he went to Mount Tĕ-Bĕg to see the relics of the first King, Dan-Gun. They told him, 'We live in this remote spot so that we may better study the mysteries of the Universe. You appear to be a trustworthy man. Here are several volumes containing the secrets that are to be handed down from generation to generation. Will you undertake to look after them?'

Yang Bong-Nĕ took the books and returned to his home. He studied hard and became well versed in the knowledge they contained. But no one would listen when he attempted to expound them, for they were mysteries that no man should hear.

Recently reprinted by Bagmun Sŏgwan; Seoul.

APPENDIX

Index of Sources

NUMBERS REFER TO THE TALES.

Index of Sources

	Korean Writings.	Chinese Characters.	
Gang Gam-Czan	강 강찬	姜邯賛	32
Ganghwa	강 화	江華	1
Gangrim Do-Ryong	강 림 도령	姜林道令	99
Gang-wŏn	강 원	江原	53, 69
Gara	가 라	駕洛	Intro.
Gayŏbwŏn	가 엽 원	迦葉原	2
Gazĕzib	가 재 집	嘉齋集	98
Gĕmudŏm	개 무 덤		58
Gĕsŏng	개 성	開城	26, 37, 79
Gil-Dal	길 달	吉達	61
Gim	김	金	30
Gim Bog-Hi	김 복히	金福姬	93
Gim Bong-Zib	김 봉집	金鳳集	91
Gim Dŏg-Nyŏng	김 덕령	金德齡	33
Gim Dong-Hŭl	김 동흘	金東屹	98
Gim Du-Hŏn	김 두헌	金斗憲	45
Gim Du-Ri	김 두리	金斗理	70, 88
Gim Gi-Hwan	김 기환	金琪驩	33, 52, 63
Gim Gi-Tĕg	김 기택	金淇澤	8, 15, 85
Gim Han-Yong	김 한용	金翰容	73
Gimhゝ	김 해	金海	73
Gim Hyŏn	김 현	金現	48
Gim Hyŏn-Czung	김 현충	金賢忠	98
Gim Hyŏng-Man	김 형안	金亨萬	47
Gim Sŏng-Bal	김 성발	金成發	51
Gim Tĕ-O	김 태오	金泰午	83
Gim Yang-Ha	김 양하	金良瑕	22, 95
Gim Yun-Gi	깅 윤기	金允基	92
Godal	고 달	高達	37
Gog-San	곡 산	谷山	98
Goguryŏ	고 구려	高句麗	Intro., 2
Go Han-Sŭng	고 한승	高漢承	26

	Korean Writings.	Chinese Characters.	
Miryang	밀양	密陽	59
Modun	모둔	毛屯	2
Mogpo	목포	木浦	57
Mo Yun-Sug	모윤숙	毛允淑	75
mŏngmŏng	멍멍		91
Mudŭng	무등	無等	33
Mug-Gŏ	묵거	默居	2
Mu-Gol	무골	武骨	2
Mu-Hag	무학	無學	37
Mun Czang-Zun	문창죤	文昌俊	68
Munczŏn	문쳔	蚊川	61
Mungyŏng	문경	聞慶	98
Myŏngczŏn	명쳔	明川	98
Nagczŏn	낙쳔	洛川	98
Nagdong	낙동	洛東	59
Namyang	남양	南陽	57
Obong	오봉	五峯	98
Ogczŏn	옥쳔	沃川	25
Ognyŏn-dong	옥연동	玉蓮洞	63
O Hwa-Su	오화수	吳和壽	3, 86
Ondoru Yawa (Korean Nights, written in Japanese by the present author, Zŏng In-Sŏb, 1927, Tokyo)		温突夜話	For., 1, 3, 7, 8, 9, 11, 13, 27, 36, 44, 45, 46, 47, 48, 49, 53, 54, 59, 60, 62, 64, 65, 66, 67, 68, 69, 71, 72, 74, 76, 77, 97, 98, 99
O Sĕng	오생	吳生	99
O Sŏg-Gŏn	오석건	吳碩根	66
Osŏng Buwŏn-Gun	오성부원군	悟城府院君	49
O Zin-Yŏng	오친영	吳珍泳	57, 77

Index of Sources

	Korean Writings.	Chinese Characters.	
Tong-yŏng	통영	統營	8, 15, 23, 32, 33, 52, 63, 70, 85, 88, 93
Tĕbĕg	태백	太白	1, 2
Tĕzŏn	태전	太田	25
Tobni	톱니		12
Tug-Zĕ	특재	特才	98
T'ang		唐	Intro.
T'ao Ch'ien		陶潛	Intro.
Ubalsu	우발수	優渤水	2
Uldon	울도		98
Ulsan	울산	蔚山	58
Ungsim	웅심	熊心	2
Un-Sa	운사	雲師	1
Unsu Sŏnsĕng	운수선생	雲水先生	99
U-Sa	우사	雨師	1
Ŭnzin	은진	恩津	80
Virgin Po Sui		白水素女	Intro.
Wakan Sanzai Zukai		和漢三才圖會	Intro.
Wang	왕	王	99
Wang Gŭm	왕금	王儉	1
Wangsimni	왕십리	往十里	37
Wang Yŏn-Hŭi	왕연희	王然喜	99
Wŏlbong	월봉	月峯	98
Wŏlmol-zŏng	월몰정	月沒亭	51
Yagye	야계	野溪	99
yang	양	兩	30, 73, 77, 94, 98, 99
yangban	양반	兩班	22, 58, 60
Yang Bong-Hwan	양봉환	梁鳳丸	99
Yang Bong-Nĕ	양봉래	楊蓬來	99
Yang Mun-Dŭg	양문득	楊文得	99

	Korean Writings.	Chinese Characters.	
Yangsan	양산	梁山	17, 21, 35, 72
Yangzu	양주	楊州	32
Yi	이	李	29, 30, 35, 37, 58
Yi Chien Chih		夷堅志	Intro.
Yi Hŏn-Gu	이헌구	李軒求	53
Yi Sang-Hwa	이상화	李相夏	14, 19, 40
Yi Sang-Sa	이상사	李上舍	59
Yi Sun-Sin	이순신	李舜臣	42
Yi Ŭn-Sang	이은상	李殷相	16, 43
Yi Yŏn-Ho	이연호	李演浩	97
Yongdam	용담	龍潭	7
Yŏm U-Gyŏng	염우경	廉又京	90
Yŏngczŏn	영천	永川	58
Yŏngnam	영남	嶺南	57
Yŏngnam-nu	영남누	嶺南樓	49
Yŏngwŏl	영월	寧越	53
Yŏnhŭi	연희	延禧	For.
Yŏni	연이	連伊	28
Yu	유	柳	98
Yu Czun-Sŏb	유춘섭	柳春燮	24
Yugdo-gug	육도국	咩島國	98
Yu Hwa	유화	柳花	2
Yun	윤	尹	59
Yun Bĕg-Nam	윤백남	尹白南	54
Yun Gwŏn	윤권	尹瓘	36
Yuyang	유양	唯陽	98
Zang	장	張	35
Zang-gun-su	장군수	將軍水	72
Zanghŭng	장흥	長興	45
Zang-Sŏn	장선	長釗	97
Zangsu	장수	長水	32
Zangzĕ	장재	長在	27

Index of Sources

Index of Subjects

(Numbers refer to Tales)

world, 3, 4, 10, 12, 13, 14, 17, 24, 50, 54, 73, 98

Index of Subjects

laurel, 8, 99
leaf, 16, 72
leek, 6, 74
lotus, 19, 27, 59, 63, 97
maiden-hair tree, 55
millet, 6, 8, 95
moss, 74
mugwort, 1
onion, 10
peach, 99
pear, 44
persimmon, 45, 76, 77, 79, 84
pine, 11, 55, 60, 71, 99
plum, 37
pumpkin, 11, 36
radish, 72
rape, 28
reed, 59
rice, 3, 6, 12, 13, 14, 16, 19, 27, 30, 44,
    49, 50, 57, 58, 64, 67, 68, 71, 72, 73,
    77, 85, 87, 89, 98, 99
rose, 97
sandalwood, 1
sesame, 3
strawberry, 68
sweet potato, 44
tobacco, 54, 64, 93
tree, 3, 16, 17, 31, 54, 65, 71, 75, 77
vegetable, 28, 89
walnut, 64
water-melon, 99
wheat, 55
willow, 28, 66, 72
wood, 13, 64, 66; — (fire-wood),
    11, 45, 53, 64, 66, 71, 77

V. GEOGRAPHICAL

air, 13, 32, 33, 72, 76, 99
autumn, 48, 99
capital, 1, 2, 6, 48, 99
cave, 1, 28, 40, 72, 75, 98
cavern, 35
clay, 57, 72, 98
cliff, 54, 59, 75
cloud, 1, 80, 98, 99

cold, 4, 5, 6, 7, 22, 28, 41, 69, 99
crystal, 98
darkness, 3, 7, 8
dawn, 9
deluge, 52, 71
den, 75
desert, 43
ditch, 64
earth, 8, 9, 24
east, 2, 8, 18, 34, 37, 68, 98
eclipse, 4
field, 2, 7, 14, 28, 36, 47, 51, 71
fire, 5, 13, 28, 35, 47, 51, 69, 98
flood, 8, 35, 41, 52, 71
fog, 99
gale, 73
ground, 9, 13
gravel, 98
hot, 4, 35, 51, 69, 74
ice, 69, 71
island, 1, 8, 19, 35, 57, 98
lake, 7, 11, 19, 27, 52, 76, 97
lightning, 35, 98
Milky way, 17
moon, 3, 4, 17, 45, 48, 57, 59, 62, 93,
    98
mountain, 1, 2, 5, 7, 8, 9, 11, 12, 18,
    21, 25, 28, 29, 31, 32, 35, 36, 37,
    38, 40, 41, 44, 45, 46, 47, 48, 49,
    50, 52, 53, 55, 57, 62, 63, 64, 65,
    66, 69, 70, 71, 72, 73, 74, 75, 77,
    79, 81, 82, 91, 96, 97, 98, 99
mud, 64
night, 3, 5, 6, 8, 9, 12, 21, 24, 29, 30,
    32, 36, 37, 39, 40, 41, 45, 46, 47,
    48, 49, 52, 53, 57, 58, 59, 60, 61,
    62, 64, 65, 66, 67, 68, 70, 71, 73,
    74, 75, 76, 77, 92, 95, 97, 98
north, 5, 98
pebble, 69
peninsula, 1, 2
pool, 2
port, 57
rain, 1, 8, 16, 28, 35, 65, 73, 98
rainbow, 11, 28
river, 2, 7, 12, 18, 32, 35, 37, 38, 41,

flag, 39
flail, 67
floor, 3, 5, 32, 70
flute, 78, 98
food, 8, 11, 12, 13, 16, 19, 20, 30, 36,
  52, 54, 55, 58, 67, 68, 69, 75, 82,
  85, 89, 98, 99
garment, 62
gate, 8, 27, 28, 34, 36, 39, 40, 49, 54,
  57, 58, 61, 62, 63, 65, 72, 96, 98, 99
gold, 2, 52, 72, 75; — (golden
  beam), 99; — (golden bottle), 58;
  — (golden crown), 12, 99; —
  (golden cup), 58; — (golden
  frame), 63; — (golden frog), 2;
  — (golden hair-pin), 13; —
  (golden ring), 13
grinding stone, 65
gun, 44
hair-pin, 13, 14
hammer, 17
handkerchief, 47, 49
handmill, 65
hat, 12, 80
helmet, 72, 99
honey, 77
hook, 76
hooves, 14
horn, 14
house, 2, 3, 5, 6, 21, 53, 58
inn, 60
inkstone, 84, 99
instrument, 12
iron, 3, 12, 71, 72, 98
jacket, 13, 40, 46, 62
jade, 59
jar, 44, 52, 66, 75
jewel, 9, 62, 65, 66, 67
kettle, 26, 36, 66, 70, 93
key, 99
kitchen, 6, 13, 15, 46, 50, 66, 70, 75,
  76, 87
knife, 31, 40, 44, 73
ladder, 17, 99
ladle, 15, 70, 87
lantern, 76, 97

leather, 98
letter, 56
liver, 44, 74
mallet, 62, 64, 77
mask, 61
mast, 43
mat, 3, 70
matock, 25
measure, 2, 12
meat, 64
medicine, 21, 26, 45, 52, 54, 56, 58,
  60, 65, 66, 67, 74, 77
money, 12, 27, 30, 36, 41, 45, 46, 52,
  54, 56, 58, 60, 66, 67, 74, 77
mortar, 70
mud, 64
needle, 38, 44, 74
numbers (frequently used): (1)
  (only), 30, 95; (2) 30, 35, 38, 55,
  60, 61, 94, 96, 97; (3) 2, 3, 6,
  21, 29, 31, 32, 33, 36, 40, 44, 54,
  57, 58, 65, 72, 76, 81, 98, 99;
  (4) 71; (5) 57; (7) 5; (8) 31,
  48, 58, 88, 98; (9) 22, 72, 98;
  (10) 69, 72, 98; (12) 15, 32, 48,
  49, 58; (30) 98; (60) 20; (70) 82,
  98; (80) 98; (99) 9, 46, 60;
  (100) 64, 99; (300) 43; (360) 1;
  (500) 99; (600) 7; (1,000) 54,
  58, 73, 77, 98; (3,000) 1; (100,000)
  99
oil, 3, 66, 96, 99
package, 62
pack-carrier, 17, 70, 71, 82
palanquin, 23, 32, 57, 58, 62, 86
paper, 46
pearl, 12
penny, 25, 31, 41, 60
pet, 76
pillar, 13, 66
pillow, 29
pipe, 44, 58, 72, 83, 93
pit, 6, 78, 94
plough, 17
pocket, 31
poison, 23, 52, 60, 68, 81, 84, 98